THE PORTABLE THERAPIST

THE PORTABLE THERAPIST

by

Judith K. Stewart

BYWOOD PUBLISHING COMPANY
Brooklyn, NY

This book is dedicated to Robert, Amy, Amy, and Adam with great love.

This book is designed to provide information about the subject matter covered. The purpose of the book is to educate and entertain. The author, editor, and publisher shall not have liability or responsibility to any person or entity with respect to any loss or damage caused, directly or indirectly, by the information contained in this book.

Published by Bywood Publishing Company, Brooklyn, New York
First Edition
Cover design and illustration by Laura Marten.
Book design by Karen Byers.

Library of Congress Catalog Card Number: 91-071636
ISBN 0-9628504-0-3
Printed in the United States of America
by Hamilton Printing Company, Rensselaer, NY.

94 93 92 91   5 4 3 2 1

CONTENTS

Preface **ix**   Acknowledgements   **xiv**

PART I: THE JOURNEY BEGINS

CHAPTER 1 - GETTING STARTED: OPTIONS..3
You Don't Have To Stay In Therapy Forever **4**   Choosing A Therapist **5**   No Excuses
Necessary **8**   What Can You Expect From A Man With A Broken Leg? **10**   Start Where
You Are **10**   Getting Clear On The Problem **11**   Life Is Manageable **13**   Create Your Life
The Way You Want It Now **14**   Feeding Time **15**

CHAPTER 2 - LETTING GO: THE WILLINGNESS TO CHANGE...........................17
Think For Yourself **18**   Patterns **19**   If You're Unwilling To Change, You're Stuck In
The Rut And It Will Always Be Like This **20**   What Can You Do Today, This Minute,
To Be Happier? **22**   Your Parents Did The Best They Could **23**   You Don't Have To Live
Out Of Your Story **25**   If You Don't Rock The Boat, It Grows Barnacles On The
Bottom **25**   Growing Up Is Hard...**27**   ...Not Growing Up Is Harder **27**   You're Trapped By
Your Limits **28**   Fear Is Your Enemy **29**   Courage Is Going Ahead When You Are
Afraid **30**   Learn To Distinguish Between Criticism And Judgment **31**   Be Willing To Be
Foolish Or Wrong **32**   Take A Chance, Take A Risk **33**

CHAPTER 3 - LOOKING WITHIN: A NEW PERSPECTIVE.....................................35
I Do Windows **36**   It's All Interpretation **37**   You And Your Life Are What You
Believe **39**   Dreams **41**   Could You Be The Reason Everyone Is Picking On You? **42**   If
You Are Blaming Someone Else, You Are A Victim **43**   If You Know Everything, Have
Nothing To Learn, Are Always Right, And Consider Yourself Superior, You Will Have A
Very Difficult Life **45**   Would You Rather Be Right Than Happy? **45**   Try A Little
Humility **46**   A Life Without A Sense Of Humor Is A Tragedy **47**

CHAPTER 4 - VICTIM/TYRANT: THE GAME OF LIFE..49
You Can Be A Champion **53**   Mirror, Mirror On The Wall **55**   Transference Is **57**   All
That Judgment You Think Other People Have Of You Is Really Your Own Self-Judgment
Being Reflected Back At You **58**   Feelings Are Not Facts **59**   Feelings Don't Make
Sense **59**   Who Can You Trust? **61**   You Cannot Force Anyone To Do What You
Want **64**   I Want What I Want, When I Want It, The Way I Want It **65**

PART II: THERAPY ISSUES

CHAPTER 5 - CRISES..**69**
First Things First **70** Nothing Is As Important As Your Life **72** If You Feel Like You Don't Want To Live Anymore, Call Someone Now **73** If You Are Considering Suicide, Ask Someone To Help You Think Of Options **74** There Will Always Be Someone To Help You **75** Make Them Listen And Take You Seriously **77** If You Want To Kill Yourself, Think Of The Devastation It Would Wreak On The People Around You **78** If You Hang On, There Will Come A Day, Probably Very Soon, When You Will Think, "I'm Glad I Didn't Do That" **79** Good Grief **80** Compassionate Friend **82** Your God Can And Will Help You **83**

CHAPTER 6 - ABUSE AND VIOLENCE..**85**
Children Are Victims **86** Child Abuse **86** If Anything Or Anyone Hurts You On A Regular Basis, Get Away Now **91** Incest And Molestation **92** Rape **94** If You Have Been Raped **98**

CHAPTER 7 - ADDICTION..**99**
Don't Suffer Over Your Suffering **103** Love or Addiction **104**

CHAPTER 8 - ANGER..**107**
If You're Angry, Look At What You're Afraid Of? **108** Learn To Be Slow To Anger And Quick To Love **109**

CHAPTER 9 - FEAR..**113**
Don't Futurize **114** Nothing Is Unbearable **115** It's Never As Bad As You Think It's Going To Be **116** Conquering Fear **117** Procrastination Is Putting Off Until Tomorrow What Will Make You Anxious Today **118** Prejudice **119**

CHAPTER 10 - GUILT..**121**
Guilt Is A Learned Feeling **122** If You Feel Guilty, Look At What You Are Angry About **123** You May Think That What You've Done Is Worse Than What Anyone Else Has Done **124** Everyone Has Done Things He'd Be Ashamed To Admit **125** There Is Nothing For Which You Can't Be Forgiven **125** If You Can't Forgive Yourself, Tell Someone Else and Let Him Forgive You **126** There Is Nothing You've Done For Which You Deserve To Be Punished **128** After All, Haven't You Punished Yourself Long Enough? **129** Look At What You Can Learn From The Experience And Let It Go **130**

CHAPTER 11 - SEX..**131**
Respect Yourself **133** What's Your Secret? **134** Homosexuality **135** Adolescent Sexuality **136** It Won't Make You Crazy **138** Birth Control **139** Abortion **140**

CHAPTER 12 - FEELINGS..**143**
Live What You Feel, Not What You Are Told **144**   You Cannot Shut Off One
Feeling Without Shutting Off All The Rest **145**   Your Feelings Are Your Power
To Create **146**

PART III: ABOUT RELATIONSHIPS

CHAPTER 13 - COMMUNICATION BASICS...**151**
Distinctions In Language **152** Moo **155** Talk Less, Listen More **157**

CHAPTER 14 - LOVING YOURSELF...**159**
Love Yourself A Lot **160**   Superwoman/Superman Or Supershit? **162**   Compassion
Is A Great Gift When You Realize That Everyone Else Is Hurting, Too **163**   Our
Feelings About Others Have A Great Deal To Teach Us About Ourselves **164**   To
Build Self-Confidence, Think Of All The Things You've Done Successfully **165**
Perhaps The Most Difficult Feat You Can Achieve In This Society Is To Be An
Individual **166**   Laugh, Lighten Up And Play! It's Important **168**

CHAPTER 15 - LOVING OTHERS..**171**
If You Can't Fight, You Can't F—— **173**   You Don't Have To Take Care Of
Everyone **176**   What Can You Do For Someone Else? **178**   Give Other People What
You Want **178**   You Are More Likely To Get What You Want If You Ask Than If
You Demand **179**   People Do Have The Right To Say No To You, And You Have The
Right To Say No To Them **179**   Make A Distinction Between The Person And
The Behavior **180**   Breaking Up Is Hard To Do **181**   Don't Be Committed To The
Commitment **183**   Love May Not Be Enough **183** Perfect Mate **186**   Don't Put
Your Life On Hold **188**   Marriage Doesn't Solve Anything **189**   You Are The
Only Person You Can Change **191**   No One Can Control You Without Your
Permission **192**   Partnership **193**

CHAPTER 16 - LOVING YOUR FAMILY...**197**
Men Always, Women Always **198**   Your Family May Not Be Your Family **200**
Compassion **201**   Happy Holidays? **204**

CHAPTER 17 - LOVING YOUR BODY..**207**
Just Because You Are Learning To Be In Touch With Yourself Doesn't Mean
You're Not Sick **208**   My Wife Has PMS And A Gun **209**   Let The Pressure Off **211**

PART IV: CULTURAL REVOLUTIONARIES

CHAPTER 18 - PROFESSIONAL HUMAN..215
Support System **217** Wake Up **220** Bargain Or Burden? **221** It May Not Be Your Job **222** Choose A Goal And Commit To It **223** The Way To Be Accomplished And Competent Is To Be Committed **224** Participate In Your Life **225**

CHAPTER 19 - RESPONSIBILITY ISN'T AS BAD AS IT SOUNDS......................227
You Don't Owe Anyone Your Life **228** Never Do Anything You Wouldn't Want To See On The Front Page Of The New York Times **229** The Reason Not To Violate Your Integrity Is That Your Self-Esteem Will Suffer **229** If You Decide It's Necessary To Compromise Your Integrity To Accomplish Your Goal, Be Sure You Can Live With The Legal and Emotional Consequences **230** Honor **231** Gossip **234** Live It, Don't Talk It **236**

CHAPTER 20 - THE ROAD TO MASTERY...239
Transitions **240** Turn It Around And Make It Work For You **242** Be A Master, Not A Slave **243** If Your Heart Is Right, Your Mind Follows **244** The Answer Is Inside Of You **245** I'd Rather Be Me **247** What Can You Do For Heaven On Earth, The Planet? **248** The Tree Of Life **249**

EPILOGUE...251

WORKBOOK...253
Exercise 1: Create Your Life The Way You Want It Now **254** Exercise 2: How Much Energy Am I Spending To Maintain What I Don't Want In My Life? **258** Exercise 3: Patterns **262** Exercise 4: Creating A Family Map **268** Exercise 5: You're Trapped By Your Limits **272** Exercise 6: Exploring Your Capsule **275** Exercise 7: I Do Windows **277** Exercise 8: Dreams **279** Exercise 9: Would You Rather Be Right Than Happy? **281** Exercise 10: Who Are The Victims/Tyrants In Your Life? **283** Exercise 11: First Things First **287** Exercise 12: When Life Gets You Down, Remember The Good Times, Too **288** Exercise 13: Addictions **290** Exercise 14: Anger Is Another Name For Fear And Insecurity **291** Exercise 15: Conquering Fear **296** Exercise 16: Procrastination Is Putting Off Until Tomorrow What Will Make You Anxious Today **298** Exercise 17: Prejudice **300** Exercise 18: What Have You Done That's So Awful? **301** Exercise 19: What's Your Secret? **303** Exercise 20: To Build Self-Confidence, Think Of All The Things You've Done Successfully **304** Exercise 21: My Wife Has PMS And A Gun **305** Exercise 22: Do Your Homework **306** Exercise 23: Do It Anyway **308** Exercise 24: Honor **310**

FURTHER READING...313

INDEX...315

PREFACE

How do you explain a life and the development of a philosophy in a few pages at the beginning of a book? I suppose the simplest thing I could say is that I am a person who has experienced my own suffering. I truly know that everything I see in clients exists in some facet in me. There is nothing that you feel that I have not felt.

Primarily, I have been educated by my own experience. I have lived the message of this book. I have been in trouble. Big trouble. I have sat on the floor of my room holding on to the bed rail for fear I would fling myself out a window. I know how it feels to want to die. I know how it feels to think that everything is so fouled up the only answer is death. I have cried for days, weeks, months at a time. I have known despair, self-loathing, and the desire to have it all be over now. I have made major mistakes. I have embarrassed myself, disappointed others, suffered great guilt, and hated myself thoroughly. I have been through this process, not once but many times.

At this point in my life, I am grateful for my many "dark nights of the soul," because I can understand things much better than I could when I still thought I could do it all "the right way." I have learned that there is no right way. There is only experience and learning.

I celebrate my "failures" because they have spurred me on to learn more, to be more. I celebrate all that I have done as having been part of my evolution as a human being. I am not proud of everything I have done and been, but I accept it all, and have learned from it. It has been valuable.

I have been a therapist for 15 to 17 years, depending on where one starts to count. I started out following the psychosocial treatment plan, the rules I learned in graduate school, but quickly threw that out and started flying by the seat of my pants. I have tried and used almost every known therapeutic modality. I am not a Freudian or a Gestaltist or even a contextual psychotherapist. I simply attempt to be with a client in whatever way will prove most healing.

I have always believed that love is what heals. I also believe in doing whatever works. What works with one person is not necessarily what works with another.

I discovered early on that one can talk about anything the client can relate to and the therapeutic process will work. In other words, if what the client understands is auto mechanics, then using metaphors from auto mechanics to explain life and behavior is what will move the process along for him.

I do not always succeed. There are people for whom my brand of "magic" does not work, but, when it does, it is thrilling beyond description. It nurtures me, it fulfills me, it uplifts me.

Throughout the years, I have been absolutely determined to grow and to learn as much as I can. One of the things that I love about life is the realization that it is never done. There is always more to learn. I sincerely hope that there are no finite answers to life's questions.

I began this book last spring when I realized that, of the children in my life to whom I am closest, the four oldest would be emerging into the world. They are not my babies. They are my nephew, niece, and godchildren, to whom this book is dedicated.

I decided I would write something that would be a constant reminder of the love that surrounds them. I wanted it to be something permanent, that would be there for them when they needed it.

As I considered this, my protective instincts were at the fore. I could well understand how their mothers, recognizing that their children are now adults, felt about having to let go.

What, I wondered, if anything could I say to these young people that might make their way a little easier? How could I safeguard them from making the same mistakes I have made? What would help them understand the sometimes chaotic world in which we live?

At almost the same time, I made a decision to move to another part of the country, leaving behind treasured and beloved clients. I wished that I could also give them something to remember, to help them keep track of the things we had learned together.

Thus was born the idea of *The Portable Therapist*. I had for many years been keeping a collection of notes and thoughts. I turned these into a book that could serve as a guide for troubled times. And so *The Portable Therapist* was written with two major purposes in mind. First, to introduce and reinforce certain basic ideas which might be generally helpful in living life. Second, to be a kind of adult security blanket. It is not meant to be a substitute for therapy. It is not even intended as an adjunct to therapy. It is simply a self-help book from me to you.

There may be times when you may not be able to get to your therapist or minister or friend and could use a handy aid. *The Portable Therapist* is meant to be sort of a "cliff notes" for therapy. It is not that you don't have to read the original text, or take the course, or do the work, it is just that you may want a study guide to help.

Each day as I sat down to write, I said a prayer that I be allowed to write in a way that would be healing, comforting, and empowering. I wanted to give you something to hang on to at those moments when it is most difficult to hang on, and thereby provide a feeling and a reality that you are never alone.

You may be angry and upset about some of the ideas in this book. I hope you are. It means I did my job well. I hope it gets you moving in the direction of your own growth, or helps you continue on a voyage already in progress.

I am The Portable Therapist. Carry me with you. Let me sit on your shoulder and whisper in your ear. Use this book in whatever way is helpful to you. Read it cover to cover. Flip through it idly when you have the time. Do an exercise or meditation. Mark those sections which mean the most to you. Read the end first, or the middle. Carry it in your purse or briefcase. Keep it by your bed. Sleep with it. Put a copy in the bathroom. Use it whenever you need a hand to hold or something to lean on. It will be there. It is your book, to be used as you see fit.

ACKNOWLEDGMENTS

An author does not just sit down and write a book. There are many people involved in the process. Certainly that has been the case with *The Portable Therapist*. A therapist learns how to do therapy from his or her own therapist(s) and teachers; mine include Frank Sorensen, M.D.; The Reverend John Fitzgerald Robohm, III; Judy Ostrander, M.R.E.; Dale Ostrander; Allen Gilmore, Ph.D.; Virginia Hoover; Vince Sweeney, M.D.; Jane Donner, Ph.D.; Robert Shaw, M.D.; and Brian Regnier. Wherever I was in my training and development, they were rungs above me. From them I have learned that the essence of therapy is love. I am not sure that any of them ever said that in so many words, but that was the message, and they lived it.

They also taught me that to be willing to be honest with and about oneself is crucial to the therapeutic relationship. Ultimately, all any of us have to offer is our humanity. That is as it should be.

In addition, I would like to thank Werner Erhard and the January B 1983 Est Training, Rabbi Abraham Weissman, David Coonrad, D.C., Rev. Shirley Lemmon, and Donald, Paul, and Sadie Haynes, who have taught me about love and about life.

My editor, Lillie Mikesell, the Max Perkins of our generation, provided support, encouragement, guidance, and nurturance, without which this book would not have been written.

Karen Byers, Peggy Lingle, and Gary Skipworth gave valuable comments and input on the manuscript.

The influence and support of the International Women's Writing Guild (IWWG) has been so great in my life that I would like all who read *The Portable Therapist* to have access to information and membership. You can write to IWWG c/o Hannelore Hahn, Executive Director, IWWG, Box 810, Gracie Station, New York, NY 10028. Specifically, I would like to thank Hannelore and IWWG members Susan Baugh, Elizabeth Greenbacker, and Alice Harron Orr. My participation in the guild and association with these women has been one of the most empowering experiences in my life.

I also want to acknowledge all of my clients who have taught me and those who asked for this book. I am grateful for all that you have brought to my life individually and collectively. I love you all.

To Robb, Sandy, Walt, and Joann: thank you for sharing your children and for teaching me so much through your parenting and your friendship.

And especially to Guido, Studley, and Curley, my best friends, who hounded me into writing this book.

PART ONE
The Journey Begins

1

GETTING STARTED: OPTIONS

HOW MANY THERAPISTS DOES IT TAKE TO CHANGE A LIGHT BULB?*

Therapy may well be one of the most thrilling experiences available in life. It opens doors you did not know existed, let alone those you thought were closed. It is like getting an education in yourself and in life. It is an incredible gift to give to yourself. Although it is sometimes a painful process, and quite difficult in some ways, it is no more painful or difficult than your life. From it will come pearls, jewels of rare beauty to hold up to the light and give your life a new perspective.

Therapy does work. It is not an exact science. It may, in fact, be more of an art than a science. Psychotherapy literally means "soul healing," and for many people it is the difference between life and death. For most it is the difference between joy and despair.

Find the therapist who is right for you and luxuriate in the love, the support, and the learning that will be yours. It will be one of the most intimate and valuable relationships you will ever have. Far from being a sign of being crazy, entering therapy is evidence of courage, strength, and good sense. You will emerge wiser, happier, and more loving than you can now imagine. These are goals worthy of some time and money.

*****NONE. IT HAS TO WANT TO CHANGE*

The idea that you have to be crazy to be in therapy is crazy. In the last decade of the twentieth century, it is probably crazy not to be in therapy.

This is not to say that therapy is for everyone. It is not. It is for people who perceive that they have a problem or problems with which they need help and which they are willing to change. It is for people who know that there has to be more to life than what they currently see, and who want to find out what that is.

Like anything in life worth having, therapy is time-consuming and arduous. One young woman who had experienced family problems all of her life was told that she needed to get into therapy and stay there. Her response was, "But I could be in therapy the rest of my life!" Referring to her family and its problems, she was advised, "That would be better than ending up like them." Therapy is an opportunity to break the chain of pathology and create new patterns of behavior and relationships that are rewarding and joyful. A good therapist is like a life coach. She is someone to teach you what you do not understand about this very complicated world. If you have more pain or confusion than you can handle by yourself, if you are consistently unable to get what you want in life, then go find yourself a good coach. It is a wise investment to make in yourself, and one which will pay handsome dividends.

YOU DON'T HAVE TO STAY IN THERAPY FOREVER

Some schools of therapy say that you have to stay in therapy until they plant you. It is not your job to let your therapist collect your Medicaid. It is the therapist's job, and yours, to get you as healthy as possible as quickly as possible, and back into the world. You can resume therapy later if you feel the need.

No one gets to tell you that you have to stay in therapy. It is your life. You get to decide. A therapist may tell you that in his considered opinion it is not a good time to quit therapy. It is still your decision. If it's a mistake, you can always go back. It is your job to live your life. Your therapist is a teacher and a coach. You can choose to quit taking lessons at any point when you feel it is necessary or warranted.

The idea that you have to stay in therapy forever prevents many people from ever getting into it in the first place. If you know that you are in charge of the door, that it swings both ways and you are not locked in, it will be less frightening to start.

No one should require you to be so dependent on her that you cannot live your life equably without her. That is not therapy. It's enslavement. At that point, the therapist needs to look at her own needs and motivations. They may be quite pure: she may sincerely believe that you will run amuck without guidance. Nonetheless, it is your right to run amuck. You might even learn more that way; no one can be sure.

Resistance is always a factor in therapy. It is healthy and natural. The therapist is trained to expect it and to deal with it. There will be times when the going is rough, when you may want to quit. You learn how to recognize that and to know that you need to continue. But if you feel a strong need or desire to quit or to take a break, that is your business. You are the one who will have to deal with the consequences.

Do not let anyone intimidate you into staying in therapy longer than you want to stay. You should be allowed to leave when you choose to do so without punishment, guilt, or threats of impending doom.

The work continues all of your life, but it does not have to be in the context of formal therapy. If you believe you can't live without your therapist of twenty years, think about what that says. It is unlikely that you are that crazy or that damaged. Do you want to be that dependent? Have you been trained to think you can't make it on your own? That is not empowering.

CHOOSING A THERAPIST

Choosing a therapist can be a complicated process. Or an easy one. It depends on your needs and your circumstances.

The best way to find a good therapist is through a friend who is in therapy with someone with whom he or she has achieved results and had a positive experience. It may not mean that this is the therapist for you, but it is a good place to start. If you visit your friend's therapist and decide he or she is not right for you, ask for a referral.

It is also fine to "therapy shop." Some people will disagree with that idea, but your therapist will be one of the most important people in your life. It is essential that you choose carefully. If a potential therapist tells you that he or she does not allow therapy shopping and you must commit now, leave and go see someone else.

On the other hand, shopping for a therapist can become a self-defeating game. If you have been to more than a few therapists and cannot find anyone right for you, think about what you are doing. Make a choice and stick with it.

It is important to remember that therapists are people. They are not always right, and you may have a personality conflict with one of them. It is perfectly all right to admit it and move on to someone else. A therapist is a guide, a teacher, a coach. The best ones have had problems of their own that they have dealt with in their own therapy and training. The particular clinician's choice of approach is probably less important than how you feel about him or her and how you get along.

It is important for the two of you to bond. The therapist is going to have to play many roles for you. He or she should be kind, gentle, supportive, flexible, and concerned. It may also be necessary to be fairly tough with you at times and confront you with the issues you face. A therapist should not be a professional hand holder sympathizing with you. That will get you nowhere. Neither should a therapist be brutal, combative, seductive, baiting, or controlling.

If you find someone you think is wonderful, who is clearly caring and empowering, then hang on and go for it. You have struck pay dirt.

Just as each therapist brings an altogether unique personality to the therapeutic relationship, so too there are a number of different kinds of psychotherapy. There is no right one. There is only the one that works for you. A combination of one or more approaches may be useful and even necessary in treating what ails you.

Psychiatrists are medical doctors licensed to prescribe medication and hospitalize patients in need of round-the-clock care. They are also, although not always, psychoanalysts, meaning that they may have a pronounced Freudian point of view.

Psychologists do psychotherapy, often behavior modification, and are trained to work with learning disorders and disabilities. They also do psychological testing and give intelligence quotient (IQ) tests.

Clinical social workers are trained to see the individual in the context of the environment in which he or she lives and works. They may adopt any of the current therapies for their use. They often work in clinics, hospitals, or church settings. Many clinical social workers are in private practice.

Pastoral psychotherapists are ministers and lay people trained in combining theology with psychotherapy.

The last three groups of people all work with clients who do not require regular medication or hospitalization.

You may find your therapist in any of these four groups. A therapist's first job is to help you discover which professional will be most appropriate for you. If you are referred to another therapist, it is not a rejection. It is simply a very professional attempt to help you get the best help possible. Gender is sometimes an important issue. Some people will work better with a man, some with a woman. Trust the professional to help you make these decisions.

In addition to therapy, there are encounter groups, sensitivity training seminars, and workshops, which may all be helpful adjuncts to your therapy.

Beginning with Alcoholics Anonymous (AA), 12-step programs for almost every conceivable problem have proliferated. They are worthwhile and powerful programs. Consider adding a 12-step program to your therapeutic plan. Therapy will not cure alcoholism or drug addiction. However, a combination of therapy and AA or one of its derivatives is effective indeed.

Discuss all of these options with your therapist on an on-going basis. With all the help available, take all you can get. It will move you along that much faster.

If your therapist wants you to come two or more times a week, she is not after your money, or trying to suffocate you. She is simply trying to give you the maximum support and move you along as quickly as possible. Alcoholics Anonymous requires 90 meetings in the first 90 days. It is a strategy that is designed to support, stabilize, and strengthen you at the time you most need it. The same is true for going to therapy as often as the therapist deems important or necessary.

If your therapist wants to put you in group therapy in addition to individual sessions, it does not mean you are crazier than you thought. It means you have learned and grown enough to take advantage of the tremendous opportunities for growth that group psychotherapy involves.

Your therapist, group, or 12-step program may well be your life saver. Do not fight the life guard. No one can do anything for you that you are not willing to have done. You have to cooperate and participate.

It is useful to see whatever help you are seeking as someone giving you a rung up on a ladder. Take hold of that ladder and scurry up. Take advantage of the assistance. That's why it is there. If you stand around deciding whether or not to get on the ladder, complain your therapist is not holding it steady enough, get on but refuse to move, or think he should push you the rest of the way, nothing much is going to happen. The trick is to get a good therapist and be an active patient. Then things happen quickly and dramatically.

If you consider all of the different kinds of help available to you, it is easy to believe that somewhere out there is someone who can help you. To come from crisis and despair is like coming out of the tunnel into the dawn. It is a glorious feeling that not only something, but anything is possible. At least there is hope and help. It's all out there. Go find it.

NO EXCUSES NECESSARY

It is understandable that people who have had a hard time growing up will have problems as adults and need help. They may have been emotionally and physically battered, the children of alcoholics, or the victims of incest. As a society, we recognize many red flags which signal future trouble for a child. There are institutions, agencies, and individuals ready and waiting to intervene to make a difference for this kind of person.

You may feel, however, that you have no reason to have difficulties. You have no excuses and feel like the woman who says she was raised by Ozzie and Harriet. While you may not have had a traumatic time of growing up, or at least think you didn't, there are still reasons to expect that you may have some problems.

First of all, many psychological wounds occur as the result of very subtle behavior in the family. Just as a child who needs glasses does not know he or she cannot see properly, what went on in your family appeared normal to you, because you did not know that there was any other way. Children do not learn to make sophisticated distinctions until much later. What might look like a normal, apple-pie American family may in fact be riddled with underlying problems that leave deep scars on the children. Poor communication patterns, lack of communication, subtle emotional abuse, parental expectations, methods of handling anger and resolving conflicts, socio-economic status, benign neglect, the number and order of siblings, family values, and the real, if not expressed, relationship between the parents are just a few of the issues which may pose difficulties for the child.

It is hard to identify or even to verbalize any of these issues, again because to you they were "normal." For instance, you cannot understand why your marriage is in trouble while your parents have been married for 40 years. But are they happy or just living out the sentence they imposed on themselves? If you did not learn from them how to communicate or to resolve conflict, having a relationship will be difficult for you.

You may be living out your family's expectations and demands for achievement while not recognizing that that is what is making you unhappy. You would rather be a carpenter than an accountant, but that is not acceptable in your family. You may have been badly neglected, and therefore expect little or nothing from anyone. You do not understand why you feel isolated and alienated.

Not all psychological problems are caused by clear and dramatic trauma. Many are the result of subtle interactions in the family and the community to which no one would point and say, "Uh oh—that's a problem." All of this makes recognizing and dealing with the results that much more difficult.

Second, the culture we live in is very complex and difficult. It is not a healthy society and cannot possibly nurture healthy individuals. In fact, we are taught not to be individuals, but to be part of the herd. Any tendency toward individuality on a societal scale is punished. The world is frightening, hard to understand, and dangerous. America is a labyrinth of social and cultural mores which threaten to engulf the individual at any moment.

There are always reasons why you have the problems that you do. The reasons just may not be obvious. You may also have blocked from conscious memory quite painful and traumatic events which still influence your behavior.

Life itself is not a rose garden, and its lessons are many and difficult. Keeping a straight course requires great skill, strength, and determination. It is not surprising or shameful to want help to maintain one's equilibrium.

But best of all, you do not have to have an excuse. You are human. You are allowed to have problems, to be imperfect, to need help. You do not have to have a laundry list of traumas and tragedies. The only requirement for attention and support is that you want it.

WHAT CAN YOU EXPECT FROM A MAN WITH A BROKEN LEG?

EVERYTHING. That's right. Whatever your misfortune, it's no excuse. You have read stories about people with one leg or no legs learning to ski. Or paraplegic artists who paint with brushes in their teeth. Good for them! That's the spirit! The fact is that most people are handicapped in one way or another. It is very difficult, if not impossible, to grow up whole.

It is not impossible to do something about it. For instance, let us take two kids who come from a ghetto. One grows up to be a drug dealer or some other kind of criminal. The other works his way through college to become a professional. Both are handicapped, perhaps severely, but they handle it very differently.

So what if you have already become a criminal of some sort? You may think you have already taken yourself down the tubes. Think again. It is never too late. You can always choose, right now, how you want to live your life. Maybe the kid who grew up and went to college had an edge you did not. Maybe he got a little more from his family or his environment. Maybe he just had a stronger constitution.

That does not mean that it is too late for you. You can do or be anything you want. You just have to work at it. The message here is that we all do. You may think it is easier for other people. In some ways it may be. But so what? Who said it was supposed to be easy? That man with a broken leg can choose to lay on his back, go on welfare, be dependent, or he can choose to get on with his life, cast and all. You can have it your way. What do you want? What is your choice? Quit making excuses and just do it.

START WHERE YOU ARE

You have been through a bad time. You are hurting, angry, confused, embattled on every front. You do not know which way to turn. It feels like everything is out of control and you are not sure you can cope. Feelings are bottled up inside of you, ready to explode, which frightens you. You are at your wit's end. This is not how you thought it would be. It is definitely not what you want.

The first thing you need is some support. Start with you. *Ask yourself who and what you need.* Erase the blackboard which holds all of your complaints and troubles and write down the thing that you need most right now. Keep it simple. Just the absolute bottom line thing that you need this moment.

Next, *ask a friend or family member to listen to you.* Tell them exactly how you feel, perhaps not all of it, but enough to feel some relief. Imagine that you are a spray can. You don't want to puncture the can, just spray off a little bit at a time. If you tell them everything all at once, you may feel embarrassed or overwhelmed and then shut down altogether. Say enough to feel relieved and understood without necessarily going into every detail. Let them reassure you that this is all manageable. It can all be favorably resolved.

Finally, *listen to yourself.* What are you really saying? What would you say to a friend in similar circumstances? It might be helpful to say everything you want to say by talking into a tape recorder. Then listen to the tape, pretending it is someone else, and see what you think the answer would be.

What you need most of all is assurance that there is an answer, a cure, a fix. There is a way to resolve all of this and get your life back on track. You may be able to do it yourself, or it may be time to call in a professional. Whatever your decision, all problems can be resolved one way or another. It is not hopeless!

GETTING CLEAR ON THE PROBLEM

The second thing you need is clarity. In the midst of a crisis it is difficult to pinpoint exactly what the salient, critical point is. Everything looks like part of the crisis.

It is important to be able to focus on the problem the way a camera focuses on the object to be photographed. For instance, if you take a picture of your living room couch, you can move everything out of the way and focus the camera in such a way that the coffee table, the pile of papers on the floor, the kids' toys, and your shoes do not appear in the photo. All that is seen is the couch and the painting over it.

In the same way, focusing in on what the problem really is requires shutting out all the extraneous details. Part of what creates the problem is the feeling of being overwhelmed, not just by the problem but by the details.

As an example, let us say that your business is in trouble. You are in danger of losing it. The employees are disgruntled and fighting you every step of the way. Creditors are on your back, threatening to sue. The people who owe you money are behind and say they can't pay now. While your customers appear to be currently satisfied, vendors are refusing to ship new merchandise on credit. You will soon have nothing to sell. Your lease is up and the landlord wants to increase your rent substantially and give you a different parking place. Several pieces of expensive equipment need to be repaired or replaced. You have not had a vacation in two years. You are exhausted. Your trusted secretary who has run much of the behind-the-scenes show is pregnant and leaving in two weeks. Your top salespeople are aware of what is happening and are looking for new jobs. Two have already left. The IRS is breathing down your neck. Your stomach hurts, your head throbs, you live on coffee and scotch and never take time to eat. You walk in at 6 a.m. to discover that the coffee maker in your office is broken and will not give a drop. There is nowhere nearby to get a cup of coffee at this hour of the morning. You collapse in your chair. The absolute last straw. How can you run a business without coffee? At that moment your spouse calls, angry that you are never home. You feel like pulling out your hair.

This is the time to focus. There are at least eighteen problems in the preceding paragraph. The trauma of a crisis is that they all appear to be of equal importance. In fact, under great stress, the broken coffee maker may take on major significance. How can you get anything done without a coffee pot? That is definitely putting the coffee pot before the horse.

The point of this exercise is not to point out what the real, or biggest, problem is in this scenario. The point is to emphasize the importance of isolating the one or two biggest problems that need to be dealt with right now. You cannot take it all on at once. The trick is to attack that issue which is generating the rest. You do that by getting clear about what is a crisis issue and what is not. What has to be handled immediately right now and what can wait until tomorrow? What is major and what is minor?

You can do that in any way that works for you. Sit down with your therapist, a friend, your accountant, anyone you think can help. Make lists. Make charts. Do whatever you have to do to arrive at clarity. If you know what the problem is, it can then be handled.

LIFE IS MANAGEABLE

A thirty-five year old woman with two years of sobriety and three years of therapy became very thoughtful in a recent session. When asked what she was thinking, she looked up with tears in her eyes and asked, "Does life ever get manageable? My life has been unmanageable for so long it seems to me that it may not be possible to manage it at all."

Life is manageable. If your life feels unmanageable at the moment, take heart. You can learn to manage it. Very often people are not taught that difficult problems can be solved, or even how to handle the everyday realities of life. A good teacher can help you learn how to make life a manageable affair.

There are some very obvious things that you may not have been taught. If your life is really out of control, these are some simple guidelines that may help you. They may sound ridiculously simple, but they are a good place to start:

Go to work on time.
Stay the full time.
Do your job.
Don't get into power struggles with your boss, or co-workers.
Do what is asked and expected.
Pay your bills when they are due.
Don't spend more than you make.

If you can't pay your bills on time, communicate with the people involved. Most people can deal with anything, if they know what is going on with you. It is when you disappear and stick your head in the sand that you create the problem.

Pay attention to your needs. Set up a schedule for your personal life and stick to it. Buy groceries on Monday, do laundry on Tuesday, run errands on Wednesday, pay bills on Thursday, and clean house on Friday. Do it in whatever way it works for you. Having a schedule will help make your life workable.

Plan. Save a little money weekly for holiday gifts, vacations, and major expenditures. Remember to save monthly for those quarterly insurance or IRS payments. Buy panty hose several pairs at a time on sale so you don't have to run out in the morning to get some on the way to work. There are many items in your life with which you can use the same strategy. The clearer you can be about the demands of your life, the better you can plan for them and the more manageable life will be.

Try to balance your work and your play. Do not overdose in either area. Keep your promises. Meet or call people when you say you will. If you can't, call to let them know that you can't. It will prevent people from being upset with you.

As you emerge from the fog of depression and crisis, your life becomes much clearer. When you have learned to manage your life, you will have fewer crises and fewer reasons to be upset. Then you can begin to discover what is enjoyable about life. You can get there; it will not take long.

CREATE YOUR LIFE THE WAY YOU WANT IT NOW

There are three possible positions in life: victim, tyrant, or champion. The champion takes responsibility for his or her life, the victim and the tyrant do not. The act of being responsible allows the individual to create his or her own life consciously. We create our lives anyway. All of it. Whether it is a painful nightmare or a wonderful adventure is determined by your attitude. You can CREATE YOUR LIFE THE WAY YOU WANT IT NOW. How do you do that? By being responsible; by expecting more from yourself; by growing up; and by not living out of the drama of your past, by not "living out of your story."

You are probably saying to yourself, "What is that supposed to mean?" It means that you can take conscious control of your life right NOW. Not soon, not someday, but now.

It is easy. Really. Just sit down and give some real thought to how you want it to be. Then start making lists. *Exercises 1 and 2* in the Workbook section at the back of this book will help with this process. Take a long hard look at how much energy you are using to keep in place the things you do not want to keep. What you focus on and give great thought to is what will be in your life. Have you ever noticed that all, or most, of those things you are afraid of and do not want to have happen, do? It is because you focus on and think about them a lot. You invest a lot of emotion in them. Start focusing on and thinking a lot about the things you do want. Dream about them. Imagine how it would feel to have them. Then do everything you can on a conscious level to make those things happen.

FEEDING TIME

Nature is a wonderful and wise teacher. It will teach you everything. Animals can be particularly helpful teachers.

The sea gulls on the beach at Atlantic City will flock around anyone who is willing to feed them. It is a common pastime for visitors to the boardwalk to buy popcorn to feed the gulls. Teenagers will even feed them french fries and pizza. The gulls will eat anything.

I took an excursion there in the late fall. There were fewer people on the beaches to feed the birds, which made them all the more happy to see a friendly bag of popcorn approaching. I had, in fact, purchased two large bags in anticipation of their excitement. With bags in hand I set out to cross the beach to the edge of the water, where I could entice the gulls.

Before I reached the water, I was already being followed by eager birds aware of the smell of potential goodies. As I began to throw the pieces of popcorn in the air, more and more gulls descended, as if from nowhere, to vie for their piece of the pie. It was a game. With perhaps a hundred gulls in a circle around the popcorn, they watched anxiously, some hovering in the air for the next trajectory of goodies.

There was clearly a pecking order. There were two very large and fat ones who did not fight each other but were ready to do battle with everyone else. The other birds fought, scrambled, and outwitted one another in a game of "get the food first." Watching them was a fascinating commentary on behavior, human and animal. There were the aggressors, the connivers, the sneaky, and the determined.

The best lesson of all came from a very small, skinny little bird. It was not that he was young or disabled. He clearly just did not know how to fight for his share. Recognizing his obvious difficulty, I saw him start for an available morsel only to have it snatched away by another, faster bird. Observing this scene for several minutes, I began to try to ensure that he would get some portion of the food.

I moved as closely and protectively toward this little bird as possible. I put the food as close to him as I could, moving it closer each time. Yet it was always snatched away from him. In exasperation, I finally reached down and put a piece of popcorn directly in his beak. He dropped it. It was snatched. I carefully repeated the process. The same thing happened again. Even when the food was put directly in his mouth, he managed to lose it to another bird. It occurred to me that people often behave just like this bird did. No matter what you do, they are not going to take the help that is offered.

Pay careful attention to how you deal with what is offered you. No one can do anything for you that you are unwilling to accept. Help, healing, and health cannot be forced on you. You must participate.

2

LETTING GO: THE WILLINGNESS TO CHANGE

The first rule in therapy is: YOU COME FIRST. This is a difficult notion for most people. You may even be upset by the thought. After all, we have been trained to be selfless, not selfish; thoughtful and considerate, not demanding; givers, not takers. But that is where the trouble starts.

If you are not living your life consistent with your needs, you are not helping anyone. In fact, you are actually enslaving others and, in this situation, everyone loses. Frightening as it may sound to you, you are absolutely free to do precisely as you please. All that is required is the courage and the strength to see it through.

You cannot make anyone else happy. You can only make yourself happy. Other people are not your problem. You are. Stop living what you know or have been taught and start focusing on what YOU need in order to live your life in a healthy and enlivening manner.

Others may not like it at first. Partners, friends, even your children, who are used to you behaving in certain ways, may be upset for a while at the new you. Yes, you may actually offend and even disappoint some people in your life. How awful!

But, believe it or not, they will live, and so will you. Most amazingly, through your act of courage in defying the demands of others, you will all be happier. They will learn from your example, and they will, perhaps for the first time in their lives, have the freedom to explore and express their own needs.

Yes, it is scary. But is it any worse than having to endure a bad situation that drags you down day after day? You can start by checking your assumptions as you go along. Instead of automatically reacting to the needs and demands of others—stated or implied—step back for a moment and ask yourself: "Does this make sense? Will this work for me? What do I need in this situation? What do I want for myself?"

Go ahead, be a cultural revolutionary. It is okay to try something new. This society clearly does not work well within the existing rules. Go against what is expected and be a hero—to yourself most of all.

You will like it. Others will, too. Wouldn't it be wonderful if everyone were free to be and do what he or she wants? The world would be a much happier place. Think about it.

THINK FOR YOURSELF

Start by thinking for yourself. It sounds easy enough. I do think for myself, you're saying. Good. Then let's look at how to do more of it.

Thinking for yourself means taking a hard look at your life to determine how much you are doing according to your own truth. How much of what you want or believe is what you've been taught or are expected to think?

If you are living to satisfy other people's expectations, that is not living. That is how most people start out. Unfortunately, that is also how they tend to end up. Never having explored how they might like, want, or need life to be, they either do exactly what is expected of them or exactly the opposite. In neither case is the person making choices.

Ask yourself, "What do I really want? What do I really believe?" Start with some of your most cherished political, social, or religious beliefs. Did you really decide to believe that? Do you know that from your own experience? Or are you just accepting what you have been taught, the common "wisdom?" Think about it.

What do you believe about abortion, birth control, money, power, sex, marriage? Are you thinking for yourself? Or did someone tell you to think that? Is that what everyone else thinks?

Did you become a Republican or a Democrat because that is what your family is? Or isn't? Does everyone in your family—or in your life—have to agree about everything? Family legacies are rich and powerful. But it is not always altogether what we as individuals need. Take what works for you, and leave the rest.

Much of what gets in the way of your happiness lies in the attitudes and beliefs that were forced on you by someone else. Start to challenge everything you think or believe. You may end up in the same place. But it will be your truth, not someone else's. You can live with that.

PATTERNS

"Patterns" is a word used in therapy to describe those behaviors or events which recur in a system, an individual, a family, group, or society. The purpose of an intervention is to change patterns that don't work. A family therapist is trained to take the history of a family for several generations. He or she then "maps" or "charts" that information in a way that shows how the patterns recur from one generation to the next.

In your life, patterns are those things that you do over and over until you have learned the lesson and don't repeat them anymore. For example, a certain woman always gets involved with alcoholic men. A particular man always gets fired from his jobs. There are others patterns, such as an inability to commit, a tendency to be in financial difficulty, or an inclination to attract abusive relationships. Until we have learned the lesson of these patterns, they will recur.

Give serious thought and attention to the patterns in your own life and in the history of your family. They will tell you a great deal about you and how you function. They will tell you the areas where you need to get to work on yourself. For example, if you have been molested, it is almost a guarantee that others in your family line also have been. What causes that and how can you stop the pattern?

What are the patterns in your life? They are there. Identify them. Write them down. Use *Exercises 3 and 4* in the Workbook section to help you do this.

Take a long hard look at your patterns. What are they? What do you need to do about them? How do you feel about them? Is that how it was in your family? What do you need to learn in order to break the patterns? Are you willing to have it continue? Do you want to break it? If you know something is wrong, but cannot identify it, ask a friend to help you. Talk it over. What does he or she see?

Patterns are often subtle, insidious, and difficult to identify in the beginning. With practice and determination, recognizing them becomes easier. Keep after it. The rewards are worth the trouble.

As you identify patterns and work with them, they begin to disappear. They no longer have any power over you. You can control them by making conscious decisions about whether or not to continue them. You will attract different people because you have handled the underlying emotion, belief, or interpretation of events that held that pattern in place.

Patterns are not absolute or written in stone. They are merely a way of identifying and categorizing what happens with you, in a way that will help you work with it. Do not give the patterns power by deciding that that is the way it is and will always be. You have the power to change. The reason you identify the pattern is so that you will know what it is you need to do in order to have your life be the way you want it to be.

It is not necessarily complicated. Keep it simple. See how it is, see how you want it to be, and make the necessary changes. All that is necessary is your identification of the genesis of the pattern in yourself and in your family. Have the attendant feelings, identify the interpretation and belief that hold it in place, and you are home free. You can then establish your own chosen pattern of healthy, satisfying behavior. Be willing to change.

IF YOU'RE UNWILLING TO CHANGE, YOU'RE STUCK IN THE RUT AND IT WILL ALWAYS BE LIKE THIS

Many people come to therapy with a hidden agenda. They say they want things to change in their lives. They really don't. What they want is for the therapist to fix the problem without requiring them to change.

It doesn't work that way. Nothing is going to be any different in your life unless you are different. Change does not occur outside of you. You know that. You may not know that you know, but it will become clear if you think about it for a moment. You have changed your hair and your clothes and your job and your spouse, but all the problems are still with you. That isn't to say that those changes may not be necessary and good. But they should come as a result of internal change rather than as an attempt to avoid it. Change, real change, occurs only as a result of a change inside of you.

That may be disappointing and disheartening to hear. You may not even believe it. You may be convinced that you can do it from the outside. Keep trying. Eventually you will figure it out, because you will still be unhappy and unsatisfied.

You may also be convinced that you cannot change. You probably cannot, not in any appreciable way, by yourself. Sorry, but it's true. There is a remedy. Get yourself a good teacher, therapist, or coach (whether professional, friend, or minister) and learn how to change. Let someone help you. Then it's not only possible, it can be great fun.

We all hate change. All of us. We resist it mightily. It is frightening. It is upsetting. It shakes us up and puts us down somewhere we are not sure we want to be. Some people actually experience any kind of change as a kind of death. No wonder they are afraid of it.

In fact, some kinds of change are the death of a way of being, or thinking, or living. These changes are often necessary to the continued growth of the individual. Just as nature changes with every season, human beings need to be willing to make a transition from one phase to another. The trees always get new leaves in the spring: they are not dead in winter, but only resting to bring forth new life.

The same is true of you. Just as you grow new skin every day and slough off the old, it is the natural order of things that you should also grow and change emotionally. It is when you refuse to change, to grow, that you become stagnant and diseased. It is not change that is the problem, but the refusal to change.

As children, we develop certain maneuvers to help us cope with the world. For the most part, they work very well and are a necessary part of growing up. The problem is that a child's defense system is not designed to serve the needs of the adult. The adaptive mechanisms do not work and eventually break down, leaving the adult feeling defenseless and vulnerable.

The healthy adult will create new strategies for each new situation. A football coach uses a different play for different points in the game. If necessary, he will created an entirely new play in order to win.

Change is really that simple. It involves adapting yourself and your life strategy to the current situation. That is not so frightening. It can be lots of fun and very exciting.

Even when it is frightening or painful, it is better than stagnation. It takes strength. It takes some courage. But you've got that. After all, doesn't it take a lot of strength to hold on to the way it is? It does. Just turn that strength around and use it to build the willingness to change.

The willingness to change is the absolute key to a fulfilling and satisfying life. It is not fun to feel stuck. That rut you think is so comfortable and safe becomes boring and painful. It is actually a shallow grave. Are you willing to change?

WHAT CAN YOU DO TODAY, THIS MINUTE, TO BE HAPPIER?

It's up to you. You have a choice. Regardless of what is going on in your life, you can do something to make yourself and your life better. You may have very real reasons for being unhappy. In truth, if you look for it, there is almost always something over which to be sad, anxious, or angry. It is always possible to whip up some sort of drama. Does that make you happy? Really happy?

What are the options? What could you do this minute to make yourself happy?

Perhaps you have recently suffered the loss of a close friend or relative. You are awash in grief, guilt, and sorrow. It is hard to imagine that you will ever be happy again. No one is trying to talk you out of that. Your feelings may be entirely appropriate to the situation.

Even in the midst of a truly troubled situation, though, you can still make the choice to do something to lighten it up and be happier. Go to a funny movie. Make homemade ice cream. Do something exhilarating that you have been postponing: white water rafting, or parasailing. Go to a concert in the park, listen to beautiful music, and sit surrounded by happy picnickers. There is something that you can do right now to take your mind off your troubles. You don't have to sit and stew in a sea of sorrow. You can make a choice to work with yourself in such a way that this depression will pass more quickly, if not easily.

Ask yourself if what you're upset about deserves as much attention as you are giving it. Is it really that big a problem, or is it part of a soap opera in which you are playing a role? Would you feel better if you gave up the drama? It's up to you. You have a choice. It's hard to see that you have an option when you are in the middle of the drama, but you do. You always have the freedom to change your mind, your point of view, and your attitude.

If you are upset because your spouse is not behaving as expected, examine whether there is really a problem or whether you are using that as an excuse to keep distance between you.

Are you really miserable and unhappy at work? Are you helpless to change the situation? Or is your martyrdom about your job how you control your family while reaping the benefits of being a victim? Do you really not have any friends? Or are you shutting everyone out?

Are you in desperate financial trouble and truly overwhelmed by it? It is possible that being financially strapped lets you avoid taking care of or being responsible to or for others. You get lots of sympathy. Have you done this long enough? Are you ready for it to change? What can you do this minute to correct the situation? There are remedies. Find them.

Unless you are wedded to your unhappiness, there is something you can do NOW to climb out of the "slough of despond." The choice is up to you. Sorrow and misery. Happiness and joy. What's your choice?

You can start by looking at who you're blaming for your troubles. Are you blaming one or both of your parents? They are everyone's favorite scapegoat. Are you ready for an important truth?

YOUR PARENTS DID THE BEST THEY COULD

People are sometimes reluctant to get into therapy because they think therapists blame everything on the parents. They are concerned about being disloyal and unfair to their parents.

It is obvious that your parents have a great deal to do with how you function today. They may have made many mistakes which were profoundly hurtful to you. You may have a great deal of underlying hurt and anger at them. After all, they were the most important people in your life during the most important part of your development. If you are going to grow up and be a whole, healthy person, you are going to have to deal with those feelings, therapy or no therapy.

The job in therapy is to help you understand yourself and others, to heal old wounds, to extinguish self-defeating behaviors, and to help you learn balance and responsibility. While you may need to talk about your parents and deal with all kinds of feelings about them, it is not a healthy or constructive attitude to take the position of a victim who blames your tyrannical, brutish parents.

Therapy should help you to understand all sides of the question. Yes, you have your feelings, and they are real and valid. But so did they. To begin to understand your parents and their pressures and problems will help you have more compassion for everyone, including yourself.

Parenting is a nearly impossible job. It may literally be impossible to raise a healthy child/adult in this culture at this time, if in fact it ever was possible. Think of the guilt you have about your children, or would have if you were rearing a child. How different would you be as a parent now than you would have been five or more years ago?

Yes, they made mistakes. They are only human. They may not have given you enough love. There may have been little love. But it was all they had. Chances are great they had just as difficult a time growing up as you did. Perhaps worse. Parents frequently give more than they were given. After all, they have learned from their own parent's mistakes.

You were not the only thing in their lives. They had the rest of the family, problems in the marriage or marriages, their jobs, finances, health, emotional problems of their own. They were not the super-human gods you expected them to be.

If you are still blaming your parents for your life, you have not learned the most important and basic lesson: you are responsible for you. Certainly you have feelings, which may be entirely appropriate to the situation, but if you are still blaming, with no understanding and compassion for them, and no gratitude for the things they did right, you have a long way to go.

It won't help to punish them. It's all over. It's all in the past. This is now. To spend your life hating them is a tragic waste of energy and will block your own growth and development dramatically. Be willing to forgive them and acknowledge what they did for you. They did the best they could.

YOU DON'T HAVE TO LIVE OUT OF YOUR STORY

Everyone has a hard time. Everyone. You may think some people have had it easy. They haven't.

You have a choice. You can live out of your story, the tragedy or drama of your life. You may continue to create soap opera for yourself. Most people do. Many are addicted to soap opera. Eventually, if you are smart, you will notice two things. One is that the same things keep happening to you over and over again. The second is that all of this becomes incredibly boring. Whatever it looks like early on is what it looks like later. Nothing changes. How many times do you have to do the same things before you learn?

For instance, a woman marries a man who turns out to be an alcoholic. They have a miserable life together and then divorce. Guess who she marries next? You're right. Another alcoholic. She has learned nothing. She is still living out of her story, she is still the hard luck kid. That is how patterns work.

People live out of their stories because they offer a good excuse. They allow people to not do anything about their lives. After all, they are victims. Look what the world has done to them! Other people will initially be sympathetic and understanding to their tales of woe, but eventually will get bored and decide it is too painful to stand around and watch them suffer.

Remember: what can you expect from a man with a broken leg? What is the option? The option is to create your life the way you want it now.

IF YOU DON'T ROCK THE BOAT, IT GROWS BARNACLES ON THE BOTTOM

Are you so afraid of change that you want to keep everything exactly the way it is? Does even the least little change throw you and upset you?

Are you committed to keeping everyone around you happy at all costs? Will you give ground on every issue just to keep the peace? Are you terrified that someone may disapprove of or dislike you?

Then you are a "peace-at-any-price" person. That means you may well be a good candidate for cancer. Does that sound crazy to you? Cancer patients are among the nicest people in the world. Their anger is all buried deep inside them, rarely if ever seeing the light of day. Everyone likes them. They are so nice. They never rock the boat.

If that idea doesn't frighten you, it should. Life is not always calm and peaceful, or even and unchanging. Pay attention to nature. Nature, at least in most places, changes four times a year, and during that year it is constantly evolving. In addition to seasonal changes, nature transforms moment to moment. One minute it is sunny and calm, the next the wind has come up, the clouds are darker and rolling, and it rains. Nature does not stand still. Neither should you.

If you are locked into a position of always being nice, mollifying, placating, maintaining the status quo, and keeping the peace, you are in a dangerous position indeed. All of those attitudes come with a very high price.

The price of denying your individuality, your personal needs, wants, and desires, is self-expression and growth in any arena. This is not to say that you should be embattled at all times, fighting over every detail of every issue. But if you never rock the boat, it grows barnacles on the bottom. You are the oar. Have you been out for a sail lately or have you been safely moored in your slip at the marina? That kind of existence is not only boring, it can and will result in "dis-ease."

The need to keep everything peaceful and calm comes from fear of rejection. You believe that if you do not do what others want at all times, they won't love or want you. But, if they really won't love you if you kick up just a little bit of a storm, then they don't love you anyway. That's conditional love.

It is very probable that they do in fact love you enough to let you be a little feistier. The first time or two you try it, they may react strongly and try to push you back into place. After all, you have trained them to expect you to let them have their way and never say anything. It is quite a shock to see you come alive and see you be assertive and powerful. Don't quit trying.

Stand up and rock the boat a little harder. It might be frightening at first, but you will get used to it. There's no stopping you now. Go for it. Be willing to grow up.

GROWING UP IS HARD...

What does that mean? What does it mean to be grown up and what is hard about it? It means being independent and responsible for your life and giving up victimization and drama. Sound simple? Not at all. Most people are not grown up. They are just an older version of what they have always been. We seem to learn very little, and most of that almost by accident.

A grown-up is usually defined as someone who had the stuffing knocked out of them enough to conform nicely, expect little, and work hard. A grown-up is defined as "stable," meaning that, for the most part, nothing is allowed to change and the routine is maintained in a consistent manner. That's not a grown-up, that's a zombie.

Growing up means taking absolute responsibility for your life. Whatever happens is on your shoulders. Many stable, grown-up people still have not taken responsibility for their lives. They have simply learned to follow the rules well. At one level, it seems easier to remain irresponsible and dependent; a victim. No one will really expect much from you. Growing up may actually seem the harder choice. You have no one left to blame, no one to depend on, there is no one to sympathize with you in your drama. There is only you. But by taking responsibility for your own life, there is also freedom and strength and power and joy.

If you take responsibility for your life, you can change it. You can make it whatever you want it to be. If you're thinking, "But I am responsible," look again. At some very deep level you are not. There is someone you blame; someone you expect to bail you out. Keep looking. You'll see it.

...NOT GROWING UP IS HARDER

What are the consequences of not growing up? People who are obviously not grown up are easily identifiable. The beggar, the bum, the institutionalized (except for those people with organic illnesses), and those who, late into their lives, are still living with relatives, are obviously adult children. Most of the rest of us are also not grown up, but it is harder to tell. Whether or not we grow up is entirely up to us. All it takes is strength and courage and determination.

We have a vision of children as happy and carefree. But wait a minute. Remember your childhood? It wasn't so happy and carefree. You were powerless, at the mercy of those around you and your environment. You had little or no power to affect your surroundings. That's where all those maladaptive behaviors began. No matter how benign your caretakers, it was still they who decided your fate, not you.

Most adults carry that position into early adulthood. We marry people like our parents, who, unconsciously, we expect to continue the same patterns. They usually do. Therein is the rub.

There comes a critical point, often when we are around thirty years old, when we have to decide if we want to continue this pattern. Prior to that, if we are awake at all, we notice that this isn't as good a deal as we had thought. Being a child married to a child becomes stultifying. Professions, careers, jobs are all chosen because we are reacting to or against our families.

To not grow up means to still be a child. You have no power, or very little, to affect your life except through manipulation and passive aggression. Relationships don't work or are so miserable as to be unbearable. There is little or no satisfaction in your chosen work. After all, you didn't really choose it. You either feel overwhelmed by the demands of everyone in your life, or have no one close enough to make any demands. You literally do not know how to get what you want. You probably don't even know what you want.

Substance abuse, drugs, alcohol, sugar, food, cigarettes, money: all can become problems. Your drug of choice may ultimately take your life. How many people do you know who are bitter, angry, and disappointed? The price of not growing up is being limited, a victim.

YOU'RE TRAPPED BY YOUR LIMITS

If you think you can't, think again. You can do it. You can grow up. You think you can't because you have set a limit on yourself. That limit comes through your beliefs, interpretations of events in your life, emotions, or societal sanctions. You are as powerful as you think you are.

You can be or do anything you want to be or do if you are willing to pay the price. What is the price? The price is being willing to investigate your belief system and give up limiting beliefs and personal interpretations. It is not always easy to ferret them out. The hardest beliefs to recognize are unconscious; you aren't even aware of self-imposed limits. Get busy with your lists again.

Use *Exercise 5* in the Workbook to think about and write out in detail the past events which you believe limit you. Exactly how would you like your life to be? Why it can't be that way? Do you see that all those things are interpretations you do not have to accept? Commit to having life be the way you want it to be. Be determined. Then deal with the source of your limits. If you find obstacles along the way, find a way to get beyond them. You created the obstacle. It is a function of what you think and feel. Make new interpretations. Find out what it is in you that insists on keeping you limited and get rid of it.

Men can cry. They do needlepoint. Women can travel alone. Women are capable of mechanical or physical labor. People of color can be achievers and be financially successful. Poor people can get an education. Handicapped people can lead a normal life and do normal things.

You are entitled to be, do, and have everything you want by the simple fact that you live and breathe. If you are determined to make it happen, if you know that you deserve it, you can do it. Get busy and make it happen. Refuse to be limited.

FEAR IS YOUR ENEMY

As Franklin D. Roosevelt once said, "The only thing we have to fear is fear itself." A very wise and true statement. Fear and guilt may be the two most destructive forces in the human psyche. Much pain, suffering, and pathology are based in these feelings. As long as you are pathologically fearful, as many of us are, you will be unhappy. Fear may well be the obstacle you never overcome completely.

Normal fear exists as a warning system to let you know you are doing something which may harm or endanger you. It is that healthy fear for your well-being that tells you not to walk alone at 3 a.m. on a deserted street, not to jump into an empty pool, or drink sugared drinks proffered by ministers in Guyana. It is that healthy fear that raises the hair on the back of your neck to tell you to get away from the person or the situation at hand.

Healthy fear does not tell you that all is lost, you must go hide in the corner. It is quite clear and specific about what you should or should not do. It says to you, "This is the situation, this is what you need to do about it." Healthy fear does not make you a coward, it makes you wise.

Irrational fear, which is what most of us experience most of the time, is not based in reality. It is based on the contents of the psyche, and on what the media and other people have to say.

We live in a fear-mongering culture. The story lines of our books, movies, and television shows say a great deal about the level of fear we entertain as a nation. We live with the threat of nuclear annihilation, world hunger, economic depression, natural catastrophes.

TO BE DEPENDENT IS TO BE AFRAID. If you think that your fate is up to everyone but you, naturally you are going to be afraid. You are out of control, which is terrifying for most people. Nonetheless, that is how many people live. They set up their lives so that everyone is responsible but them. Then they wonder why they are so frightened when they are surrounded by caretakers.

To the degree that you are afraid, you are unhealthy. Health can be described as the level of joy being experienced now. Joy and fear cannot cohabit. Each cancels the other.

COURAGE IS GOING AHEAD WHEN YOU ARE AFRAID

Everyone is frightened, some more, some less, but very few people are fearless. Some people are frightened by their own shadows, others only by their feelings. There are as many reasons to be frightened as there are people.

Very few fears are actually ever justified or even realistic. Transference, projection, and an all-consuming sense of inadequacy account for most of the things people fear. The issue is: what are you going to do about it?

If you let the fear stop you, you are going to be intensely frustrated and bored. You will be literally trapped by your own fear. If you're so frightened you can't get beyond the fear, get help. That's no way to live. Fear can make a prison stronger than any edifice erected by the government.

You, however, hold the key to that prison. It is courage. You may not see yourself as courageous, but you can be. You can learn to be heroic in the face of any of your fears.

We've all heard stories of people who raced into a burning building to rescue a child. Or of the person who, with Herculean strength, lifted a car off someone trapped beneath it. You could have been those people. You have that same strength and courage inside you. If you will mobilize yourself, the courage will be there.

Face the fear head on. What's the worst that could happen? Can you face that? Wait a minute, no one said that you had to like the idea of the worst case scenario. No one said you couldn't get upset if the worst happens. The question is, are you going to let it stop you? Are you really willing to let your fear control you?

What is all that fear costing you? Loneliness? Sleepless nights? Boredom? Isolation? Less success and power than you deserve? What else? What is it costing you, specifically?

Realistically, courage is defined as going ahead when you're afraid. If you wait for the fear to go away, you may never act. In order to get what you want, you must face the fear and move through it. You may still be afraid, but so what?

"So what?" is a good question to learn to ask yourself in many situations. It is particularly helpful in dealing with fear. So you're afraid. Okay. So What? What are you going to do about it?

Step out there. You'll survive. Facing your fears and going through them is one of the most exhilarating feelings in the world. It makes you realize you are strong and powerful. You are.

LEARN TO DISTINGUISH BETWEEN CRITICISM AND JUDGMENT

Taking constructive criticism is how you learn. It is a grand exercise in courage. Let your defenses down enough to listen to what someone else has to say. That doesn't mean you let anyone beat you up or criticize you constantly. You probably already do that!

Most people will believe any kind of unfair judgment made of them. That is not constructive criticism or feedback. That's just someone spouting off judgments which are probably about themselves. Learn to ignore these.

On the other hand, learn to distinguish between feedback and judgment. Judgment is worthless and often mean. Feedback opens windows in your mind to help you see yourself more clearly. Constructive criticism helps you to identify what you're doing to get in your own way. It tells you how you are shooting yourself in the foot.

The most miserable, unhappy people around refuse to listen or to learn. Consider what the other person has to say carefully, and if it fits for you, use it. If not, forget it. Know who you can trust to give you honest, kind feedback and take all she will give. If what she's saying doesn't make sense to you, tell her what you think she has said and ask her to clarify. It's not unusual for a person to miss a great piece of feedback because it's misinterpreted. Be sure you understand what is being said by feeding it back to the person saying it. That's communication. It works and it will help you a lot.

When you have experienced real communication a few times, it won't be so frightening. You'll be eager for more.

BE WILLING TO BE FOOLISH OR WRONG

Embarrass yourself as often as possible. That's how heros are born. If you live your life playing it safe, you will have a very dull life. This country has all kinds of rules about what it takes to be accepted. It varies from locality to locality, but it's all about the same thing: conformity.

We believe that if we conform to what is expected of us, we will win the approval and acceptance of others. It is important to get along with other people, but at what price? There is actually a great deal more latitude here than we tend to think or to recognize.

If others really disapprove of or dislike you, that's their problem. You do not have to follow their dictates. Yes, it is important to be thoughtful about what you say and when you say it. But the wise person knows when to be political and when to exercise some freedom. It can ultimately be very political and very wise to go against the grain. People respect those who are willing to stand up for what they believe, who are willing to say no to a tyrant, who are willing to stand alone and apart from the crowd.

Henry David Thoreau, the author of *On Walden Pond*, was willing, eager, and committed to march to a different drummer. We still admire him today because he was determined to be his own person, to listen to his own inner voice and to think for himself.

Admire yourself in this way. Do those things that will make you proud of your own conscience and strength of will. Instead of worshipping celebrities, movie stars, politicians, and people you think have "made it," you can become a person you respect and admire.

You may appear foolish or wrong to yourself or to others. But you will be alive and you will learn. Playing it safe isn't any fun. Putting your butt squarely on the line is thrilling. You will be a hero/heroine to yourself. Who else matters?

TAKE A CHANCE, TAKE A RISK

Taking a chance is another important way to learn. It's also more fun than being "cool." If you only do what you know, you won't learn much, if anything. Particularly if you're shy and timid, listen up. Taking a risk will get you some of the things you want. Be willing to be daring and outrageous. Other people actually love those qualities. Don't you admire them in others?

Risk-taking is simply doing what you want to do, going after what you want, regardless of what anyone else thinks. It's being willing to live with the judgments of others and not let those judgments—or your own—control you. You only have to give up trying to live up to what you think others will approve of and expect. Enliven yourself. It doesn't have to be a big risk. No one is saying you have to go over Niagara Falls in a barrel. That's suicidal, not daring.

But if you've dreamed of doing wonderful daring things, do them. This is the only life you have. Go for it. You won't be shot down. You will not be ostracized from the human race. You will just find out what works for you and what doesn't. Now that's not so terrible, is it? It is enlivening and exciting. Good luck. Have fun.

Think about the times in your life when you have exhibited great courage. Review your life and you will see it. There have been plenty of those times. Be proud of them and know that there are more where they came from.

3

LOOKING WITHIN:
A NEW PERSPECTIVE

Metaphorically, we all live inside a capsule of our own design. All we ever see is what's written inside our capsule. It may take a very long time for us to begin to realize that our internal reality may have absolutely nothing to do with external reality. In fact, there may be no external reality for the individual.

It is, therefore, crucial to begin to pay attention to and read what's written inside your capsule. The walls are totally covered with the hieroglyphics of your beliefs, feelings, and world view. For instance, a typical capsule might contain the following:

Girls can't...Boys don't...Real men don't...Republicans never pierce their ears...Money doesn't grow on trees...You have to work hard to get any place in this world...Still waters run deep...Men always abandon women...Men are only interested in one thing...Women are just looking for security...Be nice...Put other people first...Money and the things it will buy will make me happy...I'm nothing if I'm not SOMEBODY...All writers drink...Only bad people take drugs...The love of money is the source of all evil...Jesus died for my sins...Always be nice to your mother...Rules are meant to be broken...Education is the path to success...Women should not travel alone...The world is full of danger...Obey the rules and you won't get in trouble...Cleanliness is next to godliness...People of other races or religions are stupid, smelly, and bound for hell...Keep family business inside the family...Be respectful to your elders...Good grades mean you're smart...You can love a rich man just as easily as a poor man...Marry a professional...Food is love...Good girls don't...All politicians are dishonest...All lawyers are crooks...Psychiatrists are crazy...Rich people are snobs...Poor people are stupid or crazy or both...Change is dangerous...Original sin...Repent and be saved.

Some of these may belong in your capsule and you may have many others as well. Sit down and start a list of all your basic beliefs about yourself and the world. *Exercise 6* in the Workbook is designed to help you identify your beliefs and to help you examine them in the clear light of today. Those that work can be kept. The rest get thrown out in the spring cleaning. You can then begin to make some space to design the inside of your capsule exactly the way you want it. You don't have to accept it the way it is. By redecorating the capsule, you may enlarge it and have more room and freedom to move around.

I DO WINDOWS

The next step in cleaning and enlarging your capsule is either to uncover the boarded-up old windows, or to put in some new ones. Imagine that you are a NASA space ranger sent out into the universe many years ago with a specific set of instructions. Gradually, you find yourself hurtling through space with instructions that seem no longer to apply and you have no windows through which to see where you are going. Sound like your life? You'd better modernize that capsule forthwith!

How does one do windows in a moving spacecraft? Take the lists you have just made and go through them carefully and painstakingly, challenging each one of your beliefs. Check that belief against your reality. For example, men can—and should—cry. Women do travel alone quite safely.

Where do emotions come into this? Blocked emotions are the single biggest deterrent to putting a view in that capsule. They involve fears, guilt, shame, inhibitions, self-worth, feelings of inferiority, and negative judgments about yourself like "I'm stupid" or "I'm ugly." *Exercise 7* will help you think about the areas in your life that may be shutting out the view.

IT'S ALL INTERPRETATION

When you have cleaned your capsule and built some windows, you're ready to enlarge your view of the world. Imagine that your life is a giant prism. You're turned facing a particular angle of the prism. You are not aware of other angles or parts of the prism. Your entire life and the world are seen only from the angle of the prism through which you are looking.

What would happen if you could turn around and look through another angle? You would have a very different view. Everything would look different. With each turn, the angle of your view changes, and so does your interpretation of what you see. In the prism that you inhabit, there are an infinite number of angles and therefore an infinite number of interpretations. What you will discover as you continue to turn the prism, changing angles and viewpoints, is that your reality is all interpretation.

Stated simply, reality is not concrete. It is a function of YOUR interpretation. Think about what that realization could mean for your life. If you change your point of view, you change the interpretation. Changing the interpretation changes the experience. This concept is central to the message of this book. To understand that you can change your interpretation of you and your life and your world, simply by changing your point of view, is to know that you can transform every experience you have ever had. This is a powerful concept.

Let's go back to your original interpretation of your life, the one you developed in Exercises 6 and 7.

What was it?
What did you think it meant?
How do you feel about it?
How did it influence the way you lived your life?

Think about it and work with this concept. Sit down and write it out. Now try changing the angle. What do you see now? What is different? What have you learned? As you work with your prism, you will find that changing your point of view is not easy. It is hard to turn around at first. As you continue to work it will become easier. You can begin to learn how to change the context within which you live. The ability to transform context puts you on the road toward mastery over your life. If you want to master your life, use this concept constantly. It is one of the best tools you will ever possess.

You will learn that EVERYTHING is an interpretation. It is exciting to discover that you have the creative, intellectual, and emotional power to make an interpretation that empowers and enlivens you. You will learn that there is no intrinsic meaning in anything. It is all just someone's interpretation. In and of itself, NOTHING has any intrinsic meaning. Human beings are interpreters, meaning makers. It is one of the first things we learn to do. Something happens, we interpret it. It's automatic. We do it as babies.

The idea that everything is meaningless may at first be upsetting. It's frightening to even consider giving up all the accrued meaning of a lifetime. What would it mean to do that? NOTHING. Does it frighten you to think it means nothing? Why? There is enormous freedom in nothingness. From nothingness can come all of creation.

When you understand that there is no intrinsic meaning in anything, you have the opportunity to make a truce with life: it is how it is. It is exquisitely simple. The lesson is that if you can't change it, you can accept it. Quit fighting it. Let go and realize that it is how it is. No amount of anything is going to change that.

If your parents were abusive, neglectful, absent, insensitive, it didn't mean anything. It had nothing to do with you. That's just how they were. You have interpreted their behaviors as meaning something. What do you think the behavior meant? It didn't mean that. "But," you say, "it must have meant something. It had to have some meaning." No, it didn't. It didn't mean that they didn't love you or that you were bad, or any of the thousands of other interpretations you might have made. What they did and how they were is what happened, but it didn't mean anything.

When you got fired, when your lover broke up with you, when a loved one died, it didn't mean anything. It wasn't because you were unlovable, stupid, bad, wrong, or anything else. It is just what happened. Are you beginning to understand? This is a very difficult concept to grasp. As makers of meaning, we are loathe to give up meaning. Look at it this way. If it is all interpretation, and we assign all the meaning, then it is possible to assign meaning that is useful and empowering.

Instead of thinking that you were fired because you were incompetent and stupid, you could decide that it was because that was the wrong job for you and there are things that you need to learn elsewhere. Or you could decide that you were fired in order to realize and understand what failure is, and isn't. These are empowering interpretations. They are much more useful than, "I'm stupid and incompetent."

Let's try again. Your lover stands you up for a date. What do you think that means? What are your interpretations?

It doesn't mean that. Whatever the interpretation is, you made it up. Instead of focusing on your interpretations, and suffering over them, try to address feelings without making an interpretation. How do you feel about it? You don't like it? Okay. What do you want to do about it? Look at your options. You can wait to see if the explanation is satisfactory. You can wait to see if it happens again. You can decide that you don't want to be treated like this and look for someone else. You can have all the options you want *without* deciding you're unlovable, your lover is a turkey, men/women always act like this, or any of the other negative connotations possible.

Werner Erhard says: "Rocks are hard and water is wet." That's a brilliant statement. If you know that rocks are hard and water is wet, then you know that getting upset about it won't change anything. Apply that idea to everything in your life that you can't change.

You can begin by making a list of the interpretations you have made of all of the major events and people in your life. Next make a list of all of the possible reinterpretations of all of the above. And remember when you are upset that it is because you think it means something. What is it that you have decided it means? It doesn't mean that. It's just your interpretation. It has no intrinsic meaning. It just is what it is. Accept it and move on. Accepting reality instead of wanting it to be different will give you peace.

YOU AND YOUR LIFE ARE WHAT YOU BELIEVE

Skeptical? Pay attention. What you believe about yourself and your life is exactly what you get. It is your interpretation, so that's how it is for you. For instance, if you believe that everyone gets the flu in the winter, guess what you will get. But, you say, "Everyone does get the flu in the winter." Okay, but did you ever ask yourself why? If your answer is bad weather and germs, you're not getting this.

Let's try again. An enlightened employer asks his three salespeople to sit down and write out the highest figure they think they can earn in the next year. One puts down $100,000. One writes $50,000. The other lists $30,000. At the end of the year, what do you think their totals would be? That's right, very near the mark they wrote down to begin with. That's what they believe they can do and that's exactly what they do. That's how they interpret themselves.

Now why do people get sick in the winter? Because they KNOW they are supposed to get sick in the winter. Television ads abound with cold and flu remedies as well as pictures of people snuffling, sniffling, coughing, and trudging through rain, sleet, and snow.

One patient realized that her yearly bout with the "February flu" was the result of having had a bad case of flu when she was nine. From that time onward, she has had the flu every February. She "knew" she was going to have it and she did. When she realized the power of her beliefs, she quit being sick at all during the winter.

What you believe affects every area of your life. Your life is created out of what you know to be true. Remember, you are living in that windowless capsule from which you can only see what you believe and know. Naturally, that's what's going to show.

How many beautiful women do you know who sit home dateless on weekends? It's because they believe there is a shortage of men, or it's hard to get a date, or they are unattractive. They are living out their beliefs.

Have you ever talked to someone who is popular? Popular people expect others to like them and others do. Successful people who do well in the marketplace know they can do it. They don't sit around nursing their insecurities. They go out and make it happen. They can do that not because they are superior or have no feelings, but because they KNOW they can.

Now go back to your lists and look at what you KNOW about your life. If men always abandoned you, if women are always witches, if you can't get ahead, get busy on those beliefs. You can absolutely transform your life into what you want it to be by working with your beliefs.

DREAMS

One way to discover your beliefs and interpretations is to remember and analyze your dreams. Dreams are an important and powerful source of information about what is stored in your unconscious mind. Whether you remember your dreams or not, you do dream. You can train yourself to remember them. As you drift off to sleep at night, instruct your subconscious mind to help you remember your dreams. Immediately upon arising, jot your dreams down on paper or record them on a tape recorder. Because dreams are a product of the subconscious mind, they quickly elude the grasp of conscious reality unless you record them immediately. Keep recording materials by your bed in case you awaken in the middle of the night.

There are many ways of interpreting dreams. All may be valid and useful at a particular time. Perhaps the easiest way is to "gestalt" the dream. Gestalt therapy was developed by Fritz Perls. It became an important part of the Esalen Institute, and the human potential movement of the 60s and 70s. The Gestalt method of dream interpretation is still among the most powerful and healing of psychotherapeutic tools.

For example, a woman dreams that she is in Paris in an ancient stone tunnel filled with shops, restaurants, and other people. In one of the shops she buys a sequined lace blouse from an elderly red-headed woman. It is so beautiful she is almost in tears, because the sequins spell out the initials of her beloved. She clutches it to her breast like a great prize and then wakes up.

To gestalt this dream, one would have to be all of its parts: the marble, the tunnel, one or more of the shops and restaurants, the other people, the sequins, the lace, the blouse, the old woman, Paris, the initials, etc. The order is not necessarily important.

For instance: "I am the stone. I am hard, strong, cold, powerful enough to hold a tunnel together over a long period of time. I am smooth, clean, beautiful. I am the sequins. I am small, bright, shiny, colorful, ornamental, and delicate. I am the lace blouse. I am elegant, dressy, soft, attractive, beautiful, and very desirable. I make the woman happy. I am for special occasions only."

Exercise 8 will walk you through the steps of dream interpretation, using your own examples. As you discover your beliefs and interpretations, working with your dreams will allow you to uncover your most powerful attitudes about yourself and the world. You will begin to see yourself as the source of every condition in your life.

COULD YOU BE THE REASON EVERYONE IS PICKING ON YOU?

Do you feel like everyone you know is on your case? Is everyone giving you a hard time? Are a lot of people upset with you?

On a case-by-case basis, you may be telling yourself that they are all being mean to you for individual reasons. Person A is difficult and demanding. Person B is hysterical and easily upset. Person C doesn't understand you or how hard you are trying. Person D is an ungrateful and impossible tyrant. That may all be true. But why are they all upset with you simultaneously? Could it have anything to do with you? How are you getting all of them to pick on you? Are you a victim? Could you possibly have a part in all of this? What could your part be?

When you feel victimized, beleaguered, and embattled, consider the possibility that you may be the cause. That doesn't mean you should feel guilty and blame yourself. That won't help and it's not the point anyway. Simply ask yourself honestly "What's going on here?" "How am I feeding into this?" "Why am I attracting all this hostility and anger?" If you can't see what you are doing, talk to someone who can be objective to help you clarify the issues.

One woman complained that everyone in her life had been picking on her for six months. She was ready to quit, to throw in the towel. No one appreciated her efforts. She felt victimized and martyred. "I'm such a good person, how could anyone treat me like this?"

She is a good person. She's also playing the victim and the martyr. Few people enjoy bearing the brunt of these attitudes. Most will become tyrannical with someone playing these roles. That's their job. That's what she was asking them to do.

Are you begging people to be tyrannical and abusive to you? Why? Why would you do that and how would you do that? The woman in question, in addition to life's usual stresses, had lost a beloved brother just about the time everyone began to pick on her. Her family was very far away in another country, and although her husband attempted to be supportive, she felt very alone with her grief. Rather than deal with the grief, she chose to bury it and proceeded to fight with everyone around her. It's easier to be angry at the living than at the dead. Her behavior allowed her to express intense emotions without dealing directly with her brother's death.

In the process of piecing together the puzzle, she realized she had been so distracted that she really had not been doing her job. Perhaps the others were trying to get her attention back on what she was supposed to be doing. She also became defensive, emotional, and quick to anger. Everything that happened to her was being filtered thorough the intense emotion she felt about the loss of her brother. She was displacing this anger and sadness onto other people and situations.

Ask yourself whether you are doing the things you are supposed to do when you are supposed to do them. Are you blaming others when you can't or don't get your job done on time? Do you have your ducks in a row or are you scattered, inefficient, and ineffective for the moment? Is it possible you are flying off the handle too quickly and easily? Are you taking offense at everything anyone says?

Now ask yourself why you are doing that. What is fueling that response and behavior in you? Is this an old pattern you are acting out? Were you picked on in your family? Do you need to go home that badly? Has there been a recent loss, separation, or divorce in your life? What unresolved feelings are at play here?

Most people do not want to fight with you. They want to have a harmonious relationship with you regardless of the context. Investigate how you are making them fight with you by checking into your behavior and feelings honestly. When you no longer need to fight and be upset, you will deal with others in a way that brings forth love and peace in all of your relationships.

IF YOU ARE BLAMING SOMEONE ELSE, YOU ARE A VICTIM

Who do you blame? Your parents? Your spouse? Your boss? When you have a problem, an upset, a disappointment, whose fault is it? If you lay the responsibility for your life on anyone else, you are a victim.

The person or people you blame may really have done what you say they did. It is your responsibility to deal with the consequences. As long as you blame someone else, you will not be able to get free of the morass of feelings created for you by others. They did what they did, but your feelings are yours. Do you understand the distinction?

There is power in asking yourself, "How did I get them to do that?" While you are not responsible for the behavior of your parents, in your adult life you do help create the way others treat you. If you are convinced that everyone leaves you, guess what your current mate will do? You will force it by your behavior. There is an old saying in Alcoholics Anonymous that if a woman isn't a bitch when an alcoholic man marries her, she will be. He will see to it. The person in your life may be a bitch, or a bastard. How did you happen to pick him or her? Why do you put up with it? What do you get out of it? What's the payoff?

By asking yourself these kinds of questions, and by being willing to be responsible for yourself, your victimization can disappear and you can create the kinds of experiences and people that you want in your life. In order to do that, you must first ferret out what attitudes, emotions, and behaviors you have that require other people to behave that way toward you.

Haven't you noticed that people seem to have a built-in radar that will attract the experiences they expect? One woman says that if there is a depressed man within a thousand miles, she will find him. What is her need to be with a depressed man? What is it in her that attracts and puts up with that? In some way the people in your life mirror you. While you may not be a bitch, you may create them in your life by your behavior. If you think you deserve that kind of treatment or if you don't expect anything better or different, that is what you will get.

How is it that one person with good secretarial skills can't get a job while another with no skills wins a great sales job? The person with no skills wants a job and knows he or she deserves one. She is willing to do the work necessary to do well. The other person has a stake in being "Poor Pitiful Pearl."

If you want to be happy and powerful, you have to learn to be responsible for yourself and to give up being a victim. It is not easy to do. But it is the most rewarding and fulfilling exercise you can undertake.

IF YOU KNOW EVERYTHING, HAVE NOTHING TO LEARN, ARE ALWAYS RIGHT, AND CONSIDER YOURSELF SUPERIOR, YOU WILL HAVE A VERY DIFFICULT LIFE

One of the major distinctions made in psychopathology is whether or not the person learns. If you have nothing to learn, you are in serious trouble. You will fight with other people a lot, if not constantly. You will not get what you want or succeed at your chosen career. You will have impossible or non-existent relationships. Ultimately, you will be alone.

The less you see yourself as being like others, the more alienated and isolated you will be. All other people are beautiful, wonderful mirrors for you to reflect on yourself. ALL of them.

They may be exaggerated mirrors. That's so you can't possibly miss the point. They may be distorted mirrors, with only a little true vision of you. They may be a reverse mirror for you to see what you're not. You are not better or worse than anyone. You are just the same.

If you have the same experiences in your life over and over, with disappointment, frustration, suffering, and sadness, take a look at what you are not learning. You need someone to help you learn those lessons.

Unfortunately, the kind of person who knows everything and is always right rarely takes on a coach. After all, he already knows everything. Be humble enough, and smart enough, to recognize that the way you've been doing it doesn't work, and get someone to help you. Then sit down, shut up, and listen. You might learn something.

WOULD YOU RATHER BE RIGHT THAN HAPPY?

Do you know someone who is more concerned about being right than about being happy or getting along with people? Does always being right keep you warm at night? Does it rub your feet and bring you the paper? Does it pay your bills? Does it give you a warm circle of friends who appreciate your tact and sensitivity? Go to *Exercise 9* in the Workbook to find out just how much you are willing to sacrifice in order to be right.

There are times when you should stand up and argue that you are right about something. But rarely. No one is going to change his or her mind and you will most often just end up with injured feelings on both sides. Is it worth it? Is that what you want? Is it satisfying?

It is not an endearing trait. What is endearing is to be willing to listen to other points of view, to offer your thoughts or opinion as just that, not as the last word, and to be willing to be wrong. People love people who are willing to be wrong, to admit that they don't know absolutely everything. They will give you lots of space and understanding and they will be more able and willing to listen to you when they think you are right. When you are willing and able to consider other's feelings and opinions first, they know that you are more interested in your relationship with them than in having the last word. That is charming indeed.

Decide whether you can and want to change your priorities from being right to being happy. When you have determined the cost of this attitude, you may be willing to change it. No one loves a smart-ass know-it-all. We all feel insecure enough without having someone around who corrects us all the time.

So the question is, do you want to be right or do you want to be happy? What are you willing to give up to be happy? What would it cost you to back off and cool your jets and let someone else be right? What would it get you? Your ability to cede a point to the other side once in a while may make the difference in whether or not you can hang on to your friends or your relationships.

TRY A LITTLE HUMILITY

Everyone else is just as wonderful as you are. Consider the fact that you are arrogant because you really feel like NOTHING. Buried way down deep under all that cockiness is a person who feels absolutely worthless.

You don't like to be called arrogant. Or cocky. You probably think that this doesn't apply to you. It may not. But then again there are very few people around who don't have some of this.

Learn to listen. Consider the other person's point of view. It is not necessary to constantly tell everyone how superior you are. If you're really that superior, why do you have to remind us? Look to see what is wonderful about the other person. No matter how much you think you know about anything, other people have things to teach you.

Humility builds a bridge between you and other people. It is easier to have all kinds of relationships when you are willing to meet other people as equals. It might also give you an opportunity to delve into why you really feel so worthless. You're not. You're wonderful. You just don't know it. You really do think you are nothing so you have to build this wall of superiority around you. Start knocking it down. They took the Berlin Wall down. Start working on yours. Practicing humility will create big holes in that wall. Eventually you can knock it down.

If other people are often angry at you, there is a good possibility that you are in need of a heavy dose of humility. If you don't work at it yourself, life will produce the humbling for you. So try it. It's not that bad. You might even find you like it.

Be willing to look at your life in a new and different way. Consider the possibility that you may not now know everything. In fact, everything you know may be wrong, or at least out-dated. Things change very quickly. It is entirely possible that the things you believed or knew yesterday no longer apply.

That doesn't make you stupid or crazy. You just need to take a refresher course, a continuing education course. Listen to a new point of view. Consider new evidence. Be willing to change your game plan.

The best way to get knocked down hard and fast is to be overly cocky. Don't insist on your opinion as the last word. Someone may have something to teach you that could be very valuable. If you're arrogant enough to think you know it all, you will miss it all. It's that simple. And you will be very lonely. It's very hard to have any kind of a relationship with someone who knows everything and will not learn. Why would anyone want to try?

Get off your high horse. Get down with the rest of the plebeians and live and learn. You'll have more fun and be happier. You may even learn to laugh at yourself.

A LIFE WITHOUT A SENSE OF HUMOR IS A TRAGEDY

And boring. Everything that ever happens to you can be funny. It may be tragic. It may be hurtful beyond what you think you can bear. You may be so angry it frightens you. You may be scared witless. But you can still find something to laugh about in it.

If you can't, take a look at why. Are you enjoying the pain and suffering so much that you can't let go of it? Are you using it to punish yourself or someone else? Is it your excuse for not getting on with your life? Why are you taking it all so seriously?

It doesn't matter what it is. Lighten up. Have your tears, your anger, your disappointment, whatever it is. But learn to laugh at yourself and at life. It makes it all much easier to bear.

This is not to say that you should laugh everything off. Not at all. That's denial and refusal to have your feelings. The trick is to have all of your feelings, and still be able to laugh.

It's an old saw that laughter is the best medicine. Norman Cousins, among others, healed himself of a serious illness using laughter. You can heal your life.

Being willing and able to laugh at yourself and your predicaments will make your life much easier. It will also make other people love you and want to be around you. Don't you like people with a great sense of humor? Get one. They're free.

4

VICTIM/TYRANT: THE GAME OF LIFE

Life is a game. The name of the game is Victim and Tyrant. Everyone plays the game. Everyone plays both the victim and the tyrant. Few people are conscious of the game or of the role they are playing.

The dictionary defines a victim as "one who is harmed by or made to suffer from an act, circumstance, agency, or condition; one who is caused suffering and discomfort." Does that sound like anyone you know? Most of us can identify with that definition. A tyrant is "a ruler who exercises power in a harsh, cruel manner; an oppressor."

How do we choose whether to be a victim or a tyrant? We don't. We are both. We act out both sides of the pathology. We are both the victim and the tyrant, depending upon the other players and the situation. Victim/Tyrant is a pathological game. There are no champions, only players. It is not a consciously chosen game.

Victims and tyrants are created by a lack of conscious choice. At an unconscious level, these are the only two options available to most people for coping with life. It is automatic behavior. Not just in this culture, but for thousands of years, this has been the game of life. One team plays against the other; the victims versus the tyrants.

There are many examples of this game in your own life and in the lives of the people around you. We thrive on it. The media is full of it. But we can begin to break through the subtle screen of victim/tyrant when we start asking the right questions. For example: ask yourself how a victim gets a tyrant to do that to him. Interesting question. How did that poor pitiful person you all know get that big bad guy to beat up on him? The next question should be, "Why did/does he put up with it?" Exactly who is the victim here? Or is there one?

Is there a choice? What could it be?
Is it possible to end the game?
If we give up victim/tyrant, what happens to identity? Who are we
*   without these labels?*
How would we interact with others who are still playing the game?
Would we have any friends left?
Why would/should we end the game? We are accustomed to it.
Everyone does it.

There is a choice. It is possible to end the game. There is an identity beyond victim and tyrant that is powerful, joyful, and nurturing, to yourself and to others. Ending the game comes when it is too painful or too boring to continue. It isn't a fun game. There is a great deal of sorrow involved. Victim/tyrant is a game played by people who don't know they're powerful, but you are powerful enough to end the game and make the choice to be a champion!

Victimization is so much a part of our consciousness that the idea that we may not be victims can be very upsetting. The first time we run across the idea, which is not new, there may be a sense of disbelief that someone could be dumb enough or mean enough to think we're never victims.

Immediately all kinds of scenarios involving ourselves or people we know reel through our heads like private movies. Surely it is clear that these are instances of victimization. It is cruel to suggest otherwise.

Reactions of this kind just reinforce how powerfully we have bought into the victim/tyrant game. This very deep and powerful belief makes it difficult to realize that there may be a way to be free from being a victim. We become victims of victimization.

The idea that we may be responsible for our misfortunes is anathema.

It is impossible to understand. That we should consider forgiving the tyrants and perpetrators in our lives is somewhat less loathsome, but still crazy.

What would the world be like if each of us took responsibility for creating our own reality? We might not be responsible for everything that goes on around us, but we can certainly be responsible for how we deal with it.

What kind of world would it be if there were no victims?
What kind of world would it be if there were no tyrants?

To assume responsibility for your life and destiny is a very powerful act. With that act, anger, fear, hate, and judgment can disappear. What place do these things have in a life that is consciously created and responsibly lived?

Far from being crazy, mean, or cruel, the refusal to see anyone as a victim is an act of love for the self and of respect for all others. From this point of view, one can begin to see what is really happening on this planet. Our compassion then allows us to help others from a stance of empowerment, rather than one of sympathy and enslavement.

The biggest problem many people have in handling this concept is that they immediately assume it means that the person they have seen as a victim is being accused of wrong-doing and guilt. That is missing the point. Responsibility is not guilt. The position isn't, "I'm bad. I'm wrong. It's all my fault." Rather, it is, "This has happened. How can I deal with it so that it does not damage me or my life and I learn the lesson of experience? What is it in my consciousness that created this?" It's not, "What did I do wrong?" but, rather, "What can I do to correct a situation?" It's that simple. What is the lesson to be learned? It may be a very hard lesson, but learning it will allow for the creation of a solution. In this way, you begin to have more power and control over your life.

Victimization can appear both personal and political. Let's look at some examples. The meltdown at Chernobyl is a classic example of political victimization. Thousands of people were killed, hurt, sickened: their lives changed dramatically for the worse. I remember thinking at the time that the wind would blow west across Europe and then to America and we would all get some degree of radiation from it. But how many of us have stood up to the government and yelled and screamed about nuclear power plants? How many of us have even written our congresspeople? There is a nuclear power plant located on a fault line in California and one in Missouri. If you know about them, have you done anything? If you don't know about it, why not?

Part of the problem in victimization is that we are most often blind-sided by it. We don't see it coming. It is very hard to see our own complicity, collusion, or creation in the process. Therefore, part of the solution involves becoming more and more aware. We need to become more conscious. We need to work at that. We need to be willing to both give and receive constructive feedback. We need to work to get past dependency and passivity to take responsibility for ourselves and for our world. We can do that only by being as conscious as possible at any given point. And we will still be blind-sided because there is always more to learn. But we can choose how we deal with it.

A good friend was recently severely shafted by people he considered to be close and loving friends. Major agreements were broken in what appeared to be a very mean, if not vindictive, way. He was badly hurt both emotionally and financially. And yet he said to me, "I'm not a victim." Although he was unclear how, he knew that he had somehow participated in the creation of this event. He was experiencing all of the appropriate emotions—anger, sorrow, confusion, and personal hurt—AND he was being responsible. Instead of saying self-pityingly, "Why me?" he felt his feelings and took responsibility for them. That is not to say that he took responsibility for the actions of his friends. They were not his actions. But he did choose how to deal with it in order to get on with his life and suffer the least damage as possible, while learning what he could from the experience.

Let's make another important distinction here. While I also knew that my friend was not a victim and that he had participated in the creation of this debacle, it was not my responsibility to confront him with that. Nor was it my first, or last, reaction. He was fully aware of the situation and struggling to complete it on his own. What he needed from me, and what I wanted to give him, was sympathy, compassion, understanding, and support. I empathized with his feelings and did what I could to ameliorate the damage done. My point is, although we may realize intellectually that someone is not a victim, including ourselves, that does not mean that we are not entitled to the full range of feelings involved. We are also entitled to the non-judgmental love, understanding, and support of our friends. Just because we have not been victimized doesn't mean it doesn't hurt, or that the other people involved have not behaved badly. Interestingly, if we talked to the other individual or group, they would tell us that they feel victimized. The trick is to empower the human being, not the victimization. It doesn't help to make people feel guilty or wrong. It helps to make them feel loved and understood. That will give them the space to learn the lesson involved.

Stated simply, on-going victimization means that no one is learning anything. Are you smart enough to learn? Are you determined enough to put an end to pointless suffering? Do you want to grow and become the best, healthiest person you can be? Begin by working through your own victim/tyrant dynamics in *Exercise 10* in the Workbook.

If the answer to these questions is yes, then begin to look at life as an on-going classroom in which everyone you meet is a teacher and every experience a valuable lesson. To say "I am innocent," or "It has nothing to do with me," is to miss the point. You are innocent, terribly innocent, and still it has everything to do with you.

Innocence is a dangerous state. Insist on becoming worldly-wise and on understanding what happens to you. It is the road to freedom. To give up your innocence is to become powerful and brilliant. To be powerful and brilliant is to be a champion, not a victim or a tyrant. Which would you rather be?

YOU CAN BE A CHAMPION

The individual who chooses to go beyond victim and tyrant is a champion. She has won the game of life and is victorious over blaming and dependency. How did she do that? More importantly, how can you do that? A champion makes choices. Conscious choices. A champion conquers the quicksand of victim/tyrant by being responsible and self-reliant.

It sounds easy. It is not. The game is deeply ingrained in all of us. It is automatic for us to assume one position or the other. We have chosen sides and are suffering before we realize it.

The difference between game players and champions is that champions make a conscious effort to be aware of what they are doing. As soon as they realize they are playing the game, they quit. They refuse to see themselves as victims or tyrants. They refuse to blame others or themselves. They play a no-fault game. They choose a position of responsibility in which they know and accept their part in the game. That may sound callous, cruel, mean, or just plain impossible to you. It is not. It is empowering, enlivening, and thrilling.

How can it be your fault that someone is mean to you, or takes advantage of you, steals from you, or hurts you physically? How can it be your fault that life deals out illness, poverty, disappointment, loss, pain, and sorrow?

The problem is that you are asking the wrong question. Instead of asking whose fault it is, or who is to blame, ask what you can do about it. What can you do to change the situation or circumstances? How can you deal with the difficulty in a way that empowers you? What do you need to do for you in this situation? How is this a realization of your own beliefs? How do you feed into the situation? What have you been doing that keeps the game going? What do you need to give up or let go of in order to win? What action can you take that would make you happy and peaceful?

What makes you a champion? Consider the following list of attributes.

A champion does not sell out. A champion cannot be bought at any price. That is a very grown-up stance. Most of us can be bought fairly cheaply. If that idea offends you, think about how anxious you are to please others, to be right, to be popular, to be liked, to be loved, to be safe, to be dependent. That's what selling out means. It is putting anything ahead of yourself. Remember: YOU COME FIRST.

A champion does not have to be an adult. Children are usually champions before we teach them to be victims or tyrants. It is a learned game.

A champion refuses to compromise personal values for any reason. Any person, circumstance, or thing that requires you to play the game is not worth it.

A champion knows her feelings and therefore what is right and wrong. Integrity is a matter of feelings, not morals. A champion deals from feelings which ultimately empower and nurture everyone involved, and she therefore treats others well.

A champion doesn't care that other people are upset that she has left the game. That is their problem, not hers.

A champion is clear about what his problem is and isn't. He refuses to get involved in a game in which he has no part.

Other people admire champions, but do not necessarily like them. The champion doesn't care. He is concerned about his own feelings about himself, not about what other people think.

A champion is willing to stand all alone in the middle of the battlefield. She is self-reliant. She doesn't run for cover or duck the issue. She stands up for what she believes.

A champion does not fight unnecessary battles, but knows how to choose to fight for freedom and choice. Champions fight less than victims or tyrants because they are self-reliant and not living at the beck-and-call of anyone or anything. They are wise warriors.

Does this sound like a tall order? It is. To conquer yourself, your fears, and your dependencies may be a lifelong battle. It is the battle to wage. It is the only one you can win. Otherwise you are playing the game and tilting at windmills. It is not easy to be a champion. It is possible. It is possible for you. Are you game?

MIRROR, MIRROR ON THE WALL

"Mirror, mirror on the wall, who's the fairest of them all?" A better question would be: "Mirror, mirror on the wall, how can you best teach us all?" That's a good question, because it is a useful tool in learning to end the game and become a champion.

It is important to understand the concept of mirroring as applied to your own growth and learning. A mirror reflects back to you what you look like. It is an image that is reversed and somewhat distorted, but it is as close as we get to really knowing what we look like.

As discussed before, the people in your life act as mirrors in the same way. In one sense, we can never see anything but ourselves. Therefore, when we see something we don't like we want to distance ourselves from it. It is exactly for this reason that we need to take a close look at the things that we dislike the most and like the most. We are looking at ourselves.

That person you can't stand has a lot to teach you. Why don't you like him or her? What is it specifically that you don't like? Now identify the part of you that person represents.

Mirrors can be very painful, upsetting, and maddening. They can also be thrilling, joyous, and enlightening. What you see in others is what you are. If you didn't have part of that in you, you couldn't identify it in others. As we get older, this concept breaks down a little because of an increased ability to make distinctions and to see more clearly. It is still a valid tool for self-exploration.

It is when we are most repulsed by another that we need to look most closely. What is it that we don't want to look at in ourselves? What is it that we have disowned in our own behavior or being?

Mirroring is a very powerful tool. If you will see everyone, EVERYONE, in your life as a mirror for you, no matter how distorted or exaggerated or reversed, your learning will be exponential. You will be able to make quantum leaps in your understanding of yourself and the world.

When you have understood the connection between you and the mirrored behavior, you will be able to love that part of yourself and the other person. You will be able to give up your judgment in that area. It is an experience of being freed from your judgments and limits.

The power of our mirrors cannot be emphasized too strongly. In the beginning it is not necessary to see everything as a mirror if it is too painful or too upsetting. As you become accustomed to seeing in that way, it will become easier and even delightful. You will be grateful for the opportunity to have seen yourself in that way. You will reach a point where you wait in excited anticipation of the next mirror.

Remember, this works both ways. It is not just the things you don't like that mirror you. It is also all the things you see in others that you think are beautiful, wonderful, loving, kind, brilliant, or talented. These are also parts of you.

Recently a professor at a graduate school of psychology held up the diagnostic manual and said to the students, "Everything in here is in you." That is powerful teaching and powerful mirroring. There is no me and you. It is all me.

Ultimately, that may be what enlightenment is all about: the ability and willingness to recognize all others as ourselves. There is no distinction, no difference, no judgment. There is only learning.

TRANSFERENCE IS

Transference is the clinical term for mirroring. Essentially, it means that what you see on the inside of your capsule is what you see everywhere. Sounds simple, doesn't it? It is simple. It is also important to recognize the degree to which it influences your thinking and your relationships.

Everyone in your life is just like everyone else. Have you noticed that? You will see your therapist as being like your mother or your father or both. And you won't even recognize that that's what you're doing. You will have strong feelings about the therapist. The therapist will point out that those feelings have nothing to do with the reality of him or her as a person and more appropriately belong to the other people in your life: father, mother, sibling. That can come as quite a shock.

Hold on. There's a bigger shock. We're not through here. You do that to everyone in your life. Everyone. It is unlikely that you see any individual in your life as he or she truly is. You see people through the filmy foggy view of transference. You attribute to them feelings and attitudes that belong to people you knew when you were growing up. It's the inside of that capsule again.

There is great power in knowing and acknowledging this fact. You can then begin to separate out what feelings are really appropriate to what person. Maybe the person in question really is like you think he is. But think about it.

You find yourself afraid to go to class. You know it is your turn to speak and you are terrified. You do not want to go. Stop yourself and ask why you are so afraid. You love the teacher. She has never been mean to anyone in class, yet you are sure she is going to yell at you and humiliate you. The feelings don't fit the reality. What is going on?

Who was it who yelled at you or humiliated you in your past? The answer may surprise, shock, or sadden you. But you will have the beginning of a window in that spacecraft. The boss that you think is so fearsome may not be. You may be seeing someone else.

Wait a minute. Don't get upset. That's not crazy. It's really quite normal. Transference is! Everyone does it all the time with everyone else. The trick is to recognize and acknowledge it. That's when you have power over it. Otherwise, you will go through life never knowing for sure what you have seen or experienced.

It's easy. Ask yourself whether the feelings and reactions you are having in this situation about this person are appropriate or whether they belong somewhere else. When you've practiced this a couple of times, you'll get the hang of it. It will make a big difference.

ALL THAT JUDGMENT YOU THINK OTHER PEOPLE HAVE OF YOU IS REALLY YOUR OWN SELF-JUDGMENT BEING REFLECTED BACK AT YOU

That doesn't mean they don't judge you. They very well may. But if you could forgive yourself and judge yourself less harshly, you would attract people into your life who would see it more the way you do. Remember: the people in your life are mirrors. If the people around you are judging you, then so are you, in pretty much the same degree.

Quit worrying about what other people think of you and look at what you think of yourself. It's your judgments that really count. Others are just mirroring them back to you. Remember, all you can see is what's written on the inside of your capsule.

There is no failure. That's just another judgment. Yes, you have been taught that there is success and failure. In one sense, that is all there is. Everyone wants to be a success. No one wants to be a failure, at least not consciously. After all, success is what counts.

But is it? Have you ever seen a successful corpse? If you are really into success, you'll probably say yes. He was the richest man in the cemetery. Not really. The richest man anywhere is the man who has gained experience and turned it into wisdom.

There is no real success or failure. There is only experience. What did you learn? If you didn't learn anything, if you are not wiser for the experience, then what is the point? Money? Status?

The wise person understands that experience is the most valuable commodity around. It gives you the opportunity to become wise. If you become wise, then you may become loving of yourself and others, non-judgmental, emotionally healthy, joyful, and peaceful. Money and status do not bring these rewards. If you approach life not as something to be conquered "successfully," but as a series of adventures and lessons to be learned, it becomes rich, powerful, and heady in its every breath. Then you are a true success. Money and status can go in an instant. No one can rob you of your experience. Wisdom is yours forever.

FEELINGS ARE NOT FACTS

It is very important to remember that feelings are subjective, not objective; irrational not rational. Just because you feel something doesn't mean it's true. You don't measure the strength of the feeling against the objective reality. There is no correlation.

We create a major problem for ourselves when we believe our feelings without checking the reality. It is crucial to do reality checks. Without them, we are living in a fantasy based on feelings which may or may not have anything to do with our current life situation. Most feelings are prompted by old, unresolved conflicts at an unconscious level.

One of the first things you need to know about feelings is that they have their own kind of rationale which does not fit what most of us think of as rational or logical. They don't make sense when measured by our usual standards of logic.

Your feelings of self-worth are not based on reality, but on what you felt a long time ago. You think you are stupid, but you have a Ph.D. You think you are ugly, but everyone else sees a very attractive person. You think no one likes you, but your phone rings constantly. Or, that person you can't stand is probably a "stand-in," a representative symbol for someone in your past. Begin to ask yourself what the reality is: "This is what I feel, now what is the reality?" What you discover can be truly amazing.

FEELINGS DON'T MAKE SENSE

A problem encountered in learning to have feelings and to deal with them is that they are so counter to the way we think. That is why they are called feelings, not thoughts. Thoughts and feelings are not necessarily related in this context. They are entirely distinct and separate entities. That is one of the distinctions you can begin to make to help you understand which is which.

Feelings don't make sense. They are based on our unconscious, subjective view of the world. One of the difficulties in life is that we tend to operate as if our feelings were real. Given the *disjuncture* between feelings and reality, you can see that this could create major problems in a hurry.

Perhaps the clearest example of this is the paranoid person who thinks that everyone is against him. It is easy for the rest of us to see that his feelings don't fit the reality. We know that most people are not against him.

Although we are not really talking about paranoid projection, what "normal" people do can be just as destructive and out-of-reality: you think no one would notice if you're not there; you think you don't make a difference; you're amazed when someone asks why you didn't show up.

A woman in her sixties had lived her life with the view that no one really liked her and she had few friends. When she retired from her job, nearly a hundred people showed up for her party. It still did not dawn on her that they might really care about her. When it was pointed out that all these people had taken their time to come say goodbye to her, many with cards and gifts, it was a shock to her to realize that they thought they were her friends. As she began to take stock in other areas in her life, she realized she had many friends. She had always lived out of the belief that no one liked her. This discovery changed her life. She is softer, warmer, more open, and less angry.

What old, irrational feelings are you living with as fact?

While feelings may be expressed through thought, the reverse is rarely true. Your thoughts and feelings on any subject may, and most probably will, be extremely contradictory.

It is possible to understand a situation or behavior on a rational level while having very powerful feelings in an entirely different direction. For instance, a friend is late for an appointment with you, but shows up with a good excuse. You accept the excuse and forget about it. Thereafter, the friend is almost always late, always with a plausible excuse. You may consciously accept the behavior and think little more of it. But you see less and less of the friend and eventually the relationship dissolves entirely. When questioned about it, you will have some kind of rationalization for why you don't see him any more. You're both too busy, it's too far to travel, something reasonable. If you look deeper, you may find that you are deeply hurt and angry. Rather than confront the feelings you just disappear.

A close neighbor moves to another city or gets married. You try to stay in touch, but communication and correspondence wither fairly quickly. You have lots of reasons and excuses for yourself and for your friend. How does it really feel? "But I understand," you say. Fine, you understand. But that doesn't account for how you really feel about it.

A family member does not invite you to her wedding. You understand. After all, it was very small, quite intimate in fact, with just a few guests. You understand why you were left out. But how do you feel about that? Really feel?

These are fairly simplistic examples of the difference between thought and feeling. In life, as well as in therapy, the discrepancies can be startling as you begin to uncover the differences between your thoughts and your feelings. That's what makes it so necessary to begin to make distinctions between the two and to get in touch with your feelings. Otherwise, you are eating white bread when chocolate eclairs are available. Feelings are the richness in life, rational or not. Without them you are living in a tidy little world where not much happens consciously and you don't understand what is happening to you or to your life. Feelings have their own kind of logic. Begin to learn it. It's called basic.

WHO CAN YOU TRUST?

You. You and only you. Ultimately you are the only person you can trust. You will have to trust yourself through trusting your feelings, your gut instincts. You are the only one who is really going to have your best interests at heart at all times. Anyone else, however honest or trustworthy, is likely to have mixed emotions or hidden agendas, even if only unconsciously.

This is not to say that you can't trust other people. But you need to know what it is for which they can be trusted. Never just hand your trust over to someone else completely. It is guaranteed you will be disappointed.

It's not that other people are bad or mean or evil. It is that they are human. Your expectations and assumptions are very likely to be entirely out of line with the reality of human beings. You see them as you want them to be, or hope they will be, rather than as they are. You're doomed to disappointment.

One woman was convinced she couldn't trust any man. Men always violated her trust. When we took a closer look at what she was trusting them to do and be, we discovered fantasies that no human could live up to for even a little while. She expected and demanded every man in her life to be the knight in shining armor she was waiting and longing for. It of course became abundantly clear very quickly that each one was just another ordinary mortal. She was justified in her belief that she couldn't trust them.

There are two issues here. First, your expectations and demands may be so extravagant that no one can meet them, no matter how well intentioned. You will always end up feeling betrayed. Take a long look at what you expect from each of the people in your life. What assumptions are you making? What expectations do you have which you have not communicated to the other person or to yourself? Being clear in this area can save a lot of heartache. Remember, other people are reading their capsules, not yours.

For instance, do you think that a "friend" will always be there for you and always agree with you? These are assumptions many people have that are unrealistic and also suffocating. To maintain a friendship with you, are others always required to agree with you? What if they don't? Are you hurt? Do you feel betrayed? To require that of another person is making him a slave, not a friend.

Do you assume that because someone has an alphabet after her name she knows what she is doing and never makes a mistake? This is a very serious misconception on your part. The best doctor, lawyer, teacher, or therapist in the world can and does make mistakes. Remember that half of those people graduated at the bottom of their classes. One of the most serious mistakes people make is having blind trust in the professionals in their lives. Keep your eyes and ears open. Trust your instincts and your knowledge. You may be smarter than the professional. A second opinion is always an acceptable option.

You don't need to be paranoid. It is right and proper to think that the person you are consulting knows her business. Trust her up to that point. But if your feelings tell you this person isn't for you, or the work she is doing isn't getting the job done, trust yourself. She may be a lovely person. She may be brilliant with other people or situations. You don't have to hate her. Just be willing to retain the right to assess the situation and make up your own mind. You'll know if it is wrong for you. All you have to do is trust yourself and your feelings.

The second issue is that you can trust everyone you ever meet. You simply need to know how they can be trusted.

You have one friend, everyone does, who is always late. No matter what the occasion, the time, or the weather, he will be late. You can trust him for that. If you keep expecting him to be on time, you will be continuously frustrated and disappointed. You might even take it personally and think he does not care enough about you to be on time. Not so. This person is constitutionally unable to be on time. If you accept that and recognize that it has nothing to do with you, your feelings won't be hurt.

Another friend is always upset. Regardless of the occasion, the time, or the weather or she will show up being a "case." Every time, you react in turn by becoming upset. What a surprise. Jane showed up in a major upset and nothing got done because you had to take care of her. How do you think she will show up next time? Upset, of course. That's what she can be trusted to do. You know it, so you can plan accordingly rather than becoming upset and frustrated by your time together.

Your sister is a wonderful friend. She lends you her clothes and jewelry, and sits up nights listening to your problems. She can be trusted absolutely with your money or your things. But she always flirts with your boyfriends. How can she do that? She is your sister and your best friend. Yes, she is. She also consistently flirts with your boyfriends. Better to know it up front than to keep hoping she will change. Then you can maneuver so it's not a problem. Don't introduce them to her. You can trust that she will flirt with them, so eliminate the problem.

Check into your own expectations and assumptions to avoid being disappointed and feeling betrayed. Then know the people in your life well enough to know what it is for which they can be trusted. Then you can trust everyone and quit being a victim.

YOU CANNOT FORCE ANYONE TO DO WHAT YOU WANT

Would you want to force them? Do you want the people in your life to relate to you out of guilt or obligation or resentment? Would you want them to do things for you or with you because they don't feel free to say no to you?

What does that say about how you really view them?
What does it say about how they feel about you?

If we are going to break away from the "codependent," people-pleasing attitudes that shape this culture, we have to begin to allow other people the space to be who and what they are. That includes allowing them to brook our displeasure, to say what they really feel and want with no strings attached and no holds barred. That is a very grown-up attitude. Learn to stretch yourself, to give up your expectations and demands of others. It will help you learn to give up your expectations of yourself.

You will be free to say no to things and to people who don't fit your reality and you will be able to allow others the same freedom. Can you imagine a society in which everyone dealt from what is right for them, what is true for them, what they feel? What if everyone was free of the kind of emotional and social obligations we put on ourselves and each other? We could be free to choose our responsibilities and to honor them without guilt, blame, resentment, or martyrdom.

Would you like that? Would you like to be free to live your life as you please without worrying that you are making someone else unhappy? Would you like to feel that your friends and family do things for and with you because they choose to, not because they have to do so?

We are not poodles. We are people. We are not dependent on anyone else for anything unless we choose to be. It is possible to live without reference to anyone's approval. It might not be easy, especially at first, but it is possible.

If you give up the demands you make of others, you can give up the demands you make of yourself. Think about how that would feel. How would it feel to be free? How would it feel to know that the people you love are around because they want to be rather than because they have to be? How would it feel to be free to make those kind of choices?

It might be frightening for you to even consider the idea right now. That's how enslaved you are. There is a security in the way we operate. Slavery is a safe position. You know what is expected of you and what you expect of others. Ask yourself if that kind of security is fun, enlivening, or exciting. Is it what you want? Does it make you happy? Do you really feel secure or are you just in a rut?

When you force someone else to do something, you are also forcing yourself and will allow yourself to be forced by others. Is that how you want to live? Or, would you like to have choices?

I WANT WHAT I WANT, WHEN I WANT IT, THE WAY I WANT IT

If you are an American, this is probably your attitude. It creates a lot of problems. The inability to tolerate frustration or to delay gratification is at the root of many difficulties. That attitude affects every area of your life.

Do you know anyone who gets angry if you don't respond in the way he wants you to, instantly? Who punishes you if you don't do what she wants the way she wants it? Are you like that?

We are a nation of spoiled infants. Don't take offense. It's not a criticism, just an observation. We want everything yesterday and we are trained to expect that we should get it. After all, we're Americans.

Spend one evening watching television. How many times are the words "instant" and "easy" used? Instant acceleration. Instant coffee. Microwave this. Painless that. We have been trained to expect that life is supposed to be easy, painless, effortless, and immediate.

Many of us have not adequately learned to tolerate frustration or to delay gratification. We brook no delay and refuse to take no for an answer. It doesn't make us happy, but it doesn't seem to occur to us that it is a problem. We often just become more demanding, more angry, more self-indulgent.

We are a nation addicted to pleasure and entertainment. There is supposedly a fix for every problem. That's what advertising promises us. And we are quick to demand fulfillment of the promise. Failure to satisfy our immediate needs results in frustration, blame, and rage.

It is an attitude that results in addictions, passivity, broken relationships, conflicts in every life area, abusive behavior. Seemingly, it is not a useful attitude.

What would be a useful attitude? What would the mature person do? How does an emotionally healthy human being react to such situations? With patience. With responsibility. With a realization that what has to be done has to be done by her. With an understanding that there are no instant cures for anything. Substance abuse cures nothing. It just creates more problems. And how could it feel good if you take your anger and frustration out on a clerk, a waitress, a secretary, a child? Does it make you like yourself more? Does it make your relationship work?

What's necessary here is for a nation of adults to behave like adults. It is painful to try to learn these lessons late in life. We were supposed to master them as infants, toddlers, and children. But the lessons can be learned. Often they can only be learned when we have made such a God-awful mess of our lives that there is no choice but to learn them.

Don't wait that long. Begin to learn now. Question your own motivations for your behaviors. Control yourself even when you think you can't. Be willing to be responsible in your interactions with others and in your responses to frustration. It's up to you. You are the only one who can learn that lesson for you.

PART TWO
THERAPY ISSUES

5

CRISES

Life is not easy for anyone. There are times when we all feel despair and hopelessness. There is a story I once heard about a young girl who discovered one of life's secrets through a very difficult and painful time in her life.

She was part of a large country family. Life for her was wonderful. She loved the sunshine, inchworms, morning glories, and, most of all, her tricycle. She warmed herself on the hearth of her big, noisy family, which was playful and full of life. She had her troubles and disappointments, but mostly life was about the candy her daddy would hide in his hatband or his pocket, ruffled pinafores, her puppy, and climbing the pear tree. Her father was an avid gardener with a huge garden full of fruits, vegetables, and flowers. She thought it was the garden of Eden. After all, there were garter snakes. She had not yet discovered real sorrow, despair, or hopelessness.

That changed dramatically the fall she turned six. Her older brothers and sisters, whom she adored, scattered to the winds of marriage, war, new jobs, school, and work. Her father died suddenly and unexpectedly. Her grandfather, who played with her and her imaginary friends, died soon thereafter. Her mother was devastated and became ill. Within six months, they went from a family of nine to a family of three. Also that year, the city insisted they install indoor plumbing, which required a septic system that killed the entire garden and most of the trees her father had so carefully nurtured through the years. The summer had turned to intense rural winter in their little salt-box house.

Her mother lay in bed so ill that the child thought she might die, too. It seemed that everything around her was dying. She had no explanation or understanding for the events that rocked her young life. Even her puppy was sad: he waited on the step every afternoon for her father to come home from work. How could she make him understand when she didn't?

February was particularly bitter. One day, as she was playing outside, she noticed something growing next to the gas meter on the north side of the house. She squatted in that way that only children can, intent on discovering what this magic was. How could anything grow in the middle of February?

There beside the gas meter, peeking out of the hard, frozen ground, were a bunch of winter violets. Beautiful, delicate, soft, they had struggled through the frigid, rock-solid ground, endured the razor-sharp winds and the icy rain and bloomed despite it all. They had endured. They had won against all the obstacles. There were many days in the years after that when the thought of those violets kept her going, helped her keep struggling when it seemed the ground would never give and let her bloom. She did bloom, again and again, refusing to let the obstacles restrain her from light and life.

Winter violets remind us that after every winter there is spring, after despair there is life.

FIRST THINGS FIRST

As adults, we are fortunate to have many options available to help us in times of crisis that we may not have had as children. As you begin the process of healing, you need to decide what you are going to do first. In the midst of a crisis, everything tends to swirl around you, making it difficult to focus.

The first thing to do is to get some assistance from an appropriate professional or group. See a therapist, go to a 12-step group such as Alcoholics Anonymous or Al-Anon, or attend a support group set up for your particular problem. Seminars, while enormously helpful, are not designed to deal with particular or specific crises. They are primarily designed to teach you new strategies for dealing with life and to clear out areas of on-going difficulty. They are not the place to go in a crisis. Seminars should be considered as an adjunct to treatment, not as a primary resource.

Once you have taken steps to handle the crisis, look around at the rest of your life to see what else should be done. Typically, money and health need attention, as they have probably been largely ignored due to the heat of the crisis. Achieving clarity in your finances will help you know where you really are and what you can and can't realistically do in that sphere.

Check in with yourself. How is your health? An unhealthy body can complicate the problem and create others, since the body plays an important role in your emotional stability. During a crisis, the body is under more stress and needs extra care. Unfortunately, that is when we tend to forget that we have a body, much less that it needs attention and care. If you can't afford to go to the doctor or the dentist, there are clinics, often affiliated with universities or community agencies, where you may be able to get treatment at little or no charge.

Regardless of your financial situation, you can afford to pay attention to what you are eating and to provide healthy, nourishing, balanced meals for yourself. Fresh fruits and vegetables are usually much cheaper than junk food. Drinking water and juice is much healthier than endless cups of coffee, much less alcohol. Over-indulging in sugar products can throw the body into chemical depression expressed in much upset and crying. Pay careful attention to how much sugar you are ingesting. Of course you may have an occasional candy bar or dessert, but to live on sugar will skew your physical and emotional health so that you don't know what's really an upset and what is chemically induced.

In the same way that your body needs attention, so do your finances. Dealing with your finances may be more anxiety producing that dealing with your diet, but it may also be easier. Balance your checkbook. Sit down and list which bills are unpaid, which are due on a monthly basis, and how much money you need for yearly expenses like insurance or a vacation. Balance that amount against the amount coming in and make the appropriate adjustments.

If you are behind in your payments, sit down and make a list of what you owe right now. Decide how much is available to pay the bills. Then write a note with each bill saying that you are paying an equal amount of the monies available to each creditor as an exercise in good faith. If you do this, you cannot be sued. Public Law 95-109 states that no one may harass you regarding your debt. If you are being called, threatened, or harassed in any way, simply remind the caller of this law and of your intention to honor your debt. Tell them not to call again. If they continue to harass you, call your congressperson or your local Better Business Bureau and report them.

If you discover that you are in truly serious financial difficulty, you may want to consult with an accountant or attorney about the best way to deal with your creditors. They may recommend debt consolidation or even bankruptcy. You may need to join Debtors Anonymous. Do whatever you have to do to get the situation handled. The most important thing is to face the situation squarely and communicate about it to the people involved. If you bury your head in the sand and hope it will go away, it will just get worse.

The way to get out of a crisis is to face it. You can handle it and you can have help in handling it. It will not be long before you will be able to look back and see that it is behind you. Just get started now. If you want to do more work on this issue, see *Exercise 11* in the Workbook.

NOTHING IS AS IMPORTANT AS YOUR LIFE

Nothing! Life is very long. At some point, it will look very different. All you have to do is wait. The pain of the moment is the pain of the moment. It will pass. Nothing is forever. Not even this pain.

One of the requirements of life is that we endure the pain of the moment. We are ill-prepared to do that. In fact, we are trained to believe that we deserve to have everything the way we want it all of the time. Everything is instant in this culture, especially gratification.

Instant. Easy. Luxurious. Affordable. These are among our favorite words. Add sex, buy it on sale, charge it, have a drink, and you have a good approximation of the American lexicon. When we are in emotional pain, we think that means that something is wrong. There must be a pill, a "fix," for every possible ailment, including emotional ills. But pills don't take the pain away. They shut down the pain centers so we don't feel it. There are times when pills are appropriate and necessary. If the pain is more than we can bear, i.e., we have had a traumatic experience or are in a state of severe anxiety, there is nothing wrong with asking your doctor for medication. With medical procedures, which are always more or less traumatic physically and emotionally, we expect to be given pain medication. It's part of the process of healing. It's never necessary to suffer needlessly. It is important to understand, however, that there are some things that only time, endurance, and fortitude will heal.

Historical perspective is helpful in a time of great pain and stress. What do you remember of the Bible, the history of the founding of this country, the history of other nations? Everyone has suffered. There are terrible things that can and do happen to human beings. The loss of a spouse, a child, a parent, changes in financial and social status, a difficult marriage, war, famine, disease, feeling unloved, rejected, feeling unsuccessful. How many others can you list?

The people that we remember from history are either ennobled by their suffering, meaning that they learn from experience, or they are destroyed by it. Which would you choose? Would you be willing to let your unhappiness destroy you? Is it worth your life? Do you love the person or the thing you lost more than you love yourself? Or, have you decided that you are unloved and unlovable? Have you decided that it will always be like this and you will never be able to right the wrong?

It's natural to feel like that sometimes, even though it isn't true. Whatever is wrong will be fixed. You will get over it. Even though life can be devastating at times, it is still life. You have the choice to have your feelings, see what there is to learn from them, and let that knowledge polish you into a grand compassionate person; or you can let your experiences make you bitter and angry, and you can play the victim forever. It's your choice.

You can and will survive this. Remember, you are more important than anything else that has happened. In a very short time, you will be glad you waited. The rest of us will, too.

IF YOU FEEL LIKE YOU DON'T WANT TO LIVE ANYMORE, CALL SOMEONE NOW

You're never so alone that there is no one to call. Even if you're away from home or in another country, there is someone to call. Every city has a suicide hotline, probably several. They will talk to you and help you through this. Call a minister, a psychotherapy clinic, a medical doctor. Call a friend or even a neighbor just to come and stay with you. If you feel that you are in danger of losing control and may really do something to yourself, call 911 immediately. Don't drink, don't take any drug that has not been prescribed by your physician for a medical condition. Get on the phone and call someone for help. That means now!

There will always be a part of your that doesn't want to die. Side with that part. Ally with the part of you that wants to live even if you don't see how that's possible. If you will get some help you will be able to see possibilities fairly quickly. In the meantime, let someone protect you from you. Most adults experience a suicidal thought or feeling at some time in their lives. But if you are seriously considering doing something, if you think you might go through with it, you need help now.

It's possible that at this moment you think you are unworthy of help. After all, you've decided to die. Absolutely not true. There is NOTHING that you could do that would make you undeserving of help. NOTHING. No matter what you've done or what you think is wrong with you, it does not deserve a death sentence.

You've just reached the end of your rope. What do you do when you get to the end of your rope? Hang on and order more rope. How? By calling for help from anyone who will listen. All you have to do right now is stay alive. All those problems and obstacles you're worried about can be dealt with later. Those people you call will help you with that. Realize that it probably doesn't get any worse for you than it is right now. All you have to do is a wait a minute and it will get better. But don't wait by yourself. There are times when all of us need someone to be with us. This is certainly one of them. Pick up that phone right now and dial!

IF YOU ARE CONSIDERING SUICIDE, ASK SOMEONE TO HELP YOU THINK OF OPTIONS

There are always options. You may be just too upset to see them. One of the hallmarks of the suicidal person is that perception narrows, like tunnel vision. All options disappear, and the only solution to the problem seems to be suicide. Nothing else will do. But there are always options. Always. If you think there are none, enlist the help of a professional who can help you see ways to solve your problems that are less drastic. We want to help you think of options. It's easier for someone to bring perspective to a problem who isn't caught up in the hornet's nest of confusion and despair that you are feeling.

Can you remember back to childhood, to a time when you had a problem that seemed insoluble? Perhaps you absolutely could not seem to learn how to hit the ball in baseball. Or your favorite toy broke and you didn't have the slightest idea how to fix it. There's something like that back there if you think about it. But then some adult came along and taught you how to bator glued the toy back together. It was fixed. It wasn't even hard for her. What seemed a tragedy to you was easily fixed by someone who knew how to do it.

Believe it or not, your current situation is exactly the same. You don't see a way out. But someone who is not emotionally involved, who can be objective, can help you figure it out. She might even say, "What's the big deal?" Not unkindly, but to help you gain the perspective that's missing right now. The only person to whom it is a big deal is you. Other people may be worried or upset or even angry over whatever has happened. But they're not about to give up their lives over it. Nor would they want you to do so.

Please don't let your panic, despair, and hopelessness get the best of you. Depression is often greatly influenced by bodily processes; it may be primarily biochemical in nature. The influence of hormones or chemical imbalances can make you feel absolutely dreadful and as if you cannot cope any longer. It's a terrible shame to lose someone because he or she is chemically out of balance. But that's fairly easily fixed and is another option for you to consider.

You have one option already. That is to ask someone who is trained to do so to help you think of options.

THERE WILL ALWAYS BE SOMEONE TO HELP YOU

You just have to yell loud enough or ask enough people. There is someone out there right now who wants to help you. Human beings are a family. We are linked by life itself. This country is loaded with helping professionals, all of whom would love to get their hands on you. They live and breathe to help. Give them a chance. They might just do you some good.

In the helping professions, as in everything else, no one is perfect. The first person you contact may not be the person for you. Keep trying. Be willing to have someone help you. Don't make the job impossible.

On the other hand, the person you end up with will also not be perfect. Guaranteed. But he or she will be the perfect person for you. He or she may even help you learn that you don't have to be perfect. People who want to harm themselves are very often perfectionists. It's a tough way to live. The ideal of perfection is so illusive, it changes if you begin to approach it. You are defeated before you start. Get that monkey off your back. You deserve to live even if you are not, by your standards, perfect. No one requires that of you but you.

Your most severe critic, next to you, would be horrified and terribly sad if you hurt yourself. That same critic would probably even be willing to help you if you let him or her know you are in this much emotional trouble. Other people will understand your anguish. We have all had to do battle with our "dark nights of the soul." There are people who are available to you right now who have more compassion than you can imagine. They want to give it to you.

Just as you would give food to a hungry person and be glad for the opportunity to do so, there are many who would feed your soul with love and compassion and understanding and be glad for the opportunity. Most of us have felt what you are feeling right now. You may not believe that, but it's true. Despair is not the province of a few.

If you are really hell-bent on self-destruction, no one can stop you. But you can give someone the chance to try to help you. Be willing to be open and let this person know what you're really feeling and thinking. Be willing to really listen and hear what he or she has to say. Be willing to accept the possibility that this person really loves and cares for you. Yes, you may be a client. That doesn't mean you're a number or a "case." Most people go into the helping professions because they know what it's like to hurt, and they have a great deal of love to give. It's real. You can trust it.

It sometimes happens that, when we're most in need of help, we choose someone who mirrors our self-hate; who doesn't fulfill what we need. If that happens, ask a friend to help you find someone appropriate. But continue looking. There is someone out there to help you right now.

MAKE THEM LISTEN AND TAKE YOU SERIOUSLY

Often, when someone does commit suicide, he has told someone close to him what he is thinking or planning. Only later does this information register. Why?

The first line of defense in any human being is denial. We simply do not hear what would be too frightening or too painful to hear. Hearing problems are developed when we don't hear what we want to, or more often when what we hear is too painful. We simply block it out.

Watch people in any emergency situation. Screams will be ignored, interpreted as playfulness, laughter, or just shrugged off as a family squabble. Only if the screaming is loud, continuous, and impossible to ignore, will it eventually break through to the consciousness of the average listener that something is really wrong. Test it out for yourself. Most people simply don't want to accept that something truly frightening is happening.

In that same way, we listen selectively to what those around us have to say to us. Most suicide victims have been crying out for some period of time prior to their act. They just didn't force us to pay attention. If anyone ever says anything to you that even sounds remotely like a desire or an intention to die, PAY ATTENTION. Don't shrug it off. Better to over-react than not to react at all. If you don't get it the first time, it may be too late.

If you are in serious enough emotional trouble´ to be considering something like that, make sure somebody hears you, really hears you. Don't just drop a passing comment and hope someone gets it. Don't just talk about how someone you know is thinking of suicide or how there has been a rise in the suicide rate. The natural defense system in most people will ensure that they won't hear any of those signals as a call for help. Be as clear as you can. That may be hard for you in your present state, but you must try. Find a close friend or relative, a school counselor, your minister, anyone, and then sit them down in front of you and be as clear as you can about what you are feeling and thinking. Don't let him leave until you are satisfied that he is clear about what you are saying. You will know whether or not he is really getting the message. There will be immediate concern, and he will begin to suggest other courses of action you might take. If he says something like "You'll feel better" or "Have a nice day," he has not gotten the message.

Scream if you have to, but make someone listen and take you seriously. We have trained each other not to listen. We say dramatic things we don't really mean so that the effect of our communication is weakened. It's like the boy who cried wolf. We discount what we're hearing because we don't want to hear it, and because it usually doesn't mean anything. Begin to make a distinction between dramatic phrases and real communication. It could save your life, or that of someone you love.

IF YOU WANT TO KILL YOURSELF, THINK OF THE DEVASTATION IT WOULD WREAK ON THE PEOPLE AROUND YOU

Have you ever known anyone who committed suicide? How did you feel? What did it do to you? If your answer to that first question was yes, you have first hand experience of how it feels and the emotional consequences that a suicide has for the survivors. If your answer was no, read carefully. This is very important.

Do you know that the survivors of another person's suicide, the friends and family, have a siginificantly greater possibility of committing suicide? That means survivors are far more likely to commit suicide than those who have never experienced the suicide of a loved one.

The effects are truly devastating. The person who dies is not the only one affected. The closer the relatives or friends, the greater the risk. Family and friends are left with no way to say good-bye. If you can do it, why shouldn't they? They are left with a legacy of anger, overwhelming grief, guilt, and confusion. What are they supposed to do with that? A death from illness or accident is at least understandable. They can do their grieving and get on with their lives. With a suicide it is not so easy. Questions hang in the air for years, perhaps affecting future generations:

> *Why didn't I know?*
> *Why didn't I see it coming?*
> *Why didn't she tell me?*
> *Why didn't he ask for help?*
> *What did I do that contributed to it?*
> *What could I have done to prevent it?*

The questions, the self-blame, may be endless. Didn't you know they loved and needed you? What did they do that was so wrong that you had to kill yourself?

The loss of a friend or relative through suicide is anguish itself. It is hard to quiet that kind of guilt and grief. If you succeed in killing yourself, you are increasing their risk of suicide by 50 percent. Do you really want to do that to the people in your life? Your parents? Your spouse? Your children? Think very carefully here. You may truly believe at this moment that no one would care what happens to you. It just isn't so. You might even think they would be glad to be rid of you. Also not true. Or you might be so angry at some of them that this is the best way you can think of to get back at them. Is it really? After all, while they may grieve and hurt for a very long time, you will be dead a lot longer.

Do you fantasize about the obituary in the paper? Do you see the people at the funeral, the throngs who will come to weep and to mourn, or the pitiful few who come to pay their respects? What is your fantasy about it? Or have you not thought that far ahead?

STOP FOR A MINUTE AND TRY TO THINK ABOUT THE REAL CONSEQUENCES OF WHAT YOU ARE CONSIDERING. You will be dead. There is no way to fix that. You can't take it back. The people who you love and who love you will have a burden to carry that may eventually break them. DON'T DO IT! It is a very final solution for something that can actually be changed fairly quickly and easily. If nothing else, stay alive for the people who love and need you. They will be glad you did, and at some point, you'll be glad you did, too.

IF YOU HANG ON, THERE WILL COME A DAY, PROBABLY VERY SOON, WHEN YOU WILL THINK, "I'M GLAD I DIDN'T DO THAT"

There may be times when you don't feel like living any more. Particularly if you have been very damaged, you may not see any reason to stay alive. What's the use? It's all just pain and suffering and more disappointment. But hang in there. This is when you get up and fight. Don't ever give in to that. If you get some help and work at it, life will be joyful and worth living. You can learn how to get what you want and also how to release the pain. That's a promise. You can get through the pain. It can be done.

Life is precious, especially your life, even if you don't know that now. You have a great deal to live for and you can learn how to do that. This is just an inning, it's not the whole game.

Take a breather, be gentle with yourself, and get back in the game. Don't give up. This truly is just a mood, a phase. If you will hold on and keep yourself alive, what you're feeling now will dissipate fairly quickly.

Have you ever had a terrible physical pain, like a really bad toothache, a broken bone, a torn ligament, or some other pain that was intense and fairly long term? What did you do? You had it treated and soon you realized that you couldn't even remember the pain. At the time it seemed as though you would never feel better. But then it was over and you had to remind yourself that it hurt.

Psychological and emotional pain works the same way. It can be intense and all-consuming, but it doesn't last forever. Even if you don't have it treated, the pain acts like a wave with peaks and valleys. All you have to do is hold on and wait for the wave to break. It will.

Do things to take care of yourself exactly as if you had the flu. Take your mind off yourself. Do something that is safe and pleasurable and that doesn't involve drugs or alcohol. Give yourself a present or several presents. Drink warm milk, take hot baths, do whatever makes you feel comforted. Ask someone to hold you. It is a guarantee that there are people in your life who love you more than you do at the moment. Let them help you. Or, turn to *Exercise 12* in the Workbook and start remembering all the good times that are worth having again. Then ask someone who cares for you to do some of the exercises with you. And know that there will come a day very soon when you will walk with the wind in your hair, humming a tune, happy to be alive, if you will just wait this minute.

GOOD GRIEF

To lose someone or something you love may be devastating. When the pain is at its most intense, it is difficult to know how to handle it. It may threaten to overwhelm your sense of control. It is not unusual to feel that life has no meaning, that there is no point in going on, the pain is too great to bear. The feelings are so deep and so profound that drugs, alcohol, sex, or sleep become the outlets for managing to function in the face of such a crisis.

A wise man once said "I do my grieving and go on with my life. I let it go." In the depth of despair it may seem impossible to "let it go." It may seem that the pain, the grief, the hurt will be everlasting. There is a kind of emotional shock which accompanies such grief that may leave one gasping for air, feeling unable to recover from the blow.

There is a way to deal with the sorrow of a great loss that will allow you to eventually let go. Do your grieving. Really feel it a little bit at a time until the bulk of it is gone. With a significant loss, there will probably be occasional triggers that remind you of all the pain and the sorrow you felt at the time. But they will be brief and bearable.

Many people maintain such tight control of their feelings that outright grieving is not a possibility. There is a fear that if all the pain is felt and acknowledged you may break apart. The fact is that you are more apt to break if feelings are buried and acted out in the form of excesses in work, substance abuse, or serious depression.

Grief is good when expressed fully and purged from the emotional system. It is normal and healthy to cry, to be angry, to be frightened when confronted with a death, a separation from a loved one, a divorce, the loss of a job or a change in status. It is not normal or healthy to deny the feelings about such an event.

Cry. Cry as often and as long as you feel the need. Tears are purgative. They cleanse the body and the soul of feelings which may become dangerous if buried. Feelings will be expressed in one way or another. They will always show up. If they are buried, they will show up in forms of acting out or in illness. Let them appear. Then let them go. Be willing to feel them. They will not hurt you or overwhelm you. If you are really afraid of the intensity of your feelings, consult a therapist or your minister or priest. If you need someone to hold your hand in order to feel safe in expressing these feelings, allow yourself to have that help.

If you will cry, express your anger and loneliness, it will eventually attenuate. Nothing is forever, not even sorrow. To express feelings is not a sign of weakness. It is a sign of courage and of understanding of the human process. If friends or relatives are concerned by your obvious and open grieving, assure them that you are all right. Your willingness to explore your feelings may give them the freedom to re-think how they deal with their own feelings. Don't let their concern for you shut you down. Keep the feelings flowing.

Loss is a part of change. Change is on-going. It is a natural part of life to lose things or people we love or on whom we are dependent. To understand that process makes good grief logical.

COMPASSIONATE FRIEND

Without question, the most devastating thing that can happen to anyone is the loss of a child. It is a blow from which most people never fully recover. In *The Bereaved Parent*, Harriet Sarnoff Schiff says that 85 percent of the couples who lose a child subsequently experience extreme difficulty in their marriages. The death of a child creates so much guilt, anger, sorrow, and despair that life will truly never be the same. To deal with such an event with any equanimity at all is a triumph.

Compassionate Friend is a not-for-profit support group for parents who have experienced the loss of a child. They are people who have learned how to deal with the experience. They understand the feelings, the fears, the guilt, the despair. Their work is valuable and important. If you have lost a child, their support may be essential.

When a child dies, everyone involved feels guilty and angry. "How could I/you let this happen?" "What on earth could I have done to prevent it?" "I should have———." The recriminations of self and others seem endless. It is impossible for the human mind to reconcile how life or God could allow a child to die. What's the point? While we mourn the death of an aged person, there isn't the same sense of having been betrayed or cheated by life. They had their chance. A life cut short seems to be a senseless cruelty perpetrated on unsuspecting innocence.

If you should suffer the tragedy of losing a child, get help immediately. It is a crisis of such immensity that it is very unlikely you can handle it by yourself. Call Compassionate Friend, find a good therapist, contact your minister, priest, or rabbi. You will need all the help you can get for quite a long while. If you want to maintain your family, your marriage, your job, and your community ties, you must have help.

The consequences of such an event are serious indeed. Everyone in the family will require help and support to come through it. Each parent will blame the other, self-hate will be at an all time high. And the grief will be overwhelming. The other children will feel that you loved the lost child more, or that they should have been the one to die. They may be ignored entirely in the tidal wave of feelings that follows. There may be a very great anger at God for allowing this to happen, profoundly affecting your religious beliefs. The time that you need your faith the most may be the time it is eclipsed by rage. It is certain that your work will suffer and you may not feel like letting anyone be close to you.

The worst thing that you can do at a time like this is to shut off the support of friends, relatives, and neighbors. You will need all the love and support you can get. If you will allow it, there will be a great out-pouring by the community on your behalf. By contacting Compassionate Friend, getting into therapy, and allowing the community to support you, you will be able to get through this with as little damage as possible. Please understand that all of your other relationships will be put under very great strain as you go through this. If you want to save your marriage and allay long-term damage to the other children, you must get help. Call or write Compassionate Friend at P.O. Box 3696, Oak Brook, IL 60522-3696. Phone: 708-990-0010.

YOUR GOD CAN AND WILL HELP

A major resource for help and support is your God. Just ask. That's all you have to do. God is as close as you are. If anyone went away, it was you. You don't believe in God? Then ask Life to help you. Whatever your definition of God may be, there is something to believe in other than yourself. If you can't believe in you, or in God, then trust in the life principle, the force, or the higher power. Whatever you want to call it is up to you.

This is not hocus pocus or faith. It is fact. Many of our scientists know that there is an intelligence in life that keeps the universe organized and moving. If it can manage the universe, it can manage you.

You are not alone, abandoned, set adrift. Love and healing are as near as your willingness to ask and to accept. You must be willing to ask. You must also be willing to accept. No one, not even God, can give you anything if you won't take it. Belief is not enough. You must KNOW. Know you will be helped and you will.

Be prepared for surprises. It is true that God works in mysterious ways. The help you ask for may not come the way you envision it. For instance, if you ask God to help you with your fear, what you may get is more fear. Giving you more fear will ultimately help you do away with being afraid. That is not what you meant when you asked for help, but God is wiser than we are. God knows what you need to get past this and go on to the next level. If you ask for comfort, tenderness, support, love and strength, your God will hold your hand all the way. Love and support are already there. You are just ignoring them.

When you feel unloved and unworthy, it is hard to believe, or even to consider, that God could love you. It is almost impossible to believe that God already does love you and is right there, ready and willing to help you.

This is not about religion. Religion concerns a particular set of rituals and dogmas. This is just about your relationship with your God. You can put that in any context that is comfortable and workable for you.

If you are suffering and in great pain, frightened, out of control, you are ignoring the presence of your own spirituality and the power of the God within you. Ask that you be allowed to feel, to know that there is a Being of great power waiting to help you and guide you. The feeling will come. Let it in.

If you can acknowledge and learn to trust in a power greater than yourself, you and your life can get back on track quickly and powerfully. This is a basic tenet of any 12-step program. Alcoholics Anonymous and its sister programs work. Countless alcoholics have saved their own lives by being willing to turn their will over to their "power within." If it worked for all of them, it can work for you. Try it. It won't hurt you and it is free.

This may all seem ridiculous to you now. You may have to wait until you are absolutely sick and tired of being sick and tired, until you have reached your most outside limit, to try this. It's all right. Sometimes that is what it takes. But when you get there, when you reach the bottom of the pile, remember: your God will be there, waiting patiently.

6

ABUSE AND VIOLENCE

No one ever gets to be mean to you, not even you. One of the major problems that frequently comes up in therapy is abusive behavior. My response is: You don't have to put up with it. Ever. NEVER!

No one has the right to be mean to you in any way. You don't deserve it. You didn't cause the abuse. IT IS NOT YOUR FAULT. It doesn't matter what you have done or not done, you don't deserve to be punished or abused, and no one has the right to do that to you.

If this is happening to you at all, more than once, mentally or physically, your self-esteem is at a dangerously low level. Get help now. Don't wait until you can't stand it anymore, because that time may never arrive.

Ask yourself, "Why am I putting up with this?" Then say no. You're allowed to say "NO!" and mean it. Do it now.

Are you abusing yourself? With drugs...with alcohol..with sugar...with cigarettes...or even with exercise? Excess in any area is abusive. Moderation in all things is an old and practical rule.

Wake up and take a close look at what you are doing to yourself, or allowing to be done to you. Maybe someone has convinced you that you deserve this kind of treatment, or that's the way it's done, or that it's normal. Absolutely not!

CHILDREN ARE VICTIMS

We discuss at some length in this book the idea that we are not victims. We have the power to decide our destinies and to choose our state of being. We can choose to be happy and content or miserable and sad. We can make a conscious choice about how to respond to the things that happen to us, and we can take responsibility by looking at what attitude created the situation.

Children, however, are victims. They do not have the freedom to walk away, or to say no to brutality and abuse. They are dependent on their parents and other people in their environment. They are, in that sense, powerless. They are the victims of their circumstances.

It is unfair, as an adult, to blame yourself for what happened to you as a child. Blaming yourself is an unwieldy burden that does not belong to you. Children tend to blame themselves for the things that go on in the family. It is not your fault that your parents divorced. It is not your fault that anyone died or otherwise abandoned you. It is not your fault that you were abused or molested or brutalized.

Babies are born to adults who have already created a life drama that they are playing out. The child is innocent of any part in that drama. Some well-meaning person may suggest that you had some responsibility for what happened, perhaps in the form of an unconscious desire. That is not helpful. It only adds more guilt to an already overburdened psyche. You are completely innocent of any culpability in the drama of your life as a child.

Only as an adult will you truly have the opportunity to make choices about how to view what happened then and how to deal with it now. You do have the option to forgive yourself and others and get on with your life. You can do that best by not blaming anyone, you or them, but by understanding and accepting what happened without feeling guilty. None of it was your fault. While you were a victim then, you do not have to be one now. You were innocent then and you are innocent now. You can let it go without a backward glance. It is part of your past, not your present.

CHILD ABUSE

When we think of child abuse we tend to think of gross physical abuse:

battering that causes serious damage. It's not that simple. If a child is about to do something that is dangerous after being told not to, it may be appropriate to slap the child's hand while explaining why you are doing it. Otherwise, it is NEVER appropriate, useful, or healthy to hit a child.

How do you feel when you get hit? Does it make you feel good about yourself? How do you feel about the person who hit you? What kind of revenge fantasies do you have? Think about what it's like to be three feet tall and hit by a giant. Would it make you feel secure? Safe? Loved? What interpretation of yourself and the world might you make? An adult who hits a child in anger only knows how to solve problems through violence. That's how that person was treated as a child. You can count on it!

There are whole sections of this country where the parenting ethic is still "Spare the rod, spoil the child." It is shocking to find "parent paddles" in southern and western gift stores. Would you really want to receive a gift that helps you beat your child? What kind of mentality is that? Does it work? Did it ever?

Children who are spanked, beaten, and whipped learn to obey. They also learn to be sneaky, angry, frightened, and victimized. They learn that the world is a fearsome place where they will be punished for what comes naturally to them. They learn to shut down their feelings, to trust no one, to defy authority, and to create a pattern in which they are forever in trouble. They also grow up to abuse others, or to be so afraid of their own hostility that they allow everyone to walk all over them.

Is that how you were treated? Is that how you treat your child? No one learns anything from violence except more violence or passivity. The classic language is "fight or flight." Children are powerless to do either. They must take what is dished out and keep quiet about it. They are people who eventually, with any luck, show up in therapy with deep-seated problems.

Of course it is horrible to be brutalized as a child in the ways that we read about in the papers. But there are other horrors which are more subtle, more insidious and just as damaging to the psyche. It may be worthwhile to list these behaviors, some of which you may not even be aware of, as falling under the category of child abuse. They include:

Whipping a child with a belt.

Slapping a child in the face.

Terrorizing a child with threats about what will happen if he's not "good." (How does a child know what an adult considers good?)

The wild rage of a parent out of control for reasons which have nothing to do with the child.

Threatening to send a child to an orphanage if she doesn't shape up.

Threatening to abandon the child.

Constantly screaming at a child that he is not good enough, or careless, stupid, clumsy, fat, or ugly.

Giving a child a gift and then telling her how you had to sacrifice for it and how she really doesn't deserve the gift or appreciate it.

Coming home, flopping in a chair, and telling the child how it's all his fault you have to work so hard.

Telling children they are the reason for your misery and unhappiness.

Describing, often and in detail, the nightmare of the child's birth, how it was hot, how you were in labor for 72 hours, and how you had convulsions and nearly died.

Talking about how "bad" the child is as if the child were not in the room.

Always over-riding the child's decisions and desires.

Letting your children know they're too stupid to know what's best for them.

Telling the child you will love him if only he _____ (fill in the blank).

Telling the child she could do better no matter what she has done.

Being rough with the child.

Dealing with a child as if he is a chore to get done rather than a beloved person to be nurtured and cared for.

Being so moody or irrational and unpredictable that the

child lives in fear and never knows what to expect.

Taking your frustrations, anger, and anxieties out on the child.

Never being affectionate.

Being cold, distant, uncommunicative.

Threatening the child with dire consequences for breaking something or making a mess.

Giving a child everything she wants one minute, and nothing the next.

Ignoring a child's pleas for attention and getting angry when the child doesn't quit trying to get your attention.

Shutting a child out, literally or figuratively; telling her "Don't bother mother or father."

Expecting or demanding that a child take care of you and your feelings.

Coming home drunk and expecting the child to take care of you.

Telling the child all of your problems.

Discussing finances in front of the child so that he worries and feels insecure.

Automatically saying no without even listening to the request.

Over-reacting to typical childish pranks. A child is not immoral for sneaking a cigarette in the garage.

Telling children that if daddy really loved them he would come home from work.

Enlisting the child to be on your side against your spouse.

The list could go on but you get the idea. Anything that damages a child's self-esteem or sense of security is abusive. Almost every parent has struck out at a child in anger. Children can drive you to distraction. But there is a major distinction between one or two instances of loss of control, after which an apology was made and explanation given, and the consistent destruction of a human being through physical, verbal, and emotional means.

People hit babies. They beat up on and scream at toddlers, and children do not understand what is going on. They do not understand that the parent has his or her own problems. The child takes it personally. He thinks it's all his fault. There must be something wrong with her, she's bad. A child who is abused will grow up and find other people to continue the pattern through further abuse.

A baby who cries constantly, who refuses to be comforted or quieted, can drive a parent crazy in short order. Get help. Many cities have hotlines for such emergencies. Call a friend, a neighbor, a family member and tell them you need help.

Put the child in the crib and walk out for a few minutes. Collect your cool. Ask your spouse to take over for a while. Take the child to a doctor to find out if there is anything wrong that makes the child cry all the time.

Remember, babies do not manipulate. They are simply attempting to communicate in the only way they can. They are saying something is wrong and they need help. Find out what the problem is and solve it. Don't apply adult motives to children. They don't apply. Children want love, attention, and the freedom to explore the world. If they feel a lack of love, they will give you hell in order to get your attention. The more attention you give them, the less they will require.

If you have a difficult child, what are you doing to elicit this behavior? What is going on in your life or in your marriage to which the child is reacting?

If you were abused as a child, get yourself in therapy now! You need help to heal the deep wounds and scars with which you still live. If you are abusive, if you take your anger out on your children, get help. Go to individual therapy, go to family therapy, take a parenting course, read books on parenting. Recognize that you're the one with the problem, not the child. You're the adult. You are responsible for what goes on between you.

If we don't stop the cycle of child abuse, we are in for bigger trouble than we can imagine. Every generation escalates the pattern. The tragedy is that most parents, however abusive, really love their children. Unfortunately, the child doesn't know that. Do you tell your children that you love them? Or do you hurt them frequently? Do you pay attention without being driven to it, but because you want to spend time with them?

Think about how you were treated as a child. What worked and what didn't? How would you like to have been treated? Think about your child. What specific needs does your child have? What can you provide emotionally?

A woman in her sixties, who had been abusive with her own children, was hugging her granddaughter and suddenly felt so sorry she hadn't been affectionate with her children. She realized she had missed a great deal. Is that how you want to feel when you are sixty? You can avoid it by learning the lesson now. Give your child at least as much love and affection as you do your dog. They are treasures. If you're honest with yourself, you will know that they are your greatest love. Let them know that. Soon they will be gone out into the world, and you will have lost your chance to enjoy the precious love of a child.

More importantly, your children will have lost out forever. Childhood cannot be recaptured and there is never a way to make up for what they missed as children. Give it to them now.

IF ANYTHING OR ANYONE HURTS YOU ON A REGULAR BASIS, GET AWAY NOW

You can't MAKE anything work. You can't make anyone love you. And you certainly can't make anyone love you the way you want to be loved. Of course it is necessary to work at anything you do or at any relationship you have. There is, however, a limit. Whether it's a person, place or thing, there comes a point when you have to decide whether what you're going through is worth it.

It's interesting to note that when people deal with money they are generally very careful with their investments. They attempt to get the best deal possible for their money. Not so when it comes to the expenditure of emotion and life energy.

Try to take a hard, clear, dispassionate view of the situation. If it hurts, if it is a constant source of pain and frustration, why are you hanging on? Let go. Do you want to be that masochistic? Do you really need to suffer that much and that often? Some things just don't work out, and no amount of anything is going to fix them. Learn to accept that you're better off without the pain. This is a very hard piece of wisdom to come by, and it's a major part of growing up to learn this lesson.

We all hate change. All of us. But it is constant, ever present. What worked yesterday or last year probably doesn't work now. THINGS CHANGE. We don't like it but it's true. You may have learned everything there is to learn in this situation. It's hard to let go. It is, nonetheless, necessary.

The fact is you don't need anything or anyone that badly. What you do need is to protect your own peace, happiness, and self esteem. It doesn't matter who or what it is: relative, spouse, best friend, job, city/location, hairdresser, or mechanic. If you're constantly unhappy with it, you don't owe it anything. Nothing.

You do owe it to yourself to make the very hard decisions that protect your well-being. Remember: YOU COME FIRST. Write it or them off. Sound cold or hard? It's not nearly as hard as staying with something or someone that hurts you that much.

It doesn't matter whose fault it is. Quit trying to figure it out and listen to your feelings. They will tell you very clearly what you need to do for you. Then do it. And don't feel guilty about it.

INCEST AND MOLESTATION

Incest and molestation are complicated problems. Incest occurs when an adult family member sexually molests a child. Molestation occurs when anyone outside the family molests a child. Both are very common, increasingly so. If you have been the victim of either or both, just reading the words may trigger your emotions.

It is estimated that one in four American women have been molested. What that means is that the actual figure is much higher. In other words, a majority of women have been molested. What is less publicized and less apparent is that boys are the object of molestation nearly as often as girls.

If you have been molested, you may be very much aware of the memories. Other people block the memory entirely and it doesn't show up until they've been in therapy for a while. If you have very difficult relationships, difficulty with sex, are afraid of men or women, you may have been molested.

You need to know that it was not your fault. You may have been threatened and bribed, and then threatened some more. There was probably no one to turn to. Your cries for help may have gone unheeded. You were probably too ashamed to tell anyone, or too scared. IT WAS NOT YOUR FAULT.

Children are sexy, not sexual. They do not invite sexual behavior from anyone. It is the adult's problem. Intense rage, shame, a sense of betrayal, fear, and lack of trust characterize the victim. Low self-esteem, alcoholism and drug abuse, sexual acting out, and a desire to get even follow.

A woman who was sexually abused by her brother was not sorry to see him die years later of prostate cancer. She felt that he had been duly punished. This level of rage is not unusual. It is understandable. To take a child's innocence prematurely and against his or her will is a serious matter indeed.

If you are a parent, spend time thinking about every possible way to protect your child from being molested. If you were molested, you know the signals. If your child begins to behave strangely, doesn't want to go to school, to Uncle Johnny's, or to the neighbor's, be suspicious. Either take your child to and from school and play, or see that he/she travels in groups of other children.

Know everyone who is involved with your child. See to it that your baby is not left alone with anyone who is not above reproach. Talk to the child about the sanctity of his or her body. Make it safe for the child to tell you anything that happens. Always listen. If you discover that the child has been molested, remove that person from your child's life. As the parent, it is your responsibility to see to it that it doesn't happen again.

Some common ploys pedophiles use are promises of candy, money, trips to the zoo, the video arcade, the amusement park. They might say that their wife is sick and they need the child to come home with them and help. Or they may say that you are sick and they've come to collect the child from school on your behalf. Make it clear to your child that only you or one or two other designated people will come for the child. Your child is never to get in a car with a stranger. NEVER!

It's important not to frighten the child, but you must inform him or her. Help your children be street savvy. Tell them that if anyone touches them in specific places, they are to say no, and to tell you immediately. If you know who molested the child, don't hesitate to call the police and take legal action. Do you want the same thing to happen to another child?

If you have molested a child, within the family or otherwise, please get help to resolve your problem. Do you recognize it as a problem? It is very likely that you were molested as a child and are following the pattern. Do you remember how you felt? Do you live with guilt, remorse, and shame for what you've done?

One of the best things about therapy is that therapists are trained to see all behavior within the context in which it occurs. They are objective, nonjudgmental. They are not there to assign blame, but to help each person get the help they need to heal their wounds and get on with a healthier life. If you are living with the feelings attendant to being a molester and having been molested, let someone help you with that. Your therapist can help you understand why you did what you did so you won't have to do it anymore. You're not a terrible person who doesn't deserve to live. You need help. Get it now.

The sexual abuse of children is a tragedy with tragic results. Make it your responsibility to do what you can to end the cycle.

RAPE

In this country someone is raped every three minutes. Some rapes are anonymous, others are committed by someone known to the victim. In either case, rape is one of the most traumatic events in a woman's life. It is important to understand some of the basic attitudes about rape.

In the film "The Accused," starring Jodie Foster, a brilliant survey of current attitudes about rape emerges as the drama unfolds. In the movie, a young woman is hanging out in a place that is clearly not safe for women in the best of circumstances. She gets drunk and begins to dance with one of the patrons. The dance gets out of hand and she is gang-raped in public, with no one coming to her assistance. The pervasive attitude is that, through her dress and behavior, she was "asking for it." That doesn't mean she should have gotten "it." No one deserves that.

Her judgment was poor. She had not learned enough to know that it is not safe to wear skimpy clothing and be seductive in a situation involving men, drugs, and alcohol. But she shouldn't have had to be raped to learn. It should be safe for a woman to wear anything she chooses without being a target for unwanted sexual advances. No human being should ever be forced to have sex.

Society's attitude, however, is often, if not always, "she was asking for it." As the title of the movie suggests, it is the woman who is accused of wrong doing. While most enlightened people will recognize that this is a terrible criminal act, it is likely that they harbor some notion that the woman was somehow at fault. It's interesting that we don't seem to apply the same rules to robbery or murder. Somehow, women who are raped deserve less sympathy than other victims of crime.

Boyfriends and husbands often have a very difficult time when their loved ones are raped. While they may know better, they blame the woman for the assault. Relationships may break up as a result. Even treatment by the police and hospital staff, at a time when a woman needs great care and tenderness, may demonstrate uneducated attitudes. One gynecologist actually said to a patient, "They rape 'em, we scrape 'em." The rape may just be the beginning of the trauma. The attitudes of the people around the woman may be even more hurtful than the rape itself.

One woman who had been in therapy for three years finally confided that she had been raped—ten years before. She had never told anyone. She had carried the anger, the fear, the shame all alone, because she had bought the idea that it was all her fault.

WOMEN ALWAYS THINK IT'S THEIR FAULT. "If I just hadn't _____." There are a million fillers for that blank. One of the things that a rape crisis center does is help the woman understand that it was not her fault. She is not to blame. She has a right to be furious, enraged, heart-sick, and frightened. Rape leaves an indelible emotional scar which will never be erased. The pain can be healed, but the scar will always be there.

One 19-year-old was working as a go-go dancer in a bar in Brooklyn. Her car broke down and two of the patrons offered to give her a ride home. Instead of taking her home, they took her to their apartment, where they raped her. When she resisted, they shot her in the stomach with a flare gun.

A 14-year-old girl was walking home from a party just a couple of blocks from home. A car full of teen-age boys caught up with her and gang raped her. She never told her parents.

Housewives are accosted in grocery store parking lots. An attacker breaks into the room of an 80-year-old woman in a seniors' apartment building, rapes her, and leaves her for dead. Children are molested and abused all the time. Note that we do not call it rape. They rarely tell anyone.

How can anyone possibly believe that children, housewives on errands, and old women in the sanctity of their apartments, were "asking for it?" No one wants to deal with the real issues inherent in this crime. It is a crime of power, not of passion.

If you have been raped, these words may be hurtful to you. Go ahead and cry. Cry for yourself and for all the women in the world who have had to endure this grotesque experience. Understand that all women in this situation feel it is their fault. They endure great shame. They are enraged but have no avenue for the healthy expression of that rage. They are frightened that it will happen again and they may never again feel safe. It is a crime worthy of everyone's tears. But there are also ways of protecting yourself and fighting back. Particularly with the diseases rampant today, it is important to fight back. If that does not work, know that you are not guilty. You did not deserve it. And you have a right to be hopping mad about it.

Here are a few practical suggestions to help you protect yourself and your children:

> *Scream your lungs out.*
> *Scream as loud as you can, yelling "FIRE," not "help."*
> > *People will respond faster.*
> *If your attacker is much bigger than you, or is armed,*
> > *you may not be able to stop it.*
> *Be smart about how you fight back.*
> *Have a good dead bolt lock on your door.*
> *Do not admit anyone you do not know to your home.*
> *If someone you know arrives unexpectedly at your front*
> > *door drunk, don't open the door.*
> *At night, park in well-lighted areas and have a buddy go*
> > *to the car with you.*

Don't go camping by yourself.

If you can't get over being frightened, carry mace in your hand, not in your purse.

Don't go in unlighted places alone.

Jog with a partner on well-traveled busy paths.

Never, never take a stranger home for any reason. Don't go to his home.

If you don't know a date well, meet him at the restaurant or at the movie until you feel safe with him. Don't take him home with you if you don't feel ready. Any man who hassles you about that is not a man you want to date.

Get all the information you can about your potential date. A business card with both an office and a home number are essential. Check it out. It could be a fake.

Tell your friends where you are going and with whom. Give them the name and address of the person. Have them check in with you.

Stay sober. If you are sober you will have more control of the situation and can get away faster.

Never leave your under-age daughter alone with any man of whom you are not absolutely sure. Even if you feel sure that she is safe, it is a good idea to have someone else present at the same time.

A knee applied to a man's groin is a powerful weapon. Teach your daughter how to use it.

Make sure you meet and get to know any boy your daughter goes out with and his parents.

Assure your daughter that if anything should happen, you want to know about it immediately. You will help her with it.

Take your children to and from their activities.

Take your children seriously if they tell you someone has molested them.

IF YOU HAVE BEEN RAPED

Call and visit a rape crisis center immediately. They will be very helpful. You will need help to deal with the admixture of feelings you will have. They can teach you how to protect yourself and to feel powerful in the world once again. They understand the crime very well and will be absolutely on your side. Many of them are women who have had the same experience and they will be there for you.

If you feel that you can't tell your family, be sure to tell someone else. Get some help with it. Rape is one of the worst things that can happen to a woman, mentally and physically.

Go to a therapist and talk it all out. Be determined to heal the damage. You are not required to just take it and live with it. You have been done great harm. You deserve help.

Get yourself to a doctor. Have an examination that will help you deal with the physical side effects. The rape crisis center will refer you to a doctor who will be sympathetic and understanding. Try to figure out what happened so that it won't happen again. Most importantly, forgive yourself. You didn't do anything wrong. You don't deserve to suffer or to be punished for what happened to you.

Be determined that nothing like that will ever happen to you again. It might help you to work with the rape crisis center helping other women. Or participate in ways that will change laws and attitudes toward rape. It will help you feel powerful. It is a positive way to deal with your anger.

This is a very brief treatment of a very complicated issue. For more information, contact your local rape crisis center or the National Organization for Women.

Rape never makes sense. As "The Accused" makes so powerfully clear, regardless of a woman's behavior, no one has the right to treat anyone else that brutally. They certainly deserve to answer for the damage they have caused.

7

ADDICTION

Much is being said, done, and written in the name of addiction at this time. The notion of co-dependence has exploded into a national phenomena spawning 12-step programs for every possible problem from alcohol to incest.

The Portable Therapist employs the language of co-dependence occasionally, only because it is popular and understood by the general reader. Everyone knows, or thinks she knows, what co-dependence is. Co-dependence is actually a pop-psych word for a much deeper, underlying condition.

Co-dependence is not discussed in any depth in this book because it is the tip of the iceberg. It is not the primary addiction. Addiction is a symptom of deeper, underlying pathology. If almost everyone has a problem requiring a 12-step program, then clearly there is something else going on here. Twelve-step programs are powerful healing tools, but they are not the answer to everything.

Addiction has become a catchword, signifying little, much as depression has become the word we use to mean we don't feel good in any of a thousand ways, large and small. So what has spawned this proliferation of programs for addiction and co-dependence treatment? It is the recognition that most of us have a problem. It is not just a few people in this country who are ill, maladapted, or addicted.

There are many ways in which addictive behavior is manifested. What causes so many people to identify themselves as addicts of one sort or another? What is at the root of so much unhappiness and self-destructiveness?

Take a look at the world around you. This is a sado-masochistic culture. That is the real definition of co-dependence. It is the meaning of victim-tyrant. The reason other language is used is that no one wants to think that we are all sadists and masochists. Think about it. Sadists and masochists are dependent on each other. One plays victim, the other tyrant.

It helps if you can remove the judgment around the language. We think of sado-masochism as involving people who walk around in black leather and chains. That's the caricature of sado-masochism. S&M sex is the extreme end of the scale.

Perhaps a more appropriate and acceptable way to talk about the current rise in self-destructive behaviors is to say that we are a culture deeply addicted to suffering. Can you recognize that in yourself? In others?

This is a culture in which we are taught that to be fully alive is dangerous. If we get too boisterous, too rowdy, feel too sexual, too excited by any of life's wonders, we are told to get back in line. Calm down. Be quiet. Be good. We are taught to kill off our own life force and are required to succeed at doing so. The churches, the government, the schools, our social etiquette, our judgments of ourselves and each other, all combine to teach us to be good, quiet, obedient, and not to be too full of anything, especially ourselves.

The movie "It's a Wonderful Life," a Christmas favorite, is a very moving story. It is also a sad commentary, and a very telling one, on how we require ourselves and each other to give up our dreams, "settle down," and be responsible.

The young man in the story gives up his dreams of college, travel, and adventure, to run the family business and have a family of his own. There is nothing wrong with that decision if it is really his choice. For most it is not. There are no options.

The idea that someone might want to go off to Pago Pago and be a carpenter is heresy, crazy, and irresponsible. How many dreams have you been reasoned out of realizing?

We are taught that life is about suffering, pain, sorrow, and not getting what you want. Of course, no one always gets what she wants. And sometimes getting what you want does have the consequence of interfering with the wishes and needs of others. Otherwise, it should be your absolute right to go after your wildest dreams.

Our ancestors did. They came to this country full of dreams. They went west. They built empires, explored new territories. What happened to our wanderlust, our willingness to do something different than everyone else? When did it become unacceptable to want to be free?

No wonder there is so much suffering and so much addiction. Very few people are really making choices about their lives. We follow the pattern, the tradition. We do what we are told to do and what is expected. Boring! So we look for a way out. We go for a drink, a piece of food, a cigarette, a drug; we shop, we have sex—again. What feelings are we covering up?

What feeling are you refusing to have when you reach for your substance of choice? Let yourself feel it! If you have doubts about whether or not you are addicted to suffering, do *Exercise 13* in the Workbook.

Although our constitution guarantees our right to the "pursuit of happiness," most people don't even see it as a goal. How can we be happy in a system that requires two people to work to maintain a decent standard of living? How can we be happy when financial success is punished by outrageous taxes? What kind of system requires a fishing license and has rules about how you can fish? Is there anything in this country that is not regulated?

If you answered, "I'm not," you'd better believe you are. You are controlled by the demand that you suffer. It is a cultural requirement. Have you noticed that if you call one of your friends or family to share good news, the conversation immediately drifts to who's suffering over what? Pay attention next time; it happens all the time.

If you get happy, what will you and your friends have to share? No one has a stake in your getting and staying happy. If that sounds cruel and uncaring, test it out. What people really do most of the time they get together is complain about what's wrong with their lives. Do you know people who are always upset over their awful jobs, their lousy spouses, their obnoxious kids, their failing health, crabgrass, bills, car trouble, even the weather? They never have anything good to say. It is a misery to be around them or to talk to them. How much of that do you do?

Do you think that you have to have a dramatic, overwhelming problem in order to get the attention of others? Do you always have one? Do you think that you can only grow through suffering, pain, and sorrow? There are patients who think that if they didn't cry in their session, nothing happened. That really tells the whole story.

Does television news tell you all the wonderful things that went on in the world that day? No. It tells you that there is great suffering and much of which to be afraid. Good victim. Take a look at yourself, your family, your friends, your culture. You are not addicted to a substance, you are addicted to suffering. Your substance of choice, including anxiety and depression, is your way of continuing your suffering. It is something else over which to suffer.

If you notice, sometimes you learn wonderful things about yourself and the world when good things happen. You take a trip, you do something new and fun, you accidentally laugh with friends for hours on end. What did you learn from that? Is it possible to learn from play, from light-heartedness, from joy? You bet it is. And it's a lot more fun.

NEWS FLASH: You can choose to be happy. Right now. Right this minute. You can quit being poor, pitiful Pearl (or Paul), on your bed of pain, and choose to be happy this minute. You can create joy for yourself. How do you do that?

By taking charge of your life. Right now. Get out all those lists you've been making and look to see where you are not making your own decisions. Dig deep down and be honest with yourself about how you want to live your life. Don't refer to anyone else in this decision; only your thoughts and dreams are to be considered. What would it look like to live your life full out? You can balance your picture against reality later if you choose to do so. But at least let yourself know what it is you really want.

Joy is a result of freedom. Freedom is the result of courage. Courage is the result of passion. Be passionate, about everything except suffering. Passion means living as if you mean it. You can choose not to wander through life drugged to the gills with suffering just to get through it.

You can be a cultural revolutionary. You can choose to be happy and not suffer. You can refuse to have people in your life who insist that you suffer. It will be hard work, but you can conquer your addiction to suffering. What would you give to be happy, to be at peace, to be free?

If you find that you are not ready to give up your suffering, then you simply have not suffered enough yet. The time will come when you will be sick and tired of being sick and tired. Until then, you will just have to continue to enjoy your suffering. Clinically, it's called "secondary gain." That is not intended to be mean, but to point out that at some level you do enjoy your suffering.

Have the courage to give yourself freedom and joy. You have it in you to do that. It has just been educated and acculturated out of you.

Let's refuse to be slaves in any way, particularly to suffering. If we refuse to suffer, many ills, national and international, will disappear. If we refuse to be addicted to suffering in any way, we can, one by one, create a critical mass that will change the world. If that sounds grandiose, think what a few brave individuals did in Philadelphia in the 1770s. They were willing to put everything on the line to create a free society. We can re-create it.

Put your foot down now and refuse to be a slave to anyone or anything. Work on yourself until that is absolute truth at every level of your being. If enough of us make that kind of commitment, we can make a difference. We can change the world.

DON'T SUFFER OVER YOUR SUFFERING

If that sounds redundant to you, it is. It is working overtime on your suffering. Something happens that you don't like. You are upset, hurt, disappointed. You have all kinds of feelings, which qualify as suffering. You may cry, get angry, have a drink, yell at the kids and the dog. This may all be appropriate to your feelings about the situation. Most of us, however, take it a step farther.

We are upset that we are upset. In addition to our hurt feelings about the issue at hand, we are angry that life has betrayed us. We did not get what we wanted. It's so unfair. We've been so good and tried so hard and it didn't work out. We pout, we stomp around, we go to bed and replay the whole movie in our heads.

That's suffering over our suffering. It's apparently not enough to have something real over which to suffer. We then suffer over the idea that life has been cruel enough to make us suffer. It is the ultimate victim position. It can't be my responsibility. Life did this to me. It is the adult version of the child's game: "Nobody likes me. Everybody hates me. I'm going to eat some worms." Eating worms does not alter the situation.

It is useful to know how to put a limit on suffering. Assess what has happened. Acknowledge and express your feelings. Decide what positive action you need to take in view of this event. Then do it. You have had your feelings and the problem has been handled. For all intents and purposes, it is over.

On a camping trip, a bear rips your tent (in your absence!), eats your food, and generally tears everything up. The campsite is a mess. You can't stay in the tent, you have no food left, and you're afraid the bear will come back. You pack up and go home disappointed and disgusted. Your weekend has been ruined.

You have your feelings about it. You buy new camping equipment and plan a trip to a different part of the park on the next available weekend. You have a great story to tell your friends. You have had an adventure. You have learned not to leave food in your tent. Not a bad experience, all in all.

A committed sufferer will go on endlessly about what a trauma it was. You'll never have another tent like that one. It belonged to your grandfather, the great white hunter. Your kids are afraid to go camping again. This experience has ruined camping for you. It will never be the same and you may never go again. That's suffering over your suffering! There is enough suffering without creating more. Set a limit on it.

LOVE OR ADDICTION?

Addiction isn't always to a substance. It may also be to a person or to a behavior.

If your lover has made it clear he or she wants out of the relationship and has broken up, separated from or divorced you, why are you still hanging on? In many situations, it is normal to hang on, to fight for the relationship. It is tough to believe that it is over and it may not be. This may be a phase. But if it has been any real length of time since your lover left you and you are still trying to hang on, still chasing him or her, still longing every night and every morning, you need to ask yourself what is going on.

Illustrations of this kind of addictive "love" abound. There is the man who keeps going back, actually running back, every time his girl friend calls, even though she treats him very badly and always ends up breaking up with him. All of his friends and hers know she will do it again, but he keeps going back.

Or the woman who has been divorced for years but still clings to the hope that any minute he's going to come back to her. He's around for the children, and she confuses that with interest in her. She spent years during the marriage complaining about every facet of his personality and behavior, and constantly complaining to her friends about his treatment of her. But the minute he left, she swore she loved him and couldn't imagine living without him. What's going on here?

Then there is the couple who have been married thirty years or more. During that time the woman has been treated badly, the man has been consistently unfaithful, never at home, emotionally abusive, and withholding. As soon as the children are grown, he decides to leave, and he divorces her. Then the real battle begins. She chases him constantly, begging him to come back to her. He moves across the country. She follows. She will track him down wherever he goes and begin the drama all over again. He tells everyone what a victim he is, of her unreasoning demands and of her desire to have him back. She continues to harass him, living in hope and nourishing her sorrow. They are both addicted to the drama. If he really didn't want her around, he could make that clear enough to make her go away. Observers can see an obvious pattern of mixed signals. He uses her for what he needs, giving her reasons to be hopeful that it will work out in her favor. He is not a victim and neither is she. They are both addicted.

If you are caught in such a pattern of addiction, you would benefit from the help of a professional. There is something very unhealthy going on in your feelings regarding this relationship. Why would you keep going back for more abuse? Why are you creating a relationship in which you are constantly being rejected? Is this another way to abuse yourself? Is it a way to covertly express your anger at your partner? Do you want him to come back so you can dump him and be the one who left?

Go get someone to help you get out of this addictive relationship, so that you can get on with your life. Then find someone who will love and want you. Addiction and love are not the same thing. You need someone to help you learn the difference.

8

ANGER

What goes on in the world, even in your most intimate relationships, may have very little or nothing to do with you. That may be hard to believe but it's true. When other people are being difficult, angry, abusive, insensitive, or anything else that you don't like, stand up for yourself. Let them know that you will not allow them to make you the object of their anger or abuse. But don't take it personally. Remember, everyone really lives inside his or her own little capsule and ultimately is reacting to the contents. You are not in that capsule. You are in yours. When other people are reacting to theirs, you are not reacting to them, you are reacting to the contents of yours. Confusing? Look at this way.

No one can see outside of herself. We go around reacting against each other rather than to each other, and interpreting it all in a very personal way. For example, that person you know who gets angry all the time is just very angry. You just happen to be in the line of fire. Get out of the way. The other person, for whom you can't seem to do anything right, who is always hurt and upset, is just putting his stuff on you. Don't take it. Protect yourself.

IT HAS NOTHING TO DO WITH YOU. If it is a close relationship, you might want to point out that you think the anger or the upset is about something other than your behavior. If the person is wise, he will investigate his own capsule. In any case, it's not your fault. You might want to listen to what he has to say, on the off chance that you might be getting some valuable feedback, or to serve as a needed sounding board. But do so from a very dispassionate stance.

What is there to learn here? Not "It's my fault." If you keep coming up with "It's all my fault," that's what is written on the inside of your capsule. Work on it. Find out why you believe that, and then let it go. If you will quit taking everything so personally, you will be free of a lot of your anger, pain, suffering, and guilt. Line it all up where it belongs—yours, mine, and ours—and see it for what it is. This is another way that you begin to install windows in your capsule.

IF YOU ARE ANGRY, LOOK AT WHAT YOU'RE AFRAID OF

Some kinds of anger are a result of fear. When you feel angry, dig down inside yourself and find out what is frightening you. Human beings are inclined to substitute one feeling for another. For some people, it is easier to get angry than to feel vulnerable.

An easy example is jealousy. When you see your lover with someone else, it may make you very angry. Beneath that anger is the fear that you will be rejected or abandoned. The anger may be real and justified, but it is fueled by fear. What if you knew you could survive abandonment? What if you knew that the relationship is strong and you can trust your partner? Then anger would be less prominent and perhaps unnecessary.

We are very frightened people. We have trained ourselves to be. We put our self-worth up on the block to be auctioned off for approval, acceptance, love. Love seems to emanate from somewhere outside ourselves. Our security is tied up in others. Of course we're going to feel insecure with that kind of emotional architecture.

Do you have any personal strength and power, or is it all on lend-lease? Why are you so afraid? What is it that you fear most? What is it without which you could not live? Answer these questions honestly. If you are very frightened, you don't know that you are powerful.

What is your definition of power? Redefine the word for yourself. It is entirely possible that you still feel like a dependent child. Do you? In what way? That kind of dependency creates a great deal of anger. What do you do that reinforces that feeling? What could you do differently? What's the truth? Are you really that dependent or do you just feel that you are? What would you have to give up in order to feel independent? Identify your own power. What is its source? In what ways do you use it? In what areas do you deny it?

Start really working with your fears. Fish each one out and look at it in depth and in detail. As you do so, many will disappear and you will be less angry with yourself and with others. You can conquer fear and "madness." For more work in this area, go to *Exercise 14* in the Workbook.

LEARN TO BE SLOW TO ANGER AND QUICK TO LOVE

If you are angry a lot and fight with everyone, are you requiring that other people be responsible to and for you? Is everyone supposed to know how to handle you to keep you from being upset? Why should that be their job? Why should they bother? They can go find people who will be responsible for themselves and not require that kind of dependency.

If your problems are always someone else's fault, be very careful. Who do you blame and for what? Why hasn't it occurred to you that it might be your responsibility? It is important for you to learn this lesson because BLAMERS END UP ALONE.

Frustration is part of life. You don't always get what you want. If your attitude is "I want what I want when I want it," you will have a hard time and alienate a lot of people. Who told you you're supposed to get what you want when you want it? Where did you get that idea? How realistic is it? No one wants to be the brunt of someone's anger and blame. Why should anyone want that? Someone has said that experience is what you get when you don't get what you thought you wanted. Learn from this experience. Learning to tolerate frustration can be agonizingly difficult for an adult. It is part of what you are supposed to learn as a child. If no one taught you that, you will have to learn or have a miserable life.

Does someone you know get angry if gratification is not immediate? It's not a lot of fun to be around, is it? It is a major component in the co-dependent personality. It is an imperious attitude that says, "If I don't get what I want right now, heads will roll." Does that make you want to do anything for that person? Does it make you want to be around them? Blamers will end up alone because no one can do anything right for them. Eventually people will quit trying.

Learn to be slow to anger and quick to love. Appreciate and acknowledge what other people do for you. Be willing to understand and empathize rather than judge. Expect everything of yourself and nothing of others. How do you do this? By giving up your expectations, demands, and judgments. By being willing to be responsible for yourself at every level of your life. By making a clear distinction between judgments and assessment or discretion. It is your expectations and demands that create your unhappiness and suffering.

It is fine to assess a situation in order to decide if it is right for you. It is fine to exercise discretion about what you do and with whom you do it. You should use both assessment and discretion to help guide your life. They are not judgments. They do not say anything is right or wrong or good or bad, but simply that it works for you or it doesn't. You can still love the people involved. You have just chosen to do it from a distance. That is your privilege.

But does it make sense to be angry at them? You are into dance clubs or church or water skiing. Does that make it wrong for your friends or loved ones not to like those things? It certainly shouldn't make you angry. It is not something to fight about. It is not a sin to disagree.

If the people in your life are required to agree with you about everything, or if they require that of you, the relationships will be stultifying and boring. There are many families in which everyone is required to like mashed potatoes. Any disagreement is seen as a break in the ranks. What would you do in that kind of situation? Would you want to be around people who require that you agree about everything? Or, would you want to run away from them as far and as fast as possible?

If you will love yourself and the people in your life without expectation or demand, without a need to control or a demand for agreement, you will rarely be angry. If your loved one doesn't like mashed potatoes, offer him a baked potato. Ask him for a bite. You might learn something. If you hate water skiing, go along and sit on the bank or beach and read. Let your lover and friends go to the dance club or to church alone. You don't have to be joined at the hip. It is healthy to do things alone and to have separate interests.

As you begin to love yourself, the need to control others will diminish. It is fear that requires control of others. As you get rid of fear, love will replace it and more fear will disappear. Anger will dissipate and the need to control will be a thing of the past. You will be slow to anger and quick to love.

9

FEAR

What is the worst thing that could happen to you? Would you survive it? It may not seem that you could, but, with very few exceptions, you could survive just about anything.

When you can calm down long enough to take a realistic look at the situation, things become much less frightening and anxiety-producing. If you're living in your head with all your fantasies of the terrible things that might happen, you're naturally going to be miserable. The roof isn't going to fall in. The enemies are not currently invading. You will not be killed for standing up for yourself. Your worst fears rarely materialize. But dwelling on them can immobilize you and put life more or less permanently on hold.

What are you so afraid of that it paralyzes you? Looking stupid? Having someone think ill of you? Offending someone? Making a mistake? Being disliked? All of those things may and probably will happen. They're not so terrible. They're just life. You cannot go through life without making some mistakes, being disliked by someone, upsetting someone.

Someone may disapprove of you. In fact, lots of people may disapprove of you. They have to have someone to judge. Don't let that stop you or frighten you. You might lose someone or something that you love. You might be ill or injured. You might lose your job. It's true that all of those things could happen. In a long life there is likely to be a fair amount of pain and disappointment. Sitting around worrying about it, being endlessly anxious and terrified, just makes it all that much worse. You're having the pain before anything real has happened.

It is difficult to get hold of anxiety and control it. It has many determinants, conscious and unconscious. You may never be entirely aware of what creates your anxiety. When you become terribly anxious, remind yourself of the reality. What's real and what's just your fear talking? You can begin to make these distinctions. It's that easy. Decide whether you're listening to your fear or whether there is really something fearsome you need to handle. There very rarely is. Most of the things you worry about never happen. Learn to take control of your fear. Then you will master the anxiety rather than allow it to master you.

DON'T FUTURIZE

This moment is all you have to deal with right now. All those things you're worrying about haven't happened yet. Wait and see what happens. You can plan. You can prepare. Both are important functions of the healthy adult. But you cannot predict the future. Even psychics can't predict the future. They say they can, but they really can't, because everything changes. They just see future possibilities. It can all change in a moment.

Quit worrying about it. The worry just helps make it a reality. Focus on this moment. You are warm, dry, and well-fed. You have a roof over your head. Even if you don't, worrying about isn't going to help.

Be clear about the truth of your situation. Be realistic. But quit worrying about the future. Stop yourself right here and notice that what you're so upset about has to do with what may or may not happen at some point in a future you have yet to see. You don't know what's going to happen.

The moment really does take care of itself. You will note that all of the things you've worried about that really did happen, you survived. It might not have been fun. You probably didn't like it. But you survived. Dying is ultimately the worst that could happen. You can cope with the rest. Calm down, take hold of yourself, and live in the moment.

NOTHING IS UNBEARABLE

You just think it is or will be. Take it a step at a time. Break it down into the tiniest increments possible and deal with those. You can get through this. You can and will survive it. When you start panicking, taking big deep breaths will help you calm down. Try to isolate what it is you're most afraid of instead of being globally frightened. What is the real underlying fear? Is that really likely to happen? Would you survive it? You might think you wouldn't but you would.

The body and the psyche are both very strong. They are designed to support your life and they will do it. Count on it. You are stronger than you think you are.

Is there anything you can do to prevent the things which frighten you so? Take action. Do what you can. Consult the appropriate professional or ask for help from a friend. You don't have to do it alone. Don't just curl up in the corner and wait for the roof to cave in. Do what you can.

If you are so frightened that you want to curl up in a corner, turn the lights off and hide, see your doctor and get some medication. It's all right to do that. It may be necessary and important. Let yourself have whatever you need to get through this. There is support and help available. Take it. If you can't call a friend or a relative, try the local hotlines—every city has them.

Don't turn to alcohol or drugs. They will just make the problem worse. You will have less of you available to handle the problem. Don't abuse your medication. Take it as prescribed. If it isn't doing the trick, tell your doctor and ask for something else.

When you're really terrified, especially if you're afraid you'll lose control and hurt yourself, tell someone. Call a friend or family member and go be with them. This is a very appropriate time to call your therapist. A good therapist will want you to call if you're out of control. They want to help you with that. If no one is available at this particular moment, go to a hospital emergency room or an AA meeting. Go be with people who will help you if you need it. It doesn't really matter much who it is as long as you have someone to help and support you as you go through this. Just make sure it's someone who has some compassion and understanding.

There are public places where that is possible. The hospital emergency room can medicate you, let you talk to a consulting psychiatrist, or just give you a safe environment to be in until the mood passes. People in AA meetings will understand what you're feeling and will be able to sympathize. They've been there. Even if alcohol or drugs aren't your problem, the people attending a 12-step meeting will be there for you if you need them. Now get going. Do what you know you have to do now.

IT'S NEVER AS BAD AS YOU THINK IT'S GOING TO BE

Have you ever noticed that all the horrible fantasies you've had about how a particular situation is going to turn out never actually materialized? Think about it. What goes on in your fantasy is much worse than almost anything that ever actually happens. It's very useful to get hold of this idea. If you start to worry or panic, you can grab onto yourself and remember that that's just your mind talking to you. It won't really be that way.

How often have you worried that you'd have an accident, or embarrass yourself at a party, or do the wrong thing, or that no one would like you, or you'd get fired? You have all kinds of catastrophic fantasies that never come true. The plane doesn't crash. Your children and pets are ultimately safe. Your mate doesn't leave you and you don't get fired. You spend a lot of time and energy worrying about things that don't happen. Quit futurizing. You don't know what's going to happen. Don't help create it by giving it so much energy.

Anxiety has become a natural facet of the twentieth century. We live in what has been called The Age of Anxiety. You don't have to partake of anxiety to the degree that you do. You can begin to control it. You just haven't known that you have that power. But you do.

Live in the moment. What's wrong this moment? If nothing is wrong, then be happy and enjoy yourself. If something is wrong, deal with it. You can. You always do. Whatever happens, you will be able to deal with it, so quit worrying about it.

This moment is the only one you have to live right now. Hang on to right now and know that nothing is going to be as bad as you are afraid it will be. Begin to conquer your fear and anxiety by living each moment as it comes instead of trying to control the future. This is the future.

CONQUERING FEAR

The way to conquer your fear is to get clear about what's real and what's not. Do the people in your life constantly caution you about all the frightening things in the world? How is your fear being reinforced? Do you dwell on your fears at great length? Do you almost always feel anxious about something? Aside from the unconscious determinants of your fear, which are many and varied, there are two dynamics which keep your fear in place.

First, TO BE DEPENDENT IS TO BE AFRAID. To what degree and in what ways have you turned your power over to others? Most people have it set up something like this: Spouse/relationship maintains emotional security. Job/profession/clients enable financial status. House/apartment represents physical safety. Getting along, being liked, not making waves allows social stability.

The problem with this scenario is that you are not in charge of them, you are dependent on them, at least in your mind. If your mate leaves you, you will lose your emotional security. If you do something someone else doesn't like, you will lose a friend and a source of support. You worry that if you lose your job, you will be insolvent, destitute. The worst thing of all to lose is your home. Why? Because you think you'll never get another one.

Second, YOU DON'T KNOW WHO YOU ARE. You are frightened because you don't know that you can handle whatever comes up. You don't trust yourself to replace whatever it is that is lost. You don't know that you are powerful.

A client was once evicted from her apartment due to a legal battle with the landlord. She lost the battle. She behaved as if she had lost the war. She was inconsolable. She had visions of becoming a bag lady. Almost as soon as she had acknowledged this fear, she began to laugh. She recognized that this was her unconscious fear, but she KNEW that she would never let that happen. She knew she was powerful enough to prevent it, and she would.

The keys to becoming fearless are:
1. Dealing with the contents of your psyche and routing out the reasons for irrational fears;
2. Giving up dependency on other people, or institutions, and being willing to be responsible for your life;

3.   Knowing that you are powerful and can and will handle
      whatever comes. You are also powerful enough to know
      that certain kinds of things will never happen to you.

When you become responsible at the deepest level for your life and acknowledge your power to control your destiny, you are no longer at the mercy of economics, politics, or nature. You will handle it all, no matter what comes. Knowing that you can handle anything that happens to you or to the world is a feeling of intense joy and peace. All the security and power you will ever require are within you. When you know that, really KNOW it, life can become an adventure rather than a nightmare.

This may be a long process. It may take you years to rout out all the fear and come to terms with your power. It is more than worth the work and the attention necessary to change your fears into powerful dreams of a life responsibly lived. You are powerful enough to conquer your fear. Use Workbook *Exercise 15* to help you. Get started now. Those years will pass anyway.

PROCRASTINATION IS PUTTING OFF UNTIL TOMORROW WHAT WILL MAKE YOU ANXIOUS TODAY

If you do what you need to do today, you don't have to be anxious about it. Part of doing your homework is taking care of the needs of the moment. If you put off paying your bills, mowing the lawn, doing the laundry, or writing the report, it all just piles up and makes you more and more anxious while creating a number of problems. If you pay your bills late, you will damage your credit rating and have to pay late fees. You understand the consequences of your procrastination. You've experienced them many times.

You may not be aware of the anxiety and stress procrastination creates for you, or that you have the power to change that. It's really very simple. The secret is to do things when they are supposed to be done. That may be self-evident, but not at all easy for you to do. Why?

Let's look at the most powerful dynamic fueling the procrastination. When you postpone everything until the last minute, or even long after it's due, you create anxiety for yourself and problems and upset for others. People are angry and frustrated with you and there may be very real penalties.

This is not a minor issue. You already know that. You need to examine your motives. Why would you create a cycle of self-defeating behavior that frustrates you and everyone else?

What was it like at home for you? What was your family life like? Were your parents often angry? Were you in trouble a lot? Did your home environment create a lot of stress and anxiety for you? Was one parent alcoholic? Or both? Did you live under the constant threat of parental disapproval, anger, or abuse? That's why you procrastinate. You create anxiety, upset, stress, and angry people in your life. You're at home. It's just like it was then. But you don't have to live there anymore. Take this opportunity to really explore these questions in depth in Workbook *Exercise 16*. They're important.

You can create a harmonious life with a minimum of stress and anxiety. Take a long look at how you're recreating your past in the present and decide whether you want to continue to do that. If you don't, deal with the feelings you have about that and begin to let go. You don't deserve to be punished or have that kind of stress in your life. You didn't deserve it then, and you don't have to create it for yourself now. That was your parents' craziness. You don't have to continue it in your life any longer than this moment.

To have less anxiety and stress, organize your life in such a way that things get done in a timely manner. Then you can have a life that works rather than being constantly afraid that you're going to be in trouble. You may still have the fear of being in trouble, perhaps often, but if you've got your ducks in a row, you can reassure yourself that those are old feelings and you don't have to listen. Everything is fine.

PREJUDICE

Are you prejudiced? No? Look again. It is very likely that you have prejudice in one or more areas. Prejudice is based on fear and we are all afraid. The most common prejudice in this country is against people of color. It is a prejudice, like all others, based on ignorance. The only difference between people of color and anyone else is the color of their skin. They are just as bright, just as capable, just as lovable as any other human being. Perhaps less obvious, but just as common, are prejudices against:

Fat people
Homosexuals
Catholics, Jews, Protestants, Muslims
Foreigners
Poor people
Rich people
Anyone or any group that is "different"

It all comes back to judgment. Each of us has a judgment about the people we know. It is unlikely to be in their favor. Even more powerful are our judgments about those we don't know.

Spend some time with *Exercise 17* in the Workbook to help locate and identify your particular prejudices. Are your beliefs true, accurate, based on observable fact? Or are they based on fear, self-hate, and the need to always have someone to hate and dislike? Do you have a need to think of someone as below or beneath you? Why?

Why are you so afraid? What could an individual from this group, or the group itself, do to you? Are you afraid to see yourself in them? Do you need to feel better than others? Why? What is it that could convince you that you are better or different from others? You may be different, however the basic similarities are what is important. Do you practice reverse discrimination? Do you hate white people, or skinny people, or heterosexuals? Why? What do you get out of that? Look deep into your soul and your heart and find what is there.

Now it is more important than ever that we deal with our prejudice. Some of it is so ingrained that it is automatic. But you can lift yourself into the realm of rational thinking and get beyond what you have been taught.

You cannot learn truly to love yourself until you are able to love all others. As long as we have prejudice, we will have hate and fear. As long as we have hate and fear, we will have violence and war.

Have you had enough of violence and war? Are you ready for peace in your heart, if not on earth? Then work doggedly with your prejudice. Rout out the reasons for your fear and prejudice. Tear down the walls that separate you from your brothers and sisters and, ultimately, from yourself.

10

GUILT

Do you blame yourself for everything? Do you always think it's your fault, no matter what happens? There are people who blame themselves for the rain. Or for the lack of rain.

Ultimately, there are only two ways of relating to the world: we blame ourselves or we blame others. You may do both. But you will have a primary mode of dealing with placing responsibility where you think it belongs. Ideally, there are other choices. But we are not talking about an ideal world, we're talking about the real one. What people could do and what they do are usually unrelated. In the area of guilt, we make a choice in one direction or the other.

From a developmental viewpoint this makes some sense. As children, we come into conflict with the parenting figures fairly early. To be dependent and helpless creates anger. That anger has to go somewhere. When the child is frustrated, confused, and frightened, it has be someone's fault. An unconscious choice is made to turn the anger on the self. The anger then appears as guilt and self-blame.

For a child, it is the safe choice. It would be terrifying to blame parents. If it's their fault and the child is dependent, there is no one left to trust or depend upon. If, however, he/she blames the self, there may be some hope. If it's all your fault, you may be able to do something to change the situation. If the blame lies elsewhere, there's very little that can be done. You can't fire your parents.

You're not a child any more. Begin to work to turn this around and accept responsibilty for yourself. It's actually a fairly healthy and helpful stance to take. People who blame others have very difficult lives. That is not to say that you should cling trenchantly to your guilt. Guilt is a terribly painful emotion. It is important to recognize that, in a very real sense, turning the anger on yourself may have been a bright thing to do at the time. It is now time to let it go.

Work with this on a daily basis. Notice how often you automatically blame yourself. Everything is not your fault. It can't be. By looking at your self-blame regularly, you will begin to notice how irrational it is. Guilt is a learned behavior you can begin to extinguish. Pay attention to what you feel and think in each situation in your life and then notice what the reality is. It cannot be your fault that the dog pooped on the rug, any more than the weather is your sole responsibility. Don't just react. Think!

GUILT IS A LEARNED FEELING

Start unlearning it. We are taught to be guilty. We are not born with guilt. Watch babies. They are not guilty. They are not self-conscious. They are just busy being babies. It doesn't occur to them, until we teach them, that they are doing anything wrong. I watched a young mother chastise her eight- or nine-month-old child for getting dirty while playing in the dirt, saying "That's not lady like." It starts even earlier than that. We are taught that much of what we do is bad or wrong and that we should feel guilty and do the "right" thing. A baby, however, has no concept of right or wrong. These are also learned concepts.

Begin to approach life like a child. See it with fresh eyes. Explore and experience the way a child does. Don't attach meaning or judgment to your experiences. You will begin to see that right and wrong, good and bad, are arbitrary distinctions made by the people involved. Erase those distinctions. See the experience for what it is. How delightful! How freeing!

You can begin to teach yourself to be less guilty, to live your life like an innocent child. You may eventually be able to erase your guilt entirely. When you know, really know, that everything you do is for the experience of what you can learn, guilt will have no place in your life. You can then do all kinds of things the rest of the world might think are crazy, or inappropriate, or bad. So what? You're having a good time. They're not.

Animals do not have guilt. They are just members of their species. Puppies eat their own feces. They don't think it's bad. It's just something else to chew. Kittens approach everything they find as a hockey puck. They're not worried about breaking anything. They just play.

Birds don't worry about whether they are doing a good job flying. They fly. They don't feel guilty for eating the worm. They're hungry. They have no right or wrong. Bunnies do not have remorse for eating out of your garden. You planted it for them, right?

Work at becoming child-like. Go with your instincts. You have more than enough inhibitions to prevent you from doing anything really crazy. But if you're lucky, and work really hard, you might do some really outrageous things and not feel the least bit guilty. Wouldn't that be grand?

IF YOU FEEL GUILTY, LOOK AT WHAT YOU'RE ANGRY ABOUT

Guilt is often created by internalized anger. It works like this: You feel angry about something or at someone. At an unconscious level, it is not acceptable for you to be angry in this situation, or maybe ever. You then convert the anger to guilt.

Dig down under the guilt and find out what's there. Is it really guilt? Have you done something you feel guilty about, or are you just guilty of being angry? Look hard. Be honest with yourself.

For most of us, it is often socially unacceptable to be angry. Or at least it is unacceptable to us. Why? Would you rather feel bad about yourself? Apparently. It's like the pressure cooker with the steam building up under the lid. Admit it. You are mad. You probably have a right to be mad. Your anger may very well be justified in this situation. Recognize it. Acknowledge it. Deal with it. Let it go. That's the formula.

When you have done all that, the guilt and anger will disappear. The next time you're feeling guilty, remember that you may just be angry. It's much healthier to be angry and admit it than to walk around being guilty. It feels better, too.

YOU MAY THINK THAT WHAT YOU'VE DONE IS WORSE THAN WHATEVER ANYONE ELSE HAS DONE

That makes you very special. We all want to be special and unique in some way. But are you sure you want to be special in that way? Are you sure you're really the worst person who ever lived? Do you really think you're worse than Bluebeard or Henry VIII or Jack the Ripper? Hold your own version of the inquisition. You're not Hitler's clone. Does this put it in a little perspective?

But you're absolutely sure you're the worst person you know. Maybe you are, but that's doubtful, too. You probably just don't know the people around you very well, or you're too busy judging yourself to pay much attention to them. In fact, your own self-judgment may make it dangerous for them to open up to you. Try working *Exercise 18* for some perspective on this issue first.

Then tell your friends what you have done. You will be amazed by their reactions. It will open up a lot of space between you. Most adults are a great deal more understanding than you are giving them credit for being. They will most likely respond with tales of their own dark side. They need to tell someone, too.

What you may discover is that EVERYONE ELSE THINKS HE'S THE WORST. There is actually a mighty worldwide competition for the Olympic worst: worst person, worst parent, worst student. The categories are endless. How many times have you said "I'm the world's worst ...?" It's a big world. It would be hard for everyone to be the worst.

Isn't it interesting that we are quick to claim the prize of "worst" as ours? But to proclaim that we might be the best at anything would be considered arrogant, grandiose, immodest, narcissistic. Why is it all right to say you're bad but not that you're good? That's how crazy the world is.

If everyone thinks he's the worst, where does that leave you? In heavy competition. And in great company. Lighten up. At least you're not alone!

EVERYONE HAS DONE THINGS HE'D BE ASHAMED TO ADMIT

Consider this: In a culture that's based on right and wrong, it would be impossible not to transgress. Impossible. As long as you think there is a right, there will be a wrong. Given how most of our minds work, you will never measure up and will almost always see yourself as wrong.

On the other hand, if you erase right and wrong and just see yourself as being and experiencing, where does guilt go? Right out the window with right and wrong, where it belongs!

No one escapes this polarity unscathed. A very old woman I knew frequently discussed how guilty she felt that she had been flip and inconsiderate with her mother as an adolescent. Although she had raised many children, and knew thoughtlessness to be the hallmark of adolescence, she could not apply it to herself. She was "bad."

A man in his forties carried terrible, albeit subconscious, guilt and shame over the theft of a candy bar when he was a young boy. At that moment, he had convinced himself that he was bad, and thirty-four years later he was still punishing himself in a variety of ways. It is very sad to see what we do to ourselves in the name of right, wrong, good, and bad. There has to be a way out of this box, and we must find it.

Recognizing that we are all in the same box together helps. You are not the only one. Let's agree to begin to cut each other some slack. We can learn to judge ourselves and each other less harshly. We can give up the sharp black and white edges of right and wrong and create a lot of color. We're really all just students in the school of life. We all have hard lessons. Let's support each other in learning them instead of punishing and judging.

It's time for us to handle this and not pass it on to the next generation. Perhaps we can just let them be.

THERE IS NOTHING FOR WHICH YOU CAN'T BE FORGIVEN

The question is: Are you willing to forgive yourself? Other people will forgive you. Perhaps not the people directly involved, although they too might surprise you. But other people are not your problem. You are.

No matter how awful you think you or your deeds may be, it can all be forgiven. How many times will you have to hear this before you finally give it up? You did what you did. No amount of suffering is going to change it. You've suffered, you've punished yourself, and you've had excoriating pain. Unfortunately, there is no correlation between guilt or remorse and erasing the deed itself. All you can do is attempt to rectify the situation to the degree that you can, and then forgive yourself.

It may not be easy to do, but it can be done. If you're still feeling guilty about something that can't be changed, you need to investigate why. Are you beating a dead horse? It's over. It's part of the past. It lives only in your heart and mind and in those of the other people involved. You can't do anything about how they choose to deal with it. That is their choice. You are not responsible for that. If they're wise, they have learned a lot from the experience. If not, that's their problem.

Does that sound cold and callous to you? If so, you are being overly responsible and perhaps more than a little masochistic. Begin to call a spade a spade. Be willing to stand on your own truth and allow others their truth. If they are choosing to be victims, let them go. There's nothing you can do about it.

You can quit being a victim of your own guilt. Most of the things you've done that you feel so terrible about were a defense of some sort that you needed at the time. At some level, probably unconscious, you may have felt that your survival was involved. It may have been whatever you've done was a better option than suicide.

Some of you will think this is all self-serving. Too bad. That's how harshly you judge yourself. It's actually the beginning of understanding. When you understand what you have done, you will be able to forgive yourself. If you cannot forgive yourself, at least be willing to learn to understand your behavior.

IF YOU CAN'T FORGIVE YOURSELF, TELL SOMEONE ELSE AND LET HIM FORGIVE YOU

Telling someone who will not judge you about something of which you are ashamed will help put it in perspective. If you can't seem to get yourself out of the bad-wrong-guilty range, ask for help. Just telling someone else takes it out of the realm of a guilty secret and brings it out into the light. To come from darkness into daylight creates a whole different atmosphere.

It is extremely unlikely that you are very realistic in your view of your guilt. Having another person's input will help you see it for what it really is. He can help you see the reality of the situation because he is not involved and therefore able to be more objective.

Choose carefully. Don't tell just anyone. Be sure that the person you tell has enough love, compassion, insight, and experience not to judge you. If the person you choose to tell does judge you, don't take the opinion as the final word. You have just managed to choose a mirror of your own feelings. Simply keep looking until you find the person who can really help you with your burden. You should feel lighter after sharing with your friends, not heavier.

If there's no one close to you with whom you feel safe to unburden yourself, go to a therapist, a counselor, a minister, or a priest. They are trained to help you through this. Again, choose wisely. Don't just go in and bare your soul. Spend a few sessions getting a feel for where this helper really is with judgment. If your instincts tell you it isn't right, move on. But continue to look.

Don't get hung up on the inability of others to forgive you. All you can do is acknowledge what you've done, acknowledge their feelings, apologize, and do what you can to make amends. Beyond that it is their problem. They may just be stuck in the process of learning their lesson. You can't help them with that any more than you have. They may still enjoy their feelings of victimization too much to give them up. There are actually people who never forgive anything. You, however, can forgive them for their unwillingness to forgive you. Then you can let them go. They are part of your past. They have nothing to do with you now.

There is someone close by who is available to help you. Ask him to forgive you. Be willing to accept his absolution. In doing so, he can help you find your own.

Search your heart to discover whether you're willing to let this go or if you still need to hang on to your guilt and suffering. If you still need to feel bad, go get help to feel better. It doesn't have to be like this. Regardless of what you've done, you can forgive yourself. You just think you have committed an unforgivable sin. You haven't. You can be forgiven and learn to forgive yourself. You don't have to punish yourself.

THERE IS NOTHING YOU'VE DONE FOR WHICH YOU DESERVE TO BE PUNISHED

No matter what you've done for which you are afraid of being punished, you don't deserve punishment. That may sound crazy to you. Society says you must be punished. Your own conscience is probably already punishing you. So where do I get the idea that nothing you do deserves punishment?

First, we have already discussed that there is no right or wrong. If there is no absolute right or wrong, then what have you done wrong? "But I've sinned," you might say. According to whom? How? If you need to, go back and review the section on interpretation. It's important. It's not just rhetoric or philosophy.

Second, the purpose of all experience is the opportunity to gain wisdom. Stop and take a look at what there is to learn. Quite a lot. Would you do it again? Not if you learned the lesson. Are you wiser, more compassionate? Do you understand more about people and life? Good. Then why would you punish yourself for growing? You've simply had an experience from which you gained wisdom.

It is reality that you will do those things you have judged. This is the truth. Be very careful about what you say you would NEVER do. Because it is precisely that thing you will do. You almost have to do it. If you can't get rid of the judgment any other way, you will have to experience it.

Think about it. How many "I'd never do thats" have you already done? Interesting, isn't it? Now look at the ones you haven't done and start handling your judgments so you don't have to go through that.

When you look at other people, do you think, "How awful?" Or do you think, "There but for the grace of God go I?" If it's the former, get to work on your judgments. They apply to you.

Finally, the reason you don't deserve to be punished is that you will punish yourself more harshly than anyone else would. Yes, there may be legal penalties, or societal ostracism, but they will be nothing compared to what you will do to yourself.

Make a quick equation of your "crime" compared to the punishment you have already meted out for yourself. Are they equal? Or have you punished yourself more severely than the crime warrants? Probably. You certainly don't deserve any more punishment. Have some compassion for you. Start forgiving yourself.

AFTER ALL, HAVEN'T YOU PUNISHED YOURSELF ENOUGH?

It might feel really good to let yourself off the hook. How much longer do you think you should suffer for what you've done? Forever?

Look at the toll your guilt and self-punishment have taken on your life. They have adversely affected you in every area: career, relationship, income, recreation, spirituality, community involvement, creativity. How much more do you have to pay for what you've done? When is it enough?

The legal system sets a limit on how much is to be paid for any particular misdeed: a $500 fine and 30 hours of community work; a $500 fine and 30 days in jail; 5 years in jail and one year probation; suspended sentence and 30 days probation. The point is, whatever the crime, there is a definite limit to the punishment.

There is even a statute of limitations which essentially says that for any crime or misdeed committed, there is only a certain length of time for which that person may be prosecuted. When that time is up, it is no longer an issue. It is over.

Consider whether you are suffering needlessly and overly long about something that should have been forgiven and forgotten long ago. Why are you still hanging on to that? What will it take to get you to forgive yourself and give up the punishment?

Guilt and self-punishment become very crazy business. They will make you crazy. They can literally ruin your life. Have you done anything that terrible? You haven't done anything anyone else hasn't done.

Part of the value of group therapy or a seminar experience is the opportunity to discover that you are just like everyone else. If you put a thousand people in a hotel ballroom for a seminar, 999 of them will have skeletons in their closets. The other one is lying. Everyone has skeletons in the closet. So how much longer do you think you need to suffer and punish yourself? Set a limit on it. If that limit has already been reached, give it up.

LOOK AT WHAT YOU CAN LEARN FROM THE EXPERIENCE AND LET IT GO

What wisdom do you have now that you didn't have before this happened? What have you learned? How can you use this to change your attitudes?

The issue isn't what you do, but how you deal with what you do. If you treat it like an insurmountable obstacle and give up, you lose. You will be stuck with it until you can overcome the obstacle. On the other hand, if you recognize that you did not get the result you wanted and don't like the result you did get, you can regroup and figure out how to get what you want.

If, for instance, you plan to climb a mountain, you make a plan, collect supplies, assemble a team. On the way up, you realize that your plan is faulty, or that you don't have the necessary supplies, or the team is too weak to make it.

Do you struggle on, hoping you can make it anyway? Do you quit and go home? Do you get mad and blame someone else? Do you feel like a failure and vow never to climb another mountain?

The wise person goes back down the mountain, assesses the situation, rests, regroups, and starts over again. That's what a champion does. A champion just keeps at it until she gets it right. But she is smart about it. She doesn't doggedly keep attempting to move forward. She regroups, she studies the situation, and makes a new plan. Then she tries again. And she looks to see what she can learn from her mistakes.

There is a huge difference between learning from your mistakes and obsessing endlessly on how stupid you are. You're not stupid. You didn't fail. You just haven't learned the lesson yet. Keep trying.

Most experiences in life are not a timed exercise. You get to try and try again until you get it right. A wonderful, powerful, loving man was successful in every avenue of his life except relationships. He couldn't seem to choose the right woman to make a marriage work. Finally, in his late thirties, he found and married a woman with whom he has had a wonderful, fulfilling marriage.

It took him three or four tries, but he finally got it right. No one held it against him. MOST importantly, he did not hold it against himself. He learned from each experience and went on to the next. He finally learned enough to make it work the way he wanted it. You can to.

11

SEX

There is an amazing and incredible emphasis on sex in this culture. Everything seems to be about sex. Madison Avenue and Hollywood are sex-crazed. The way to sell anything seems to involve sex, if not violence.

In the sexual revolution of the last twenty-five years, we have come a very long way, baby. It's time to go back to center just a little and find a balance. It is wonderful and healthy that we are more open about matters sexual. But it is important to realize that perhaps the pendulum has swung too far in that direction. Somehow we seem to have given ourselves the idea that sex is the most important thing that happens.

An entire generation has proceeded on the assumption that sex is more important than a relationship, and thus seeks constant sexual gratification. The intimacy of sex has been replaced by a desire for frequency and variety. We have had a sexual carnival for the last two decades. It is time to reassess our viewpoint. Particularly with the advent of AIDS, there is an imperative need to be wise and careful.

AIDS may be the most important teacher of our lifetime. It may force all of us to get off the merry-go-round and start relating to each other as human beings rather than as sexual objects. After all, life is not meant to be lived between your legs.

The joy of sex is precisely that: the joy of sex. It is nothing more. It is not the ultimate in human achievement or experience. While sex is wonderful, it isn't everything. We have been behaving as if little else mattered. In and of itself, it doesn't mean anything. It's just sex.

Sex doesn't prove anything. It doesn't make you a man or a woman or powerful. Sexual liberation has informed us that, if we're really sexy, we will have frequent sex and multiple orgasms. It is our responsibility. If not, there is something wrong with us.

Men study sex manuals, learning how to please their partners, to make sure they have an orgasm. Women are obsessed with their bodies, for fear no one will want to make love to them. Everyone is at the gym firming up all those muscles to be the perfect image of Hollywood cheesecake, male and female. The same man who reads the manuals insists that the woman have her orgasm. If not, he has failed. Both partners feel frustrated, angry, and embarrassed if "the earth doesn't move."

What a waste of time and energy. That's not making love. That's having sex. There is a distinction. Making love is LOVING one another. Having sex is acting as if there are two machines in bed pushing each other's buttons for the desired result.

This attitude has forced our children into an early loss of their innocence. Teenage girls no longer look sweet and vulnerable. They dress like movie stars. Babies wear bikinis. Eleven-year-olds wear make-up and dress in dramatic clothing. Fifteen-year-olds of both sexes rush out to lose their virginity for fear they'll miss out and be considered nerdy. Adults make fun of and pressure anyone who isn't sleeping with anything that moves. It is considered hopelessly old-fashioned to want to be in love in order to share one's body.

What happened to being together? Loving each other? Being tender with each other without any particular purpose except to express love? What happened to loving each other with such emotional passion that "the earth moved" without straining and trying? It is wonderful for everyone that we have learned more about the mechanics of sex. To be a good sexual partner is to understand the workings of the human body and how to increase its pleasure. It is understanding that this is a shared act in which both partners participate, and it is necessary and important to consider the feelings and needs of the other. And sometimes it is just nice to love without any expectations, for the sheer pleasure of loving and being together.

Sexuality is a part of life. It is normal and natural to want to have a satisfying sexual relationship. The key word here, however, is relationship. A relationship involves responsibilities, intimacy, and commitment, not just sexual gratification. Be willing to share yourself as well as your body.

And while we are sexual beings, we are also much more than that. What else do you desire? What else are you passionate about? Take some of that passion and energy and apply it to your work, your art, your hobbies. You can be passionate about everything. Best of all, you can be passionate about loving yourself. Learn to live from your heart rather than from between your legs.

RESPECT YOURSELF

In today's sexually permissive world, it is easy to get lost. It is easy to begin to think that having anybody to go to bed with is better than no one. But take a minute to think: Is it really? What is it that you're really after here?

You may think you're after sex. After all, isn't that the gold ring on the merry-go-round? That wonderful feeling of release and relaxation? Guess again. What most folks are really looking for is intimacy.

Sex, love, and affection are very different things. They may not be at all related. That may all be very confused for you, particularly if you come from a family which was not affectionate. Sex is what two people do to have an orgasm. Love is what one person feels for another that makes the two of them want to be around each other consistent basis. Affection is the expression of the love in non-sexual and sexual ways. Making love is what people in love do. It may or may not have anything to do with sex or orgasm. Sex is better with love and affection. Being sexy and being lovable are not the same thing.

If you love yourself, you will attract someone who will also love you. You can respect yourself enough to require that the person in your bed respect you. If he or she isn't nice, respectful, or considerate, why are you hanging around? You're not that hard up. Respecting yourself may mean you go through long periods of celibacy. It's not fun. It can be physically and emotionally painful. Going to bed with strangers will ultimately be much more destructive, emotionally. Given that AIDS is around, it is also physically dangerous. If you find that you are willing to go to bed with almost anyone, you don't love you. You are attempting to find love in someone, anyone else. That's not love. It's sex.

You may be sexy and you may be lovable. What is it that you are requiring other people to respond to? Insist that they know you and like you before you let them in your bed. Consenting adults are free to make their sexual choices. Anything that doesn't hurt anyone goes. You're free to do as you please. You don't have to be a virgin waiting for your true love to come along. Do consider what you're doing. All the orgasms in the world will not make you feel good if you are being treated badly in other ways.

Look for someone who is loving, generous, tender, and willing and able to commit. Good time Charlies/Susies are fun for the moment, but is that what you're looking for? Hold off on going to bed. The longer you wait before you consummate the relationship, the better chance it has of lasting. You will get to know each other better by allowing time for intimacy and mutual respect to develop. You don't have to wait forever, just slow down enough to know who it is with whom you're getting involved.

WHAT'S YOUR SECRET?

Everyone has sexual secrets. There are as many sexual secrets as there are people. Sadly, there is great suffering over these secrets. It's as if we haven't figured out that we are sexual creatures and that sex is normal and natural. Perhaps if we accepted this as fact, there would be less molestation, incest, and rape. Whatever your sexual secret, forgive yourself. Understand the context in which it occurred and forgive yourself as many times as you need in order to make peace with what happened.

If you have been the victim of rape, incest, or molestation, you need to talk to someone. It wasn't your fault. If you have raped someone, committed incest, or molested a child, get help to understand what made you do that. You know that you feel terrible about it. It isn't easy to live with. Go find someone who can help you with that so you won't have to do it any more.

Whatever your secret may be, sharing it with someone objective and non-judgmental will help you get rid of the pain and guilt. It doesn't matter what you've done, you can be forgiven and learn to forgive yourself. Start by doing *Exercise 19* in the Workbook.

HOMOSEXUALITY

Homosexuality is simply an unconscious choice of sexual identification. Nothing more or less. It is not bad, or evil, or threatening to anyone except the homosexual. Why is it threatening to him or her? Because of the judgements that the culture has about homosexuality. Gay men and lesbians are often ashamed, or frightened, with a pervading sense of guilt or "wrong-doing." The individual may believe there is something wrong with him, that she is "crazy" or "sick." Many people try desperately to deny their own feelings and instincts. For that reason, and that reason alone, homosexuality may be a tragedy for the individual and his or her family.

It needn't be. For most homosexuals, it is a lifetime orientation. They choose a partner of the same sex. They do not do so consciously, or willingly, any more than a heterosexual person chooses to be attracted to people of the opposite sex. It is simply the way they are wired. With the sexual liberation of the last twenty years, it is a better world for gay people. It is far from easy. Gays face enormous internal pressure from their own feelings and judgments about themselves. They also face tremendous homophobia in the form of discrimination in the work place, fear and hostility from the ignorant, and violent rage in some situations. It is all unnecessary.

Homosexuals are no different from anyone else. Gay men and lesbians want what everyone else wants: to date, have fun, fall in love, have a committed relationship, a job, and a home. They are no threat to anyone.

If you are gay, give up the guilt. You haven't done anything wrong. It's not your "fault." If you are not ready to "come out," you don't have to do so. Neither are you required to hide out, be ashamed, guilty, or depressed about your situation. You are what you are. Accept yourself for that. If you can't do that, get help. There are many wonderful support groups available to the gay community.

If you have a prejudice about gay people, reconsider your position. Does it get you anything to hate them or to fear them? Does it really make sense?

Does it help anyone? Do you consider them as individuals or lump them together in a group?

If your child or other family member is gay, he or she will need your love and support more than ever. Don't turn away, judge, or punish. Your loved one can't help it. He or she is not doing it to spite you. This person will face many obstacles in the world which can be ameliorated by a loving and supportive family. There will be enough suffering without having to endure your disapproval.

ADOLESCENT SEXUALITY

No one ever talks about adolescent sexuality except in a negative and judgmental way. Especially to adolescents. Many a confused teenager emerges into the world of sexuality with little or no real and useful information.

Talk to your kids about sex. Tell them how it works, the mechanics. Tell them about menstruation, intercourse, pregnancy, disease. Talk to them about the emotional components. Tell them about the powerful feelings that go with sexual involvement. Help them make the distinctions between sex, love, and affection. Give them lots of affection so they won't have to look for it elsewhere. Teach them to come to you if there is a problem. If they say that someone has taken liberties with them, pay attention. Take them seriously. If they tell you that Uncle Johnny or the next door neighbor or the baby sitter or a teacher has touched them "funny," protect them from further encounters. It is our responsibility to protect young men and women from sexual predators.

Keep an eye open for what goes on with everyone who is around your child. There are situations you cannot prevent, but there are many that you can. You can tell when playful teasing by an adult or older adolescent has a sexual component. Quietly step in and make sure it doesn't go any farther.

Encourage your children to be open and honest with you. Let them know that they can tell you ANYTHING. You are there to help and to protect them. There are certain experiences that everyone has as a teenager. How long have you remained embarrassed by things in your adolescence that you now understand to be normal?

Adolescent girls' breasts can be a very tender subject while they are developing. Your teenage daughter needs the reassurance of knowing that not everyone develops at the same rate. Girls who develop breasts very early or very late often carry a lot of self-consciousness and shame. The understanding support of a parent can increase her self-esteem.

Adolescent girls often spend their early years being embarrassed by their periods. They are afraid someone will know that they are having a period, that their clothes will get stained, that everyone can see their sanitary pads through their clothing. Help them understand that these concerns are typical and normal for girls their age. All women, young and not-so-young, go through the same things.

Adolescent boys have nocturnal emissions, "wet dreams," and fierce hormonal changes. They often experience unwanted erections at inopportune and embarrassing moments. Skin gets oily, hair grows in new places, and emotions are fickle and fluctuating.

There really is such a thing as "growing pains," physical and emotional. Both sexes develop "phonitis" and "mall fever." It's part of the package.

It is normal and healthy to play spin the bottle and post office. It is normal to go steady and break up and go steady with someone else the next day. Some people are late bloomers who may not have a date until they blossom in college. That's okay, too. It is normal to have sudden "funny" feelings for no reason, and to develop crushes on older people, teachers, or coaches. It is normal to want to be alone with the Walkman one minute, and then to crave attention and company the next. It is normal for teenagers to "travel in packs." Most do at some time or another. It is not normal or healthy, however, for teenagers to drink or to take drugs.

Explain all this and anything else you can think of to them. They need help to understand the consequences of the hormones raging inside of them as well as the social pressures fomenting outside of them. Give them as much freedom as possible while protecting them from their own impulses and lack of judgment.

Two of the young people to whom this book is dedicated were given "safe" graduation parties. The two sets of parents, in different parts of the country, organized with other parents from the respective schools two gigantic all-night senior bashes. They had games, dancing, music, and food galore.

What they were attempting to guarantee was a special night that wouldn't end up with the graduating teenagers out drinking and driving in the communities.

To the degree that you can, protect your children from the consequences of their ages throughout their growing up. Kids get in trouble when they have too much freedom and too little real attention. Pay close attention. Give them lots of attention. Love them, pat them, spend time with them. Let them know you love them on a daily basis. Be there to help with any problems that may come up. Sometimes these problems may seem silly to an adult. But to your teenager they're not silly. They don't understand that this is just a phase that will pass. For them, it feels like life or death.

Spend as much time with them as you can. In the blink of an eye, they will be out in the world and gone. Give them as much love, information, and understanding as possible to take with them. They'll need it. You remember what it's like.

IT WON'T MAKE YOU CRAZY

There are many myths about masturbation. It may even shock or embarrass you to read about it. That's how much prejudice we have about the subject.

Get ready for another shock. EVERYONE DOES IT. If everyone who masturbated went crazy, or got pimples, or grew hair on his hands, therapists and dermatologists would be working overtime. They don't.

Most people carry an inordinate amount of shame and self-loathing for what amounts to an instinct. The sexual drive is the most basic and powerful drive in human beings. It is part of the survival instinct. In this culture, young people are expected to postpone sexual partnering long after their hormones begin to cry out for another. What else are you supposed to do? Spend your life in a cold shower?

It is natural and healthy to want to relieve yourself of pent-up sexual urges. To refrain from doing so can, and does, lead to excessive aggression and hostility. Feeling guilty and ashamed of it complicates the problem. Do you hold off as long as possible, enduring much physical anguish, then give in with great guilt? There is nothing wrong or perverse about it. Unless you are locked in your room an extraordinary amount of time, you are simply behaving like a normal human being.

Watch a baby. A baby left alone while its diaper is being changed will naturally reach to touch itself. It doesn't know yet that there is anything wrong with that. It will touch itself for a few minutes with a look of absolute bliss on its little face. That is normal behavior for an infant.

It is also normal behavior for an adult deprived of an adequate, normal sexual outlet. Don't agonize over it. It is not a sin and it is not wrong. Anyone who believes that is very repressed.

Masturbation is certainly better than going to bed with someone you don't know or don't like. That kind of relief isn't necessarily a relief and may be dangerous in a number of ways. It can damage your self-esteem or bring you a social disease. With the wrong person, it can be a nightmare not soon forgotten.

If you are an adolescent, you can give up the idea that you are a terrible person who does things no one else does. You're not. Everyone does it, but no one ever talks about it. People will confess to the most dreadful of deeds, sometimes at the drop of a hat, but they will not easily or openly admit or discuss masturbation. This lack of communications in what is supposed to be a sexually open society is an indication of the guilt and shame we all still feel about it. At the very least we would be embarrassed to have anyone know we really do it.

Take heart. It's all right. You are not going to end up on a back ward somewhere, crazy, pimply, hairy-handed, and cross-eyed. You'll just be a little bit less cranky than you would be otherwise.

BIRTH CONTROL

Unless it is against your religious beliefs, if you are having sex, use birth control. Unless you want to face an unwanted pregnancy or forced marriage, be responsible enough to protect yourself, whether you are male or female.

If you are a man, come prepared. Don't leave it up to the woman. It is also your responsibility. Support her in taking the time to be responsible.

If you are a woman, protect yourself. Any man who gives you trouble about taking the time to be protected does not deserve to share your bed. If he's not willing to share the responsibility, or to support you in doing what you need to do for yourself, what are you doing with him? Do you think he's going to be responsible and supportive in any other way?

Educate yourself about contraception and the workings of the human body. Know what works for you and what doesn't. Then use it. Don't leave it in your purse or the dresser drawer. Use it.

Condoms, diaphragms, foam, and the pill are all available. Choose what is best for you and have it available. If you are a "fertile turtle," you may want to use more than one form at a time.

A word to the wise: coitus interruptus does not work as contraception. There is sperm in the man's lubrication. In other words, a man does not have to reach orgasm to emit sperm. It is there all along. Many a couple has been surprised by this fact.

Particularly with the presence of AIDS, it is vital to the well-being of both partners to use condoms. They are inexpensive and easy to obtain. Don't be stupid. Protect yourself from this disease. Again, if the man refuses to wear one, you can refuse to participate. Make it very clear in an up-front discussion that you will require the proper protection. Then stand by your statement.

Put your "safety net" in your purse or your pocket and don't leave home without it.

ABORTION

Religious and political debates have raged over the subject of abortion for at least the last 20 years. It is a loaded issue. Almost no one is neutral about it.

To have to decide whether or not to terminate a pregnancy is an agonizing decision. If it is against your religious beliefs, it may be upsetting to even have the thought. Even if your intellectual position regarding abortion says that it's a woman's right, making the decision to actually have an abortion is very painful. Just because it's your right doesn't make it easy.

Whatever your decision, it must be made from the dictates of your own conscience. No one has the right to tell you what to do or what is right, either way. You are the only one who has to live with the consequences. It is your decision.

Women choose to have abortions for a myriad of reasons: the health of the mother, the age of the mother, financial circumstances, the size of the existing family, fetal damage or imperfection, bad timing. At an emotional level, no one wants to advocate abortion. Intellectually, it may be the only option that makes any sense.

Whether you are "pro-life" or "pro-choice," your reasoning is real and powerful. You are entitled to make that choice for yourself. Your choice should be respected.

There is an attitude in the world that we should have the right to legislate personal decisions. There is no freedom in that. Everyone should have the right to make his or her own decisions about everything. Equally. To think that we can make a law saying that a woman does not have the right to have an abortion is dangerous and ludicrous. It is the church and the state interfering where they don't belong. It is just as crazy as saying that all women are required to terminate pregnancies under certain conditions. How would a pro-lifer feel if such a law was passed? To decide to bring a life into the world, to take on that responsibility, is an intensely personal decision. No one has the right to make anyone do that which is against her own best interest or her moral, religious, and political beliefs. This country was founded on the desire for personal religious freedom. That is what this issue is about. If your religion says abortion is wrong, you don't have to have one. But if terminating a pregnancy is within the range of your morality and ethics, then you should have the right to do so.

Why should any woman whose life, circumstance, or family is not ready for a child or another child be forced to have it? That attitude makes no sense at all. Children do not fare well in this society. The welfare system is bulging at the seams from the weight of children someone wasn't ready to have. These unwanted children show up in therapy or in the courts having been beaten, neglected, molested, starved, drug addicted, abandoned, and emotionally abused.

Don't fool yourself. Unwanted children know they are unwanted. Whether it is ever verbalized or not, the child knows it. Would you like to think that you are the reason your unhappy parents had to get married? Would you like to be blamed for that?

If it is a sin to abort a fetus, consider whether it might also be a sin to bring a child into the world who will not be loved, sheltered, nourished, or educated. How can it be right to force the child and the family to endure economic and emotional privation?

If you are attempting to decide what to do about your pregnancy, understand that it is your decision and yours alone. If you have a mate, it is a decision the two of you must make. No one else is concerned or involved. You are the one who has to live with the consequences.

If you have had an abortion, you know what the consequences are. You know that it is not a decision easily or hastily made. You know the sadness, the guilt, the sense of loss and deprivation that results. You know what it did to your relationship. Forgive yourself. Let it go. You made the best decision you could at the time.

Some women will rush right out and get pregnant again to assuage their sense of guilt and anguish. That is also their choice. But it is possible to learn that you do not have to be the slave of your body or your guilt.

Please understand the issue here is not that abortion is right. The issue is that it is your right to decide how you want to handle the situation. It is cruel to stand outside an abortion clinic with signs and slogans damning the woman who has made her choice. It was an agonizing choice and she is anxious and sad. She doesn't need help to feel guilty. No one stands outside a delivery room protesting the right to have a child.

Legislation ending the right to an abortion will not end abortion. It will just force women into the black market of illegal, dangerous, murderous abortionists. Let's re-establish the principles upon which this country was founded and allow everyone to follow the dictates of her own heart and soul.

12

FEELINGS

Have you ever had a piece of a popcorn hull stuck between your gum and your tooth? A splinter under your fingernail? Or, a tiny pebble in your shoe? It hurt, didn't it? It probably nearly drove you crazy. However, when you ferreted it out, the popcorn hull was not the size of a walnut, the splinter was not a branch, and the pebble was so small you wondered how it could have caused so much pain.

That's how feelings work. You hold your feelings in, creating all kinds of side effects, including immense physical pain, because you just know that what ever is under there is going to be absolutely overwhelming. When you finally get to it, it isn't overwhelming at all. It is just a little pea under the mattress.

The classic example of this is the patient who comes in with a terrible headache. Classically, headaches are a function of repressed anger. It usually turns out that the patient has had a feeling that was unacceptable or frightening, for which he or she felt there was no time or space. In the process of denying the feelings, great pressure is exerted, creating physical symptoms. When the event is unearthed, it turns out that the feeling attached to the event is truly minor compared to the amount of energy expended to deny it. Very often, the worst headache, when analyzed, requires only a few minutes of crying to release the pressure.

LIVE WHAT YOU FEEL, NOT WHAT YOU ARE TOLD

One of the major problems in this culture is that many people live out of their heads instead of their hearts. We attempt to be a very intellectual and scientific culture. We try to reason and figure everything out. There is nothing wrong with that, except that as a culture we carry it much too far. We need to balance that intellect with feeling. Knowledge is important. Terribly important. But there are different kinds of knowledge.

What about knowing yourself? When one deals from feelings, things become very simple very quickly. Confusion is really a function of trying to think through a problem when the feelings are already very clear. We try to force ourselves and others into pre-made molds that don't fit. The pain becomes excruciating very quickly. Is it any wonder that we have the level of substance abuse that we do in this country? No. That's just another way to try to kill off feelings. Although it works to some degree, the price is very high.

Consider for a moment the notion that if life's problems were approached with feelings fully intact, this would be a very different world. How would the world be different? Think about Hiroshima and Nagasaki; prejudice in any form; hurting other people in any way; hurting yourself; destroying the environment. If we all dealt from our feelings, these examples might have a very different result. We might all stand up and in one powerful voice demand that things change. We might each be willing to do whatever we can on an individual basis, however small, to be more loving to each other and to the planet.

Add to the already heavy mix of science and reason the basic human desire to please and to be accepted, and you have a culture in which everyone loses. There is no life in that recipe.

If you are busy being rational and reasonable and pleasing everyone else, doing what you are told, where are YOU in that? It is an absolute truth that if you do what you feel, really feel, you will always do what is right.

Your feelings will never lead you astray. Even if it appears for a time that you have made a mistake, you will eventually realize that "mistake" is precisely what you needed to do in order to learn and grow.

Your feelings will never tell you to go get drunk, or to have a little coke, or to wrong yourself or another. It's your mind that tells you to do these things. And the chances are great that someone else has told you, encouraged you, and bullied you into it.

Just pull back a moment, get in touch with your feelings, and you'll know what to do. You may not know how to get in touch with your feelings. If you don't, find a good therapist and let him or her teach you. You will never regret it.

YOU CANNOT SHUT OFF ONE FEELING WITHOUT SHUTTING OFF ALL THE REST

If you are attempting to control your anger, fear, or pain by denying it, pushing it away, or shutting it off, then you are also shutting down the rest of your feelings. To the degree that you shut down any feeling, the rest are also shut down. So you may be able to block out the pain, but your joy, excitement, and love will also be turned off. They are all on the same switch. Like a dimmer switch on a chandelier, all the lights go down at the same degree at the same time.

It would be interesting for you to explore why you think you have to dim out. Are you afraid of your feelings? Are your afraid your anger will rage out of control and you will hurt someone? Will your pain overwhelm you? Would it kill you to feel your alienation and loneliness? Give some real thought to this. The answers should be very revealing.

In fact, feelings operate in an entirely different manner than most people think. It is the degree to which those feelings are held back that they become explosive and dangerous. If you can learn to release your feelings on a regular, as needed, as felt, basis, there will be no danger of being over-whelmed. If you are really afraid that you can't handle your feelings, seek out a friend, counselor, minister, therapist, or transformational psychology seminar to help you. You don't have to do it by yourself.

And you are not crazy! There are many prohibitions against the overt expression of feelings in this society. It is considered unseemly, not "cool," out of control, even weak. Look at what we do to ourselves. Our judgments of ourselves and others kill off the most valuable asset we have: our ability to feel.

This isn't to say that you should go around the world taking your feelings out on others. Not at all. They are your feelings and you alone are responsible for them. But you are certainly entitled to have them, even when others might deem them inappropriate. That is their problem. We have become a nation of zombies. Let's start turning that switch back the other way and get those lights on again. I promise you that if you do, you will most likely discover that it's like the pebble in your shoe.

YOUR FEELINGS ARE YOUR POWER TO CREATE

All creativity is a combination of thought and feeling. To the degree that you have your feelings shut down, you cannot create.

The most frequent problem encountered in psychotherapy is that the individual is completely out of touch with his feelings. The feelings are buried and bottled up, often for years. CONTENTS UNDER PRESSURE. Eventually the person will blow a gasket. Feelings have to erupt somewhere. It's like a river that overflows its tributaries because the natural channels have been blocked. Feelings will come out in behavioral disturbances, psychosomatic or psychogenic illness, deep depression, or substance abuse. But they will come out. Isn't it better to learn how to have them and to ally with them and make them work for you?

For instance, someone appears in therapy saying she can't seem to maintain a satisfying relationship with a person of the opposite sex. She is attractive, likable, and concerned to know what is wrong with her. Nothing. She just has some wires crossed. She has deeply buried, unconscious conflicts with the parent of the opposite sex, and perhaps also of the same sex, that come out inappropriately when applied to a current relationship. She has attendant attitudes and interpretations of herself that prevent the nurturing of intimacy. It's like hooking up the air conditioner to the night light. It will blow the circuits. Or trying to run the washing machine from the blender motor. It just won't work. It's hooked up all wrong. The power lines are literally crossed. It is not possible to create a relationship with your power shut down. The same is true for your job, career, sports, creative pursuits, and your spirituality. Feelings are the key to everything.

If there is an area in your life that doesn't work, that is very problematic or painful, it is a very clear indication of unexpressed feeling.

You cannot create or bring into your life the people, things, and situations that you desire, as long as your feelings are unavailable. Before you panic, this isn't tragic. You are not emotionally deformed. You just have not learned how to have your feelings. It can be remedied fairly easily. You just need to go to feeling school, otherwise known as therapy.

PART THREE
ABOUT RELATIONSHIPS

13

COMMUNICATION BASICS

Most communication is simply, "I love you. Will you love me?" But, you say, "It is not. That can't be. We're talking about contract law, structural engineering, politics, food. None of that is about love. How ridiculous!"

But wait a minute. What we talk about is not necessarily what we're talking about. There is a level of communication called "process." It is what the brilliant family therapist Virginia Satir has called "metacommunication," the communication that is going on under, around, and above what we are talking about.

Ninety percent of communication is nonverbal. Have you noticed how difficult it is to get something clear with another person? It is quite nearly impossible. If you can remember that, whatever the issue, the person is really saying, "I love you, will you love me?" then negotiations, conversations, and relationships of all kinds will go smoothly. If all communications are "I love you. Will you love me?" then what happens when people are upset with each other? Most upsets occur because someone interprets the communication as "You don't love me, you're going away." It may look like the conflict is about money, time, sex, an attitude, power, fairness, equality, or any of the other things we think we fight about. That may be the content. But the process or metacommunication is some version of "You don't love me, you're going away."

If you approach the conflicts in your life conscious of the possibility of this interpretation, it will become very clear that that's what they're really about. Either you or the other person, or both, have interpreted the other's behavior to mean "You don't love me." A process level of "You don't love me," may include "You don't respect my feelings," or "You treat me like I'm powerless."

With that understanding, it becomes a snap to resolve conflicts. All you have to do is confess your part or gently ask the other person if that might be what is underlying his feelings about the issue. He might deny it at first but with a little help and love on your part, he will be able to see what kinds of interpretations he has made.

When we have decided that someone's behavior toward us means he or she doesn't love us, we become frightened. It is also entirely possible that we have made that interpretation because we are already frightened and insecure. Love cannot be seen through fear. Neither your love for the other person nor hers for you can be felt and acknowledged when there is fear involved.

Why are you so afraid? Why do you need others to love you so much that the idea that they might not panics you? Because you don't love you.

Of course it's upsetting when someone we have been close to or on whom we have been dependent in some way changes the nature of the relationship. It does not have to be devastating. If you love yourself, you will know you can survive it. You will be wise enough to recognize that it may be time or past time for a change in the nature of the relationship.

If you love yourself you will be able to see the love of the other person regardless of the issue or of how the relationship changes. Then your communications can be "I love you and me. Will you love you and me?" Things are a lot easier that way.

DISTINCTIONS IN LANGUAGE

The English language is very limited in how it addresses love. There is only one word for love although there are many levels, kinds, varieties, and intensities. The language requires explanation of what kind of love is involved: familial, platonic, romantic, maternal, or patriotic.

In addition to the limitation of the language, each person hears the language through his or her own idiosyncratic set of interpretations. While there are some clear, agreed-upon meanings, what one person will do with that set of meanings is entirely different than what another will do.

It is for this reason that the reader must be very careful in the interpretation of the concepts in this book. Much care has been taken to make each concept as clear as possible, but the human being is a self-serving creature and will make a determination based on what he wants to think is being said.

There are two invaluable opportunities in working with the language of this book. The first is to begin to realize just how you interpret language. What do you put on what is being said that is not really there?

The second opportunity for you is to begin to make distinctions between an empowering interpretation and an interpretation that is in the service of ongoing self-destructiveness. This problem can be seen clearly in the following example.

At a number of different places and in a number of different ways in this book, you are being exhorted to "Do what you want to do." Let's look at just a few of the possible interpretations people have come up with and then explain exactly what is meant.

Interpretations: "That's a dangerous idea. It flies in the face of all reality and social order." "That's selfish, unfeeling, narcissistic, inconsiderate. It does not take into account one's responsibilities in life."

"Good, that means that I can continue to do precisely what I want, which has created such problems in my life. After all, I want that drink. I feel like having a tantrum with my boss. Clearly, I have been given permission to function with no controls at all. I am free to live with my wildest hedonistic urgings and feel justified."

"Fabulous. I have just been given permission to continue to be lazy and undisciplined. If I don't want to work, I won't. I can do whatever I want to do or feel like doing without reference to anyone's rights, feelings, or needs."

Meaning: "Do what you want to do" means feel what it is you really want and then do it in a responsible way. Certainly you can have another drink or not go to work or throw tantrums. You probably already do that. To tell you to do more of that is not empowering or healing.

"Do what you want to do" means look deep inside yourself and find what it is you NEED to do for yourself. It means find that healthy, true, independent spirit and let it guide you to do what is good and right for you.

If you really do that, you will not have that drink, however much you want to, because there is something more important that you want. Ultimately, what you want is your own transcendence over destructive behavior.

It is possible that what you decide you need and want is contrary to public and social order. You may be living or working in a situation that is part of your pattern of self-destructiveness. If that is the case, then you may have to extricate yourself, whatever the social cost or judgment of others.

Doing what you want and need to do from your deepest feelings and understanding of life is never destructive or narcissistic. It is the noblest, most honorable recognition of the real-life force within you that urges you on to your greatest growth and potential. Only a society sick with the rules and prejudices of enslavement would consider that selfish.

Doing what you want to do may come to mean for you that you honor yourself, your body, and all others as the miraculous expressions of life that they are. It may mean that you do the hard things precluded by an immature interpretation of what "want" means.

You may refuse to gossip, to take advantage of anyone in any way, to lower the sights of your goals and dreams of what you and the world can be, to prostitute yourself for any advantage or benefit whatsoever. It may mean that you love all others as you would want to be loved, putting aside all petty needs, desires, or grievances to be a champion in the game of life.

Your interpretation of all of the concepts in this book needs to be in that vein and at that level. *What is always being discussed is the attainment of that which is healthiest and most ennobling in your experience of yourself and of the world.*

Any other interpretation is self deception and will only serve to continue to reinforce the patterns you are trying to break. To learn to make distinctions in language and in experience can transform every aspect of your life.

MOO

How well do you communicate? The communication patterns exhibited by you and the people around you can tell you a great deal. Communication styles are often used by psychotherapists as a diagnostic tool to determine how a client functions.

Among other things, communication facilitates getting what we want and the kinds of relationships we have. If you are dissatisfied in either area, listen to yourself and others as an indication of the problem. For example, suppose someone says to you, "Moo," which you somehow are supposed to interpret as that person's desire for a chocolate ice cream cone. You may think this is a silly example, but, unfortunately, it is not far from the way many people try to get what they want.

Can you remember when you were very young and had to point or make up a word that you hoped stood for what you wanted? And you had to keep at it until the grown-ups figured it out? You may still be doing that today in a more grown-up way.

"I saw a cow today" is an improvement over "Moo," but not much. "I noticed that the ice cream store was open as I passed by" is yet another improvement. At least the desired ice cream is mentioned. Do you think, though, that most people would figure out that the person wanted ice cream?

"After dinner, I'd love to go get some ice cream. Would you like to come?" This is a clear and appropriate communication.

Given how much crazy communication goes on, it is a wonder that we understand each other as well as we do. One client remembered her family as making little or no sense to her as she was growing up. She used to wonder if perhaps her family was a little crazy. Of course, she discounted that until she made a trip home while in therapy and discovered that, indeed, they did not make any sense and that the communication was crazy.

"We never go anywhere" is a complaint, not a request. It is also not a statement of intention.

"I'm tired of staying home all the time. I'm going to go to the beach this weekend. You are welcome to come if you like." That kind of statement puts the power and the control squarely in your hands and makes the situation clear for everyone.

Make clear statements and clear requests that identify either the problem or the desire or both. At the very least you will know that you have done your best to communicate. The other person will hear your very clear statement/request and respond accordingly.

"But I've told them a million times. I've begged and screamed, cried and yelled, and they just don't listen." Maybe they don't, but have you considered that they aren't hearing you because you are not really communicating? "Do not use my razor!" is much more direct than "I wish you guys wouldn't get into my things," or "I nicked the hell out of myself this morning because SOMEONE shaved their underarms with my razor." Can you see the difference?

There are three distinct ways to learn about your communication.

1. *Listen to yourself. Closely.*
2. *Listen to others. Closely.*
3. *Notice whether you're getting the results you want or not.*
   If you're not, spruce up that communication.

Therapy can help a great deal in restoring healthy communication patterns. There are also many seminars and books that deal specifically with communication. Partake of some of them. Remember that you are on the inside of that capsule, so that almost everything you say or hear is going to be distorted. The least you can do is attempt to be clear in what you are communicating. The other person may still distort it, but it will be a distortion of what you originally intended, not a distortion of a distortion.

If you find that your communication is way off the mark, empower yourself to speak clearly and frankly, with the knowledge that it is your right to speak your mind. It's all right to ask for what you want. You are allowed to tell others what you really mean. That's probably the only way they're going to understand you.

There are times when you are afraid to do anything for fear that it will be wrong. That's because no one has been clear with you about what is acceptable and what is not, and you haven't asked in a way that made it clear. That's how important communication is: it affects everything.

Clear, straight communication is a way out of the trap of frustration and unhappiness created by feeling that you are being ignored. If someone else gets upset because you haven't done what he wants you to do, ask what it is that he wanted, and then help him see that the communication was not clear to you. Give him permission to be direct with you. Just this change will work miracles in your life. You and everyone around you will be more satisfied, happier, and less fearful and frustrated, especially if you learn to listen.

TALK LESS, LISTEN MORE

There are many advantages to talking less and listening more. A primary advantage is that other people will think you are charming. They will love to talk to you, and they will tell others what a brilliant conversationalist you are.

Listening is a lost art. Everyone is anxious to get his point across, express his opinion, display his brilliance. Let him. Most people are starved for attention. It is possible, if not probable, that in a person's whole life, no one has ever really listened or paid attention to her. Her friends and family would be insulted by this idea. It is nonetheless probably true.

There is an interesting side note to this. The person to whom you most don't want to listen is the person who most desperately needs your attention. The boorish, the opinionated, the braggart, the needy-whiny, all really only want you to listen to and acknowledge them.

If you will REALLY listen to someone, understand what she is saying, not just pretend to listen and to understand, you can provide a lasting healing for her. At the sight of you, she will brighten, soften, and calm down. Here, at last, is that wonderful person who really understands me. How healing would it be for you to feel really heard and understood?

The reason someone corners you at a party and goes on at length about something you could care less about is that he wants to be acknowledged. He needs to feel that what he says and thinks and feels matters. If you will treat him to some real listening, he may learn to do the same for others. At the very least, somewhere in his very hungry heart and soul, he will be touched by your love and attention.

You already know what you think and feel. It might be very useful and interesting to know the same about others. If you listen carefully, you will learn a great deal about what makes people tick, what they want and need, what their concerns are and the myriad of ways in which we are all alike. That could be pretty valuable.

Listening allows you to feel more connected and intimate with others. What is it that keeps you so distracted that you can't listen? Why are you so anxious to be heard rather than to hear? We all crave attention. What could be more wonderful than having undivided attention? It is healing, it is comforting, it is empowering.

14

LOVING YOURSELF

You've already learned that loving you is important. Loving is an important part of any relationship. It is a vital message from you to you. The degree to which you love yourself is the degree to which your life will get better. So prove it to yourself.

What would you do for someone else you loved? Give them presents? Take them nice places? Nurture them? You can do that for you. Particularly if you are going through a difficult time, emotionally or just generally, take a little extra care of yourself. Begin to act like you matter. You do.

Given that you are not well-schooled in nurturing yourself, here are some beginning steps for what you might do for yourself:

> *Buy yourself some nice cologne or perfume and use it.*
> *Do something you always think about doing but never do.*
> *Take in a sports event.*
> *Pile up in bed with a good novel and your favorite foods*
>   *for an afternoon.*
> *Invite a friend on a picnic.*

Make some tea and sit quietly listening to your favorite
*   music (not something that will bring you down).*
Have a manicure, a pedicure, a massage.
Go to an art fair, flea market, farmer's market.
Take a hot bath with your favorite bath oil.
Have a Walter Mitty-type fantasy in which everything is the
*   way you want it, and you're the star.*

LOVE YOURSELF A LOT

The problem is that most people don't love themselves at all. You may think you do, but you don't really. Look at the things you do to yourself. What do you believe about yourself?

It's all your fault.
You're always wrong.
No one loves you or wants you.
You're ugly, too tall, too short, too fat, too thin, too stupid,
*   too uncoordinated, a no-talent nothing.*
You'd better not make waves at your job, at home, or anywhere else,
*   because you know you're just there on sufferance.*
You'd better be very good and very nice or no one will like
*   you at all.*
It's probably even your fault if it rains. Now, come on,
*   you know it is!*
You buy yourself the absolutely cheapest things you can,
*   and very little of that. After all, you don't de-*
*   serve anything really nice. Or you buy the*
*   absolute best of everything, hoping to cover up*
*   how worthless and unlovable you feel.*

Now try loving yourself, just a little. Start with eating right and wearing warm clothes in the winter. That sounds ridiculously simple. But, how often do you eat on the run, grabbing whatever is quick and easy? Do you skip meals entirely? Have you eaten a fresh green leafy vegetable in the last month? Do you dress properly for the weather? Do you carry an umbrella for the rain when indicated? Do you slip into a heavy coat, scarf, gloves, and boots for snow and bad weather? Do you make sure that you have enough money to get home from where you're going?

The way you take care of yourself now paints a picture of how you were cared for as a child. It may be painful to see how you take care of yourself now because of that connection with past caretaking.

It's valuable information. It's a way for you to understand that the precious, delicate flower in the garden (you) requires nourishing to flourish.

You may never have been truly nourished or protected. If you have had a particularly hard time up to this point, you need to begin to be nice to you. You also need to begin to require it from those around you. You have the right to ask for what you want and need.

Be the loving parent you always wanted. Treat yourself the way you wish you had been treated. You deserve and need nice things, people, and experiences in your life. Set it up that way. Refuse to accept less for yourself. Stop acting like the hired help and become the boss in your own life.

To be a human being means, in part, to suffer and to have pain. You know how hard it has been just to get to where you are. You have done well to survive and create a niche for yourself. Now start rewarding yourself.

Start paying close attention so that you can begin to limit the kinds of experiences you don't want to have and have already had too much of. Then build in the experiences you like and want.

Choose people who are good to you, who nourish and contribute to you. If someone is just difficult or demanding or hurtful with you, you don't need that person in your life. It's that simple. If you love yourself, you won't allow it.

Create an environment for yourself that is peaceful, calm, and attractive rather than one that creates more stress. You can have candlelight, flowers, and nice things.

You can have a life and an environment that works instead of one where something is always breaking down and requiring your attention and care. Make it all work for you. Not the other way around. Remember, you're the boss.

SUPERWOMAN, SUPERMAN, OR SUPER SHIT?

Taking charge of your life means that you begin to be realistic in your expectations of yourself and others. To expect too much of yourself creates a cruel burden of demands which you will never be able to meet. You will always fall short of grandiose goals and therefore have more reason to believe that you are worthless.

This is at least part of the reason to believe that you are worthless. This is at least part of the reason for the ongoing spiral of guilt, self-hate, lack of self-confidence, and depression that you experience. Who could possibly live up to the saint-like genius image of what you're supposed to be?

To expect too little of yourself creates a personal mythology of "I can't." No one can possibly be as worthless as you think you are, either. To expect little or nothing of yourself is a major cop-out. Either way, you are setting yourself up for failure, more self-hate, and hard evidence that you really aren't good enough. There has to be a middle ground. It is important to find it.

The middle ground is found by taking a very hard, clear look at who and what you really are. It is helpful to have an objective observer assist in this process. You're almost certainly neither as awful as you think you are or as incredible as you think you have to be. You are capable of more than you think you are. You are not, however, required to win a Nobel Prize.

Outline a course of action which would give you a happy, satisfying life, without setting you up for ultimate failure. What are your aptitudes? What do you like to do? What gives you pleasure and fulfillment?

If there is something you want to do but don't have the necessary skills or know-how to do, go back to school. Get a coach in that area. But be realistic, too. If you're small, uncoordinated, and break bones easily, it is probably not wise to plan a career as a pro football player. That's unrealistic. On the other hand, just because you made a C grade in junior high school algebra doesn't mean you have to give up on science and math, or that you're too dumb to understand them. That's unrealistic, too.

You don't have to be perfect. You just have to be able to do it. Einstein, among others, did not do well in school. Grades and degrees are not necessarily an indication of what you can do. If you're determined, you'll make the grades and get the degree.

Just quit expecting yourself to be perfect. No one is always brilliant, always nice, always even-tempered, thoughtful, sensitive, kind, honest and helpful. You're not a boy/girl wonder. You're a human being. Give yourself a break.

COMPASSION IS A GREAT GIFT WHEN YOU REALIZE THAT EVERYONE ELSE IS HURTING, TOO

All people have a well-practiced facade designed to make you think they're cool. Beneath the facade is a human being just like you. Everyone wants to be liked, loved, accepted, well thought of, successful, and, most of all, safe, whatever that means to them.

Most of the time, if you will be just a little self-revealing, it will put a crack in the walls of others and they will soften up. Be understanding and be gentle. Treat them the way you would like to be treated. It works. Especially for you. Remember, if you're gentle and understanding with others, you will be more so with you.

Compassion is simply a component of unconditional love. It is loving and attempting to understand without judging. What do you think might happen if you could apply just a little compassion to all those judgments you have about you? If you will begin to love yourself a little bit, the results will astonish you. You will begin to relax, calm down, lighten up. Maybe not a lot, but noticeably. The more you give to yourself, the more you have available to give to the world.

Be gentle with yourself and with others. Quit being so demanding and judgmental. Be a little tolerant. Learn to forgive. Try to bring a little gentleness to bear on the matter. Even the crustiest person will soften up, at least a little, if you are giving and understanding. That translates to love. Very few people are unwilling to be loved. If they are, the loving thing is to leave them alone.

Be patient with the waiter, the bus driver, the clerk. You don't know what their home life is like, what demons they carry with them, what burdens they shoulder. Try to understand everyone. What motivates someone? Why is he arrogant, angry, defensive? Don't just judge people. Everyone is frightened. To help others with their struggle will help you with yours.

Everyone is hungry for love, affection, approval, and acceptance. That's what runs the world. All of our maneuvers and manipulations are designed to get love. Practice unconditional love. Give it to yourself and to others. Give it in kindness, generosity, attention, helpfulness, and thoughtfulness. A thoughtful word can make someone's day.

Love and accept people as they are, not for what you want them to be or for what they should be. Love them all: the beggar and the businessman, the rich and the poor, the glamorous and the plain. That's unconditional love. You love them no matter what they look like, what they do, or how they act. You don't judge them. Then you can begin to see the beauty and joy in life.

Do you think we would have allowed this country to be the way it is if we loved ourselves? Or the planet? Hardly. If we loved ourselves and each other, we couldn't destroy the planet. Our love would naturally extend to the environment.

What a wonderful world it would be if we all loved ourselves and each other. Sound idealistic? Maybe. But it could happen. We could make it happen.

OUR FEELINGS ABOUT OTHERS HAVE A GREAT DEAL TO TEACH US ABOUT OURSELVES

What you don't like about others, really don't like, is what you don't like about yourself. This is not always true, but you should at least consider the possibility that everyone is a mirror of some kind for you. The mirror may be exaggerated, distorted, or reversed, but it has something to do with you.

If you have already come to terms with the similarities between you and another person, you won't be bothered by them. But if what someone else does or thinks really pushes your buttons, if you absolutely can't stand that person, there's a good chance there is something important for you to learn from her about you or your immediate family.

On the other hand, comparing ourselves with others is just another way to invalidate everything about ourselves. It creates feelings of inferiority and guilt. Being envious and jealous of others always casts you in the loser's role. It is helpful to quit comparing yourself to others. Why do you need to be better than anyone else, anyway?

No one else has lived your life, or you theirs. How can you possibly compare? Any comparison requires a judgment to be made of both parties. One has to be bad in order for the other to be good; one has to be wrong for the other to be right. What difference does it make? Why do you need to do that? What do you get out of it? Are you trying to reassure yourself that you're really not that bad after all? Or that you are?

Every single person has had a very different experience in life. Everyone has unique cellular, biological, and genetic make-ups, upbringings, socio-economic backgrounds, abilities, and problems. No one is better or worse; each one is just different.

Begin to learn to judge yourself and others less. To the degree that you judge others, you will judge yourself. The way you treat yourself is the way you treat others, and vice versa. Think about this for a minute; it's pretty sobering. If you are petty, demanding, judgmental, and unforgiving with others, guess how you are with you? If you are withholding and punitive, you do it to you, too, not just to others.

Look at how you think of others. How do you treat them? Then look at how that works in your life in your behavior toward yourself. Is that really how you want to be treated? Would you want to have a relationship with someone who treated you that way?

All the love you ever needed is inside you. It's not out there in some other person or thing. Others can love you a great deal, but if you don't love yourself, you will never feel it.

Everyone wants to be loved, including you. When you think you have no more love left to give, that's when you need to dig down deep and give even more. That's when you need it the most. The way to get it is to give it. Acknowledge yourself for what you think is right with you.

TO BUILD SELF-CONFIDENCE, THINK OF ALL THE THINGS YOU'VE DONE SUCCESSFULLY

You probably spend most of your time thinking about all the things you can't do, have done wrong, or think you could never do. That's not very helpful. It may also not be true. Reality often doesn't jibe with thoughts. You think you are incompetent when the facts would strongly suggest otherwise. Why do you keep that game going? Where does it come from?

Start to look at the reality of your life. Don't listen to your mind. It will always tell you you're not good enough. That is not the truth! It's just what you think.

For instance, what about the woman who has dozens of boy friends, but thinks of herself as a wallflower? Or the man who thinks of himself as a failure, but has a wonderful wife, children, a nice home, a great job at which he does well, receiving promotions, raises, and respect? What is the truth?

Look at your life. You do and have done hundreds of things successfully. Isn't it interesting that you absolutely discount the things you do well? It was an easy school, a lenient teacher, a soft boss; the person who asked you out was just desperate; you just got lucky. Baloney!

You created your own opportunities and you did a good job. Stop negating it. Everyone can't do what you do. It's also a very cheap shot to claim that others are just stupid or crazy or desperate if they like you.

The school which honored you wasn't easy and the teacher who held you in high regard wasn't stupid. You earned the grade, the promotion, the raise. That person who asked you out or who accepted your invitation really does like you. Why do you choose to believe that you are second best? Recognize your achievements. Acknowledge yourself. To build your self-confidence today, do *Exercise 20* in the Workbook.

PERHAPS THE MOST DIFFICULT FEAT YOU CAN ACHIEVE IN THIS SOCIETY IS TO BE AN INDIVIDUAL

There are so many rules, so many shoulds, oughts, expectations, and demands of each of us that it is difficult not to lose even the last vestiges of our individuality and self-confidence. We look alike, dress alike, talk alike, and think alike. You disagree? Even if you're part of a counter-couture, you behave and think in conformity with the counter-culture.

The culture, whether we choose to be an active part of it or to rebel against it, hangs over us like a giant shadow obscuring original thought. We are slaves to the approval of others, to status, to culturally determined definitions of responsibility, creativity, and lifestyles. It is difficult indeed for the individual to break out of the box in which all the rules are written.

It is a beginning to start to question the rules. Have you? Have you wondered why you would adhere to this or that rule? Even what we want is culturally determined. Do you think Pygmies care whether they have tennis bracelets or Porsches? Probably not, because these are not status symbols for them. We allow other people and their values and judgments to determine what we think of ourselves.

Are you on automatic pilot when it comes to the rules you follow? You may not even be conscious of them, they are so deeply ingrained.

Get an education.
Get a job where you will make lots of money.
Get married. Have children.
Buy a house in the suburbs.
Do community work.
Dress according to the styles of the sub-culture.
Do what is socially approved and you will be a success.

Sound familiar? Adolescents often question these kinds of assumptions, but are quickly swept up in the maelstrom of becoming adults and conforming. People in their forties are often caught up in a desire to break out of the box and do things that are considered bizarre and are labeled unstable.

Psychiatric professionals are well-aware of the cultural differences in definitions of pathology. What is considered crazy in one culture is normal in another. Clearly, the determining factor is cultural mores and values. The idea of culturally determined roles can be traced all the way down to the individual family system. What is acceptable in one family is unacceptable in another.

What's acceptable to you? What do *you* want to do with your life? Is it acceptable to you to continue to live in the box and never question what might be outside? Or do you sometimes wonder what it's all about? What does life mean? What is the purpose? Who or what is God? What is possible for a human being? Who made up the rules? Are they the right rules? Do there have to be rules? What if there were none?

What kinds of questions, longings, dreams do you have? Do you feel suffocated by the rules and expectations of the culture, the family, work, or politics? What parts of your self, your dreams, your thinking have you shut down in order to fit into the culture? When did this happen?

This isn't about running amuck in the streets. It is about thinking for ourselves, making our own decisions, being original rather than being slaves to the common denominator of what is acceptable.

It is not unusual to discover that what is ailing many people who show up in therapy is that they have lost, or never had, a sense of their own individuality. They are following, and being forced to follow, the dictates of others. To lose one's dreams, to be unable to question or formulate personal explorations, is literally sickening. Yet it is one of the most common experiences in every culture on this planet.

The demand for conformity kills creativity. It murders genius. It emasculates the heroic in each of us. What genius are you hiding behind respectability and conformity? Every person has the capacity for genius in her own right, just by thinking for herself.

Would you like to try? Is there a voice inside you that calls you out into the moonlight of your soul to commune with who you really are? Listen. Answer the call. Be willing to at least brave the constraints of your own mind.

When was the last time you did that? It's not easy. Perhaps the most difficult feat you can achieve in this society is to be an individual. There are penalties to pay. It is not free. But what price are you already paying for conformity?

LAUGH, LIGHTEN UP, AND PLAY! IT'S IMPORTANT

Learning to make time for real fun is one of the hallmarks of a loving individual. Are you addicted to suffering? The addiction to suffering underlies all of the other addictions. It is truly the single biggest issue in America.

If we could just give up some of our suffering, we might begin to be happy. On the other hand, we are very much attached to suffering. Look at the soap opera and drama in the lives of everyone around you. The news media have refined it to a high art.

Begin to consider that life could be a wonderful adventure rather than root canal surgery. It doesn't have to be heavy and awful all the time. In fact, it is neither necessary nor healthy to be heavy and significant all the time. Even as wonderful as therapy is, it is not a twenty-four hour assignment. You might consider taking a little time off now and then to live!

It is difficult to learn balance, to keep everything in some kind of proportion. When you're hurting or in trouble, this is especially hard. But if you can and will lighten up, just a little bit, it will put a whole new complexion on the situation.

Everything, *everything*, has its funny side. If you can't have a sense of humor about yourself, you're going to have even more pain than is necessary.

Children and animals are a wonderful distraction. If you don't have any, borrow some. Or get yourself a pet. A puppy or a kitten or a fish can take your mind off yourself and your day-to-day world in a wonderfully refreshing way.

Animals don't have guilt or anxiety or morals. They just live. Dogs want to please you. Cats don't care. Fish swim. You can learn a lot from them. They can be a great comfort and a source of joy. They'll snuggle with you any time you want. Well, maybe not the fish.

Find ways to take the pressure off and let off a little steam. Work out. Pump up some endorphins. Borrow a jacuzzi. Take a walk by the river. Read a Larry McMurtry novel. Find funny friends and keep them—in the middle of a terrifying near-hurricane, a friend once called and said, "Let's do lunch." That's the kind of friend to have. It is also the kind of friend to be.

Don't worry that you're not taking your life seriously enough. It's all right to take a few minutes off from worry. The problems will still be there when you get back. Look at how much you have to be grateful for and happy about. Then laugh at yourself for making such a huge drama out of the rest. Really. Is history going to care about your troubles? Are the planets going to alter their course? Unlikely. So shake your fist in the face of all those troubles and show them they can't make you lose your sense of humor. That's loving you.

15

LOVING OTHERS

If you want to be close to someone, communicate. Tell her what is on your mind. Be honest. Really communicate what you want, think, feel, and need. Be willing to say the thing you most don't want to say.

Is it hard for you to say "I love you?"
Do you find it next to impossible to say "I need you?"
Are you afraid to communicate what you are really thinking for fear you
will upset or alienate the other person?
Do you know exactly what the problem is between you, but are unwilling
to verbalize it?

The way to get the other person to listen to you and to hear what you are saying is to make an "I" statement. For example, "When you do that, I feel judged." Say what you are feeling, not what the other person is doing. Let him know what the impact is on you, and be responsible for your feelings. It's not his fault that you feel or react the way you do.

Speaking your mind clearly and honestly allows the other person to consider whether there might be another way to behave that is more helpful, useful, or powerful. Blaming, accusing, judging, or pointing a finger is not communication. That's fighting. Do you want to fight? Or, do you want to work something out between the two of you?

There will be times when you want to fight. Go ahead. Just be sure you pull some of the punches. Don't say things you can't take back later, or that will hurt so much they will damage the relationship. Do be willing to take a strong stand on what you are saying and make sure the other person hears you. Be willing to back up and try again until you are sure she understands you. If you will make "I" statements, gently, with responsibility, the other person is less likely to become defensive.

If she becomes defensive, reassure her that you are not saying anything about her, blaming her, or criticizing her. Your intention is to clarify an issue between you, and only that. Don't say things you don't mean to placate her. It will cause problems later. Don't agree to do something you have no intention of doing. That will cause a fight.

When someone wants to talk to you about a problem, be willing to listen and to hear. Listen effectively, not selectively. Be careful to hear what the person is really saying to you, not what you are afraid she will say or what you want her to say. Tell her what you think she is saying and let her clarify. Keep working at it until you are both clear that you are giving and receiving the same message. Try to keep your defenses down and just let her say whatever she has to say.

Communication is the basis of any good, on-going relationship. It is a two-way street. You and your partner, mate, or friend must both be willing to communicate. You must also be able and willing to hear. When you allow the other person to speak his mind, regardless of what she needs to say, it creates trust. True communication creates intimacy.

It is not a sin to disagree. Say what you think, tactfully and gently. But do say what you think. It makes for lively discussion, and it makes clear that someone is home inside of you. Nothing is more boring than someone who never has an opinion and always agrees.

If you present your opinions as if they are the last word on the subject, expect a fight, or at least a deaf ear. That's not discussion, its pontificating.

Be willing to ask for what you want and need. Being passive and going along becomes boring and frustrating for everyone. If you go along rather than state an unpopular opinion or ask for what you want, you will resent and blame the other person.

A word of caution: as you are communicating, remember that the other person has feelings and is very likely to misinterpret what you are saying. She is apt to hear it much more harshly than it is said. Be tactful. Be gentle. Lay the responsibility at your own door. Don't blow her away with anger and self-righteousness. That will get you nowhere except in trouble.

Some people, especially those new to therapy, transformation, spirituality, or any of the other growth-producing disciplines, think they should "say everything, be totally honest." That is a major mistake.

Yes, you should say what you most don't want to say. But that means to say the things that are hardest for you because they are most threatening to you, not to the other person. Being "totally honest" is not really honest, it's an excuse for cruelty, meanness, and anger. Watch what you're doing. Be careful of your motivations.

If you are going to say something that will hurt the other person, what are you getting him back for? That's what you need to talk about. When you want to be that angry and punitive, you are really hurting about something. Talk about what it is that hurts and be responsible for your hurt. It's yours, not his. It is likely that he has no idea he hurt you and certainly didn't intend that. You may have just misinterpreted whatever happened.

When you start to communicate, be willing to keep backing up until you both understand. That's the key. Don't allow it to be a fight. Hold your temper and your defensiveness in check to allow the other person to calm down. If you get upset it will simply escalate.

The point is to clarify an issue, to work out a problem, not to make war. Remember that you love this person and she loves you and you have a common goal. You want to continue to be friends, if at all possible. That is usually possible if you will be responsible for yourself and say what you feel, and also be responsible for her feelings, and listen carefully to what the other person is saying in return.

IF YOU CAN'T FIGHT, YOU CAN'T F——

Strong language. As a therapist, I have used this expression often to get my client's attention, to wake them up and become aware of their own co-dependence. What does it mean to you? What's your interpretation?

It means exactly what it says. If you are a push-over, peace-at-any-price kind of person, if you never stand up for yourself, if you are an "I'll do anything, put up with anything, as long as you love me" person, you are unlikely to excite anything in others besides contempt and abuse.

If you are not having a satisfying sexual experience in your marriage or relationship, or if you cannot seem to have a relationship, that may very well be part of the reason. Exciting people have a healthy self-conceit which will not allow them to just roll over and play dead. They're interesting because there's someone home inside of them, someone who interacts on an honest basis, someone who is willing to stand up for what she needs and wants instead of just manipulating to win approval.

"If you can't fight, you can't f——" is a good description of what is popularly called "co-dependency." Most of the people in this country suffer some crippling form of co-dependence. If you are handing out or putting up with whatever comes your way in order to continue the status quo, not standing up and requiring anything in particular, much less what you want and need from the other person, that is co-dependent behavior. In other words, the expression can be interpreted as a call-to-arms for all those who allow themselves to be abused, exploited, and manipulated because they don't have the self-esteem to set a limit on what they will take.

> *Do you let people get away with outrageous things with you?*
> *Do you let yourself be manipulated, resent it mightily but go*
> *   along with it, rather than brook someone's displeasure*
> *   or have a disagreement?*

"If you can't fight, you can't f——" applies to every aspect and area of your life. It doesn't mean you should go around fighting with everyone in your life. It means that when necessary you need to be willing to stand up for yourself.

Is it next to impossible for you to say no? Think about it. Do you really say "no" most of the time you want or need to? Or do you just whine, complain, and play martyr to yourself and others?

Are you willing to pay any price to get what you want? One woman, upon being confronted with knowledge of her husband's affairs, told him, "Do what you want, but please don't embarrass me." Can you imagine how that made him feel? Clearly she didn't care as much about him as about having her apple cart upset. Naturally he embarrassed her and then left her. Other people know whether you really care about them or whether you're just hanging on out of dependency and need.

Do you live in fear that you will hurt someone's feelings? When someone pulls a power play on you, you pull one right back. If you are attacked, physically or verbally, you stand up for yourself. You don't allow yourself to be abused in any way. You ask for what you want, and require a direct answer. You refuse to work for less than you are worth. You do not allow yourself to be taken for granted.

Co-dependents and cancer patients are the nicest people in the world. Do you want to be in either group? They turn all the anger in on themselves, with predictable results.

Start learning to fight for what you want and learning to think that's okay. The reason you're so afraid to stand up for yourself is that then you will no longer be allowed to be dependent. You won't be taken care of by the person or the organization involved. There is a hook in the relationship that looks like a realistic reason to allow the abuse and manipulation to continue: you think you want or need something from that person on a concrete or material level.

For instance, a client owes you money. You are afraid that if you cut him loose, you will not get paid. Or, if you break up an abusive relationship, there will be no other relationship. You will be all alone. Or, your friends won't let you use their summer house any more. The reality is that the client, the lover, the friends make you crazy. The fact that you end up feeling ill, unhappy, getting drunk, or otherwise having a miserable time escapes you. The real hook is not the money or the relationship or the summer house. It is the fear that the person or people involved won't like you any more. For some of you, that is a horrifying thought. Being judged unacceptable or disliked is the worst thing that could happen to you.

At an unconscious level, the fear of being judged and rejected is the hook that holds you in destructive relationships. Why? What's the real underlying motive? Why are you so in need of approval?

If they judge you negatively, then you can't depend on them and you will not have the fantasy of being taken care of by them. The co-dependent is a gambler who keeps betting on what she hopes will happen regardless of the current reality. It's called "betting on the come." You hope you will eventually get what you want, to be taken care of, so you hang in no matter how awful it gets. You haven't a clue as to why you're so unhappy and frustrated. But you couldn't possibly give up the game.

When the actor Rex Harrison was accused of being callous, he responded, "So many people today want to be liked." Is that true of you? You want to be liked and popular above all else? At any cost?

If you can't fight, you will always give in and you will never get what you want. You still will not get paid by the client, the relationship will continue to be miserable, and the summer house will come at the cost of peace, joy, comfort, and self-esteem.

YOU DON'T HAVE TO TAKE CARE OF EVERYONE

You shouldn't be expected to do so. Who is it who expects you to take care of him? Who is it for whom you feel responsible? If it's anyone other than your children, or your professional charges, think about what you are doing.

Given the level of dependency in this population, caretaking becomes a major issue. The need to take care of others is often the result of a deeply denied desire to be cared for and the hope that it will win love.

Do you think that if you take care of some other person he will love you? Or do you do it automatically? Does it not occur to you that you don't have to do so and that it may even be unhealthy for both parties? To allow, or even encourage, the dependency of another adult does not force him to be responsible and to empower himself. How dependent are you on him to let you take care of him? Why do you need that? Does everyone in the system of which you are a part have to be a cripple to participate? What if you were all independent or interdependent?

Many parents expect and require their children to take care of them, physically, financially, and emotionally. The children have been reared with that expectation and don't know they don't have to do it and shouldn't. These parents are demanding, selfish, emotionally immature people. Do your parents treat you like that? Is that how you deal with your children?

Break the cycle and stand on your own. If they fall down, that is their problem. That is how they will learn to walk. If they don't learn, they will manipulate someone else into taking care of them. You are free to go.

This kind of dependency is at the core of "co-dependence." Everyone expects to be taken care of by everyone else. It is a vicious cycle of systematic infantile behavior in which no one ever has to grow up and be responsible. It is sucking the life-force from everyone involved.

No one owes anyone anything. There are no free lunches for anyone. Look at nature. Every animal works for its survival. It collects or kills its food. It is alone with the elements and other animals. It is the animal's job to survive. It does not expect that anyone is supposed to come along and give it a handout, or do it for them. Where did we get the idea that someone else is supposed to be responsible for our well-being, our feelings, our survival? Does that kind of behavior sound grown-up to you? Do you like to be around people who put all the responsibility on you? Do you do that to others?

Emotional health combines the ability and the willingness to be independent and self-sufficient. Of course we want and need other people in our lives. But if you need them for your survival, you are in trouble. The essence of being an adult is being someone who can take over and care for others when necessary, not someone who has to be cared for like a child.

There is a difference between help or support and dependency. "God helps those who help themselves" is an old saying. Do you help yourself? Do you do your part? Do you know that your survival is up to you? Or do you expect and demand someone else to handle your needs and problems for you?

It is an awesome relief to pull the leeches off your back. To allow them to continue to suck just drains you and does nothing for them. They are not learning, growing, or even living. They are just leeching. It is not mean to take leeches off, nor is it mean to refuse to be dependent. Both are attempts to reach a new level of growth and understanding. If someone doesn't like it, let him leech on someone else.

It is empowering and thrilling to give up dependency and stand on your own. It is the first step toward health and freedom.

The message here is that no one is required to take responsibility for another adult and shouldn't. If each person stands on her own, we all stand together, strong and forceful. If each person expects to be taken care of, everyone just lays in a heap. No power. No strength.

Please make the distinctions among loving, caring, strengthening, empowering, and caretaking as discussed here. What we are ultimately striving for is to be more loving to ourselves and to others. But to allow someone to be overly dependent is neither loving nor caring. It is crippling. It is more loving to kick ass, take names, and get going on your own. Let their problems be their problems and let them solve them. You've got enough to do just to live your own life.

Of course, it is appropriate to help when friends or family are in trouble. But there is a limit. Knowing that limit and setting it can be tricky. It's easy for both parties to want to continue the dependency. The wise, loving person knows when it is time to let go, and does so for the good of everyone. Such a person understands what he can do for others and what he cannot do.

WHAT CAN YOU DO FOR SOMEONE ELSE?

Take a look around. You know what you wish others would do for you. But what can you do for them? Be careful. We are not talking about what you can do to manipulate or curry favor or make points. Whatever it is you choose to do, do it because you want to do it. Because you feel like it. Because it would please you. Then it will feel right. It will feel good.

It can be something very simple or very complicated. It's up to you. Take the focus off of yourself for a minute and see what other people need. Just a word of kindness, a gentle touch, a few minutes of real focussed attention, can make a real difference in someone's life.

Do it without thought of reward or gratitude, but out of the goodness of a generous spirit and a loving heart. Give of yourself. It doesn't need to be material. Do something anonymously. Say a prayer for someone. Send someone a loving thought. Put in a good word for someone. It will make you feel wonderful about yourself. That's the point.

GIVE OTHER PEOPLE WHAT YOU WANT

What you get from other people is probably what you are putting out. That may be a hard fact to face. It is also very valuable. If you don't like what you're getting, take a look at what you're giving.

If you need tenderness, comfort, understanding, give it to others. It is a way of giving it to yourself. Every time you are tender to someone, are kind or gentle, you are giving that to yourself as well. Take it. It's yours.

If you give what you want often enough, then you become it. You become the quality of tenderness, understanding, love. Then you no longer need it from anyone else. You are it. Understand?

YOU ARE MORE LIKELY TO GET WHAT YOU WANT IF YOU ASK THAN IF YOU DEMAND

Remember, people basically want to contribute to you. It makes you feel good to help someone, even a little. It works that way for the rest of us, too. When you ask for something, remember that most people really want to give it to you, if they can. Ask sweetly. Ask nicely and politely. Let her know that you understand she has the right to say no, and if it's difficult or inconvenient, you rescind the request. Then let her answer honestly.

If you ask in an aggressive, or demanding way, or, worse, just tell the person to do what you want, or if you try to manipulate him into doing what you want, you have set up a power struggle. He may do it, but he won't like it and it won't feel good to anyone.

There may be times when it is appropriate to boss someone around. It may even be necessary. But you can usually still manage to do it nicely, allowing the other person to feel like a team player or a partner, rather than a serf.

If you are not getting what you want from other people, review how you are asking. Is it a loving request or a non-negotiable demand?

PEOPLE DO HAVE THE RIGHT TO SAY NO TO YOU, AND YOU HAVE THE RIGHT TO SAY NO TO THEM

Just as you have the right to say no to others, they also have the right to tell you no. If you don't allow others the right of refusal, they feel trapped, angry, and resentful. Would you really want anyone to do something for you that she really doesn't want to do? That's being a tyrant.

It's perfectly fine to ask for anything you want or need from anyone.

Just give him the space to say no without worrying about making you angry, disappointing you, being punished, or rejected. If you give others the space to say no, you will also be giving it to yourself.

Be clear with yourself, and with others, that if they say no it doesn't mean they don't love you or anything else. They just said no. If it really upsets you when they say no, settle yourself down and take a look at why it is so upsetting for you. What's going on with you? Do you require absolute obeisance as proof of love? Are you that demanding? Are you that dependent? That insecure? Come on, this is your reaction. Be responsible for it. Find out what the trigger is and then let it go.

There are lots of reasons in your head not to say no. They won't like you any more. You might make someone mad. You don't want to upset anyone. After all, it's not that big a deal. They've done so much for you. You owe it to them. It really is your responsibility. But deep down inside, you probably feel less than comfortable. You may feel angry or resentful or martyred.

You can't even begin to be free and your own person until you can say no when you want to. It's your right. It is necessary for you to learn this lesson. Until you do, you will always be at someone else's mercy: a victim. Is that what you want?

Go ahead. Try it. The sky won't fall. You might feel very anxious or uncomfortable for a while. But you will live. And then you will feel wonderful. When you realize that you have the power to say no and to make it stick, it is a GREAT feeling. It gives you the courage to say no more often.

It is not bad or wrong or mean to say no. You are simply taking care of yourself. You come first. Remember?

It may be difficult for the people around you to believe that you are saying no. They may not be able to hear it. After all, you have trained them to expect you to say yes. Keep after it. They'll learn too.

MAKE A DISTINCTION BETWEEN THE PERSON AND THE BEHAVIOR

Part of learning to say no and of allowing others to say no to you is making a distinction between the person and the behavior. Unconditional love simply means loving the other person regardless of what she does. You don't judge her or her behavior, even when she says no. You recognize that she is not what she does. Behavior is not *what people are*, but what people *have done or are doing*. From this position, it is easy to love anyone. Even yourself.

That doesn't mean, however, that you have to like the behavior or put up with it. You can let the other person know that he is not allowed to behave that way with you. He may choose not to be in your life. That's fine. You still love him. You don't have to love the behavior.

This point of view also makes it easier to decide whether you want someone in your life or not. You might love her a great deal but simply find her behavior too painful and too destructive to be around. If you separate your love for the person from your feelings about her behavior, then the decision, and the choices, become clearer.

You can also let others know that, while you love them and you want them around, there are some things you will not allow. Then you work it out together. You make it very clear what you want, and help them learn what that is.

For instance, you don't have to allow anyone to smoke in your house, office, or car. Simply tell others you don't allow that. You'll be glad to have them visit, but they can't smoke. If they have to smoke, you can meet them in a restaurant, the park, or their house. See how easy it is?

BREAKING UP IS HARD TO DO

Breaking up is hard to do. Even when you know it won't work, even when you are miserably unhappy, even when you know it is wrong for both of you. Regardless of the reason for the break-up, it is still hard.

While your heart says you love this person, and you may be very attached, your head tells you to get out while the gettin's good. We choose partners based on unconscious motivations. The most common is that they represent one or, more likely, many of the characteristics common to our families, especially our mothers or fathers. Unfortunately, what you need at age nineteen or twenty may not be what you need at forty or forty-five.

As you begin to grow and to work out the unresolved issues with your family, it is possible that you will outgrow your partner. Even if the partner grows at a similar rate, you may go in very opposite directions. Or you may wake up to what is destructive in the relationship even if you have not resolved those issues and be unwilling to tolerate that behavior any more. Someone once described it as "an attack of good sense."

You will almost surely marry for largely unconscious reasons. That does not mean it can't work. You may both grow together beautifully and gain a great deal of wisdom from the experience. The problem occurs when you have come from a family with a great deal of pathology and pick someone with whom you will feel very much at home. Home may not be the healthiest or the happiest place to be.

Given all this, breaking up is painful partly due to the stress caused by growing and giving up your own need to continue those patterns. The known is always preferred to the unknown. Most of us hate the unknown and prefer to "sit in the middle of our stuff" rather than change.

By far the most difficult part of breaking up is that we have to renounce the dreams we once had of what the relationship was and could be. It is a very old saw that dreams are harder to give up than reality. After the break up, it may not be the daily reminders of your loved one that bring you sadness, but the symbols. Running across your wedding ring in the jewelry box can evoke a good crying spell.

Unfortunately, we are often wedded to what we think the person is or can be rather than to the person he or she is. Facing that reality and giving up the dream hurts. It is appropriate and realistic to feel very sad, to cry, to do your mourning. To fail to do so is denial and will prolong the process.

Of course, there is always the spectre of life-long loneliness. There will never be another love like this. Hopefully not. If you have learned the lessons, you can go on to bigger and better things.

But the fear that no one will ever want you or that you will never find anyone else looms large on the horizon. While it is normal to feel that way, it is rarely the case. In fact, it is amazing how fast people couple up again after a break-up. Although it is often too fast to have dealt with the mourning and to be clear about all the lessons, it is usually a very short time before people find the next great love.

A good rule of thumb for achieving a healthier relationship next time out is to wait at least a year after a major break up before getting back into a committed relationship. But, if you find someone you feel you truly love and can have a great relationship with, go for it. You can't mourn forever. It will just be another lesson.

DON'T BE COMMITTED TO THE COMMITMENT

Commitment is a powerful word. It is a powerful act. It is not a jail sentence. It is not a sin to break a commitment.

At the time that you make a commitment, it may make sense for you to do so. It is important to honor your word. It is more important to honor your feelings and integrity.

A commitment is not just an agreement to do or to be something. It is a stated desire on your part to fulfill something in yourself. We tend to forget that part and become committed to the commitment.

Part of living in the moment is learning to do what you need to do for you at the time. We have all been slaves to our commitments and promises. That is not only unhealthy, it makes everyone miserable. Are you an adult who makes your own decisions, or are you a child, a slave? You choose.

If you are an adult, there will be times when commitments and promises you have made become detrimental to your on-going growth. Then it is time to look at whether you are committed to the letter or the spirit of the law. If you are an adult and choose to be responsible for your life, rather than victimized and enslaved, then you must deal with the spirit of the commitment.

If keeping any agreement is detrimental to your health, spiritual or mental, or to your emotional growth, you have a right to either break the agreement/commitment, or to renegotiate it so that it allows you room to grow.

If you have the strength and the courage to do this, your life will be a powerful expression of individuality. It may not make you popular with the people involved, but, after all, life is not a popularity contest.

LOVE MAY NOT BE ENOUGH

Love may not be enough to hold a relationship together. In fact, there are times when the most loving thing one can do in a relationship is to let it go.

A tormenting and tragic aspect of romantic love is that it is possible to be in love, to love someone deeply and profoundly, and to have to face the reality that it is not a workable, compatible relationship. However much love there is, one for the other, there are too many other things in the relationship that preclude longevity.

Young people often learn this lesson in their first experiences of love. It becomes obvious to even the most romantically inclined that one can love the core of another without being able to reconcile the differences that would make it possible to be in a committed relationship.

However carefully you choose the person to whom you commit, underlying psychological forces may foil all attempts to partner successfully. The axiom that you don't really know someone until you live with him is true.

In dating, courtship, and engagement, everyone is on his or her best behavior. Even if you live together before marriage, it is not the same as being married. The door is still open. Closing that door allows all of the psychological baggage carried in the relationship to come to the fore. That is part of what makes the first year of marriage so difficult.

If you have chosen a partner who exemplifies the worst traits of one or more of your parents, it will be very difficult. It is also an opportunity to work through your feelings and behavior patterns from your family. Whether or not it works out will depend on many unpredictable factors.

Perhaps the most difficult situation of all occurs when the couple discovers that their goals are vastly different. It is important to be brutally honest with yourself and with your partner during the period of courtship and engagement.

If you want children, don't lie and say you don't. Don't tell the other person what you know she wants to hear. While you may run the risk of losing the relationship if you are honest, it is better to do it before marriage rather than risk a divorce later. Marriage in this culture at this time is very difficult. Very few marriages make it under the best of circumstances. Being dishonest with yourself or with your potential mate is almost a guarantee that it will not work long term.

In order for a marriage to work, your basic goals must be the same. If one wants to be a rock star and the other wants to have a stable, ordinary home life, the relationship will not work. If one of you wants to be a missionary in Africa and the other wants to be a socialite, it won't work. Your basic life goals and values must be very closely aligned.

If your choices of lifestyles are drastically different, a hippie and an heiress, a cowboy and a princess, a farmer and a yuppie, the chances for a successful relationship are slender indeed. These examples are obvious and perhaps even ridiculous, but they are given to make a point. The problem in most relationships is that the differences are not that clear cut.

Don't misunderstand. No two human beings are ever going to agree on everything or even most things. But the most basic issues must be fairly closely aligned. A marriage can tolerate a great deal of basic difference with compromise as the key word, but there must be at least a basis for compromise. If you each hate what the other one considers basic, there is just no chance. In other words, two squares may get along, or two circles, but you can't put a round peg in a square hole.

Coming to the realization that you are in an unworkable situation and facing it squarely can become one of the most painful experiences in life. It is at that point that you have to decide honestly and clearly whether you can work this situation out to serve both of you. If children are involved, it will be that much more difficult.

The choice that has to be made is whether to hang on to the security of marriage or to let it go in service of the growth and freedom of each other. It is not fair or loving to insist that one partner follow the dictates of the other. It is not fair or loving to you to give up what you need and want to satisfy the other person's desires.

While there are elements of both in any good marriage, to have one person doing all the leading or all the following is unhealthy. That is not a relationship, it is slavery. Even if it is done from choice and out of great love, one must stop long enough to consider whether it really works, because there will be a price to be paid in other areas of the relationship and in the lives of each of the individuals.

If you are constantly trying to fit a round peg into a square hole, both of you are going to be sore and bruised. Is that love?

Eventually one must decide what is the most loving thing to do for both people. What will produce growth in each? What will allow each the freedom to explore the world in the way he or she would choose if the partner were in agreement? The unalterable conclusion may be that the most loving thing to do is to let it go.

PERFECT MATE

If you are looking for the perfect mate, you are going to be alone for a long time. Are you looking for a mate with your head, your heart, or both? Hopefully both. If you have a list of the qualities and requirements necessary for a man or woman to be acceptable as a life-time lover, what have you done with your feelings?

Like the perfect parent and child, the perfect mate does not exist. Someone who will be a perfect mate for you does exist, but he or she will not be perfect. Are you? Does everyone you meet fall short of the mark in one way or another? Do you like 90% of the person, but the other 10% won't work? Why not? What kind of game are you playing here? Have you set yourself up to lose?

Choosing a mate is tricky. It requires a balanced combination of intellect and emotion. It is entirely possible to fall in love wildly and passionately with someone who is not a suitable mate for you. It is also possible to find someone who fits your specifications but with whom there is no "magic" or "chemistry."

Are you attempting to "computerize" your dating by looking at the resume? The resume is not the person. She or he might look great on paper but be impossible as a person.

You can't talk yourself into loving someone. You either do or you don't. In your heart you know the truth. It is a major mistake to get married for the sake of getting married. It's hard enough when you really love each other.

Do you think sex is the key element? If we are powerfully attracted to each other and have great sex, will it work? Sexual attraction does not a marriage make. Passion isn't love or commitment. Good sex comes from good communication, trust, love, depth of commitment, and partnership. If the partnership is rocky, or becomes rocky, those rocks will show up in bed immediately. Don't count on sex to save the relationship. It will be the first thing to go when it gets in trouble.

It helps to start by being friends. Get to know each other. Do you have common interests, values, and goals? Do you enjoy being together whether there is anything going on sexually or not? Can you tell each other secrets? Can you accept each other in the unconditional way that real friends do?

In a good relationship, your partner should be your best friend. That is who you want to talk to when you are in trouble or have something wonderful to share. That is the first person you think of when you want company. He or she is the person you turn to for advice, support, comfort, and encouragement. If the relationship is based on sexual attraction alone, those things will be missing. Will that be satisfying for the next 50 years?

It helps to put as much planning and thought into the choice of a mate as you would your career. So he has beautiful eyes, or she is very charming. That may be what attracts you, but consider whether the rest of the package fits. If this isn't the person for you, and you know it in your heart, be willing to wait. Someone else will be along soon.

If you turn down one person after another, take a look at what you are doing. If no one is ever good enough, if you love him but can't seem to make the commitment, or it just never works out, what's happening?

What are you afraid of?
Are you capable of intimacy?
Are you capable of commitment?
Are you afraid to let anyone really get close to you?
Do you want a guarantee that it will work?

There are no guarantees. There is only risk and commitment. If it doesn't work out, at least you will have had the experience and learned from it. If you are insisting on a guarantee, you will never do it, because no one will ever be able to make you feel safe enough. Why do you need to feel safe? A relationship is anything but safe. True intimacy requires courage to allow yourself to be truly known by another. Why do you need a guarantee?

Start asking yourself some of these questions and giving yourself straight answers. Work on yourself and clean those emotional windows so that someone can win with you in the relationship department. Do you want to be alone forever? Then get to work on yourself. There is no reason you can't have a wonderful relationship, except for your own attitudes.

DON'T PUT YOUR LIFE ON HOLD

Don't put your life on hold waiting for Mr. or Ms. right to come along. Go ahead and live your life. Do what you want to do. Why is it that you feel like nothing without a relationship? Why do you think you can't live your life without a mate?

Women are particularly inclined to sit around and wait to get married. Men don't do that as much. They get on with their work and their hobbies. They look actively and want a mate, but they still live their lives. There are women who won't change their nail polish for fear it will hurt their romantic possibilities.

Women's liberation has accomplished a great deal. But many women still feel empty and worthless, failures, if they are unmarried. A woman without a man is still a human being with a life. The point of the women's liberation movement is to teach women that they can have an identity separate and apart from their marital status. It is important to be a woman, a person, before you get married. How are you going to know who you are if you set yourself up as "just a wife?"

Be the person you want to be and you will find the person you want. Work at becoming a fully individuated adult human being. Discover you. What do you want to do? What do you like? Do the things you naturally want to do. Play tennis because you like to and maybe you'll find a great tennis partner. Do the things you enjoy. Live your life the want you want to live it. An independent spirit is a very attractive quality. Marriages break up because one partner is so dependent that the other feels suffocated. Have friends, interests, and work of your own.

If you want a mate, get out there and look. Be active and available. Most people do want a long-term committed relationship. But a relationship shouldn't be the only thing you want. Define yourself as a person. Knowing who you are and what you want for your life will help you know what kind of person you want and need. To make another human being your life is boring and unhealthy for everyone. The flip side of dependency is rage. If you or your partner is excessively dependent, there will be a great deal of anger in the relationship.

Marriage isn't life. It is an aspect of life. The chances are very great that you will get married. If you are not married now, go ahead and live your life now as you want to. You may never have an opportunity to have the kinds of adventures you can have now. Take advantage of your singleness to fully appreciate doing things exactly as you wish. When you get married, you will rarely have that chance again.

MARRIAGE DOESN'T SOLVE ANYTHING

It just creates different problems. It is entirely possible to feel even more lonely in a relationship than out of it.

Marriage, along with parenting, is hard work. Marriage isn't about living a romantic fantasy happily ever after. A good marriage requires compromise, flexibility, forgiveness, understanding, patience, cooperation, communication, and love. Because it stretches you emotionally, it is the best laboratory around for personal growth. You must constantly deal with the baggage you have carried into the marriage.

The person you marry will be a good mirror image for you. Mirrors are not always pleasant to look into. The rocks in his or her head fit the holes in yours and vice versa. That means you will have to be responsible for your own feelings and behavior without blaming them on your spouse. Marriage is a breeding ground for the victim/tyrant game. To be a champion in marriage requires extraordinary work and a commitment to the growth of both partners.

Because the rocks and holes balance out, if you are looking for perfection, you are doomed. It is guaranteed that this Greek god or goddess you have married will have feet of clay. What you loved in them before you married will be what will drive you crazy later.

One man said that his wife's independence and self-sufficient attitude were very attractive to him when they were courting. He loved the idea of having a woman who would not depend on him for her every need. After they were married, it made him feel unneeded and unnecessary. He thought she was aloof, detached, and cold. He had previously been married to a suffocatingly dependent woman. The idea of an independent female felt like a cool breeze in August. What he soon discovered was that he needed and expected the women in his life to be dependent. In that way, he felt needed and safe and knew that she would not stray. He and his second wife both did a lot of work to balance their attitudes.

Anyone who tells you he or she has no problems in his or her marriage is either lying or living in La-La land. Marriage is problematic. Two separate and distinct people are attempting to forge a life together. It is not impossible, but it is very difficult to put two capsules together. When each is reading the inside of his or her own capsule, it is hard to know what is going on with the other.

In fifteen years of marriage counseling, it has never failed that when the partners are seen individually, each will come saying, "I do all the work in the relationship." Each feels angry and victimized by the other's lack of concern and insensitivity. It is humbling to discover that the partner feels the same way. If you enter marriage with the idea that it will solve all of your problems, and that at last you will be happy, you will be sorely disappointed. Do you have the idea that when you get married all your troubles will be over? That you will never be lonely again? That your spouse will take care of you?

What is it that you want or expect from marriage? You have all kinds of fantasies about what your prince or princess will do for you. What are they? What do you expect to get? It is very likely that you are clear about what you expect and want from your spouse and from marriage. A much tougher question is "What do you expect to give?" What do you have and want to give? Give it some real thought. It's important. It is amazing that most people don't think about what they have or want to give. They just think about what they are going to get. No wonder relationships get into so much trouble so fast.

If you don't love yourself now, you will not love yourself any more after you are married. It is true that you can't love anyone else unless and until you love yourself. There will be days when you look at your spouse and think "Who is this person and what did I ever see in them?" You will be astounded that he lives in your house and shares your bed. That is when you are not loving yourself. If you remember to love yourself, you will remember to love your mate.

In marriage, as in life, there are no guarantees. The key to a good relationship is communication. If you love yourself, love your mate, and communicate, you at least have a chance. Put everything you have got into it, and, if it doesn't work, then you have nothing to regret.

Cooperation and compromise are marital necessities. Don't always insist on having your own way. Couples fight about wall paper, lamps, and carpet colors. Is it worth it? What difference does it make? Learn to choose your battles. Learn to fight only about things that really matter in the long run. Letting the other person have her way in small things is endearing and will allow her to give you space in the larger issues.

One last word. The person who leaves a marriage is rarely the person who left. What happens most often is that one of the spouses leaves the marriage emotionally. He or she does not treat the spouse or the relationship as a priority. She has pulled away emotionally in anger, or detachment. He is there in body, but not in soul. Sex becomes a thing of the past. The partner who leaves is reacting to this behavior, which has already signalled the end of the marriage.

If you or your spouse is pulling away, detaching, get in there and communicate. Talk about it, fight about it, cry together. See what you can work out. The love is still there, but it is buried under resentment, anger, and misunderstanding. Try to work it out with the understanding that it doesn't always work. Sometimes it is just over and there is nothing anyone can do about it. If that is the case, do your mourning and get on with it. But understand that the next marriage won't solve anything either.

YOU ARE THE ONLY PERSON YOU CAN CHANGE

You have no control over anyone else. Control is an illusion. If you think you have any control over anyone you are fooling yourself. Can anyone control you? No? Then what makes you think you can control them? There is an old joke that appears on t-shirts:

> Never try to teach a pig to sing.
> It is a waste of your time and it annoys the pig.

Quit trying to teach pigs to sing. Isn't that what it feels like? You keep pounding away at other people and, if anything, they just get worse. They are not going to change, especially if they think you are trying to force them. They will resent and defy you. It is human nature.

What you can do is to love them exactly the way they are. Allow them to be who and what they are and to express that in any way they choose, as long as it is not destructive to you. When you accept someone as she is, you give her the freedom to change. To want someone to change is to have a judgment that he is not acceptable as he is. If you can love and celebrate her as is, that love will be the impetus for her to grow and love herself. Unconditional love creates miracles. In that kind of loving environment, people blossom and bloom.

If you can't love someone else unconditionally, what does that say about how you feel about you? It always comes back to you. If you think it is necessary for the other people in your life to change in order for you to be happy, guess who needs to change? That's right. You. If you will change your attitudes and your interpretation of yourself and of others, things will look very different.

You are the only person you can change. To think otherwise is to be frustrated and angry. What right do you have to expect or demand that anyone else change? How do you feel when someone treats you like that? Hurt? Angry? Resentful? Does it make you think you are loved? Do you feel misunderstood and unfairly judged? How do you feel around someone who lets you know that you are just fine, however you are? It feels like sunshine in the winter. How do you feel about the person who treats you like that? You probably love him or her totally.

You can give the same kind of unconditional love to yourself and to everyone else. Then no one has to change. Everyone can simply evolve at a rate and in a way that is natural to them. If a pig wanted to sing, he'd ask for singing lessons. If the people in your life wanted to change, they would. Let them make the decision by loving them as they are. It's called living in harmony.

NO ONE CAN CONTROL YOU WITHOUT YOUR PERMISSION

In the sixties, a famous comedian made the line "The devil made me do it" a national catch phrase. People all over the country said that to each other, often amidst much hilarity.

It is not funny to blame your behavior on someone else. But everyone does. How often do you say something like, "He made me do it?" Start paying attention. Listen to yourself. You'll be amazed at how often you blame your behavior on someone else. "She would have been upset if I hadn't done it." "They'd disown me, fire me, etc."

Unless you are a child, these are very childish, and actually very dangerous things to say. They are dangerous because they indicate that you are being a victim and are not taking responsibility for your life. That is a prescription for an unhappy life. If you are married or a parent, it is a guarantee of an unhappy, unhealthy family.

No one can make you do anything without your permission. Colonel Bo Gritz says that if even one buck private had objected, had stood up for what was right to Lt. Calley, the killings at My Lai would not have occurred. But no one had the courage to stand up and be counted. There might have been repercussions. Would they have been any worse than living with the nightmare of having been a part of the mass murder of innocent villagers?

As long as you are willing to be controlled, you will be. It is much easier and safer than being responsible. It is not a lot of fun. If you are constantly blaming someone else for your action or your unhappiness, you have a serious problem. Bring it home. Lay it at your own doorstep. Then you have power.

To take it a step further, that includes blaming your parents. If you are over 30 years old, you are responsible for your life. It doesn't really matter what your parents did or didn't do. It is your life and you get to choose how to live it. If you blame it on them, you lose. Yes, what they did has a powerful effect on who and what you are. But you still have choices. And ultimately, even if what you do is a result of childhood experience, you are the responsible party. You have to pay the price. No one else. It is up to you.

PARTNERSHIP

Partnering is an important concept for every on-going relationship. It is useful and helpful to partner with your therapist, your mate, your children, your boss, your business associates, and your friends. What does "partnering" mean? What does it mean to be in a partnership?

It means that no matter what comes up, each partner is committed to the growth and nurturance of the other person. Each is committed to getting the job done rather than becoming involved in power struggles and getting his or her own way.

It means that even if the relationship comes to an end, or changes radically, each person is committed to working it out in a harmonious way which allows the love and friendship to continue, despite the changes in structure.

In any real partnership, there are hidden agendas which must be addressed and acknowledged. Transference will be a major factor which has to be dealt with by each. Every relationship in which any major goal is being pursued will have stress, misunderstanding, conflict, and insecurity.

In a partnering relationship, each person deals as honestly as possible with his own judgments, anger, resentment, fears, insecurities, and frustration. Blaming is not an option. Communication is clear and honest, with respect for the feelings of the other being paramount. The agreed-upon goal is to remember to love, empower, and nurture the other. There is an absolute agreement to resolve conflict in a way that satisfies both partners.

There are two goals. The primary goal is to work out the relationship regardless of the difficulties that arise and to deal with one another with integrity and honesty. The secondary goal is to get the job done. If the first goal is achieved, the second one will also fall into place.

In a true partnership, power is not the name of the game. It is not about having control and getting what one partner wants out of the relationship. It is seeing that both people are satisfied and fulfilled by the experience. It is a shift of paradigms from content to process.

The content of the relationship is what has to be done, what the contractual agreements are. The process is how that work gets done. In a good partnership, the process is more important than the content. It is the adult realization that what each person is really after is the experience rather than the goal. In this way, both the goal and the partners are better served than in a goal-oriented, contractual approach.

Each person takes full responsibility for the job to be done. It is an acknowledgement that the part makes up the whole. There is no power struggle, no domination of one ego over another, no insistence on a single way of operating.

A process-oriented partnership requires that each person dig down deep inside to be responsible for her own feelings, behaviors, and tasks. The other helps in that process by being non-judgmental, supportive, giving the other person what she wants and needs, and communicating honestly and openly.

Partnering then becomes a thrilling, fulfilling process in which the goals are always achieved, powerfully so. Without partnership at this level, a task-oriented relationship breaks down into a stalemate of ego, power, and control.

To operate in this way in a relationship builds trust. It is that trust that the other person values more than any goal or benefit of the partnership. It allows chasms to be bridged, conflicts to be resolved, and personal power to be increased for both.

Trust is, therefore, the basis of the partnership. It is a stated and tacit understanding and agreement that the people are the most important part of the partnership. It is an agreement that says, "I promise to put our relationship and your feelings above any possible benefit to myself; above money, power, status, or the insecurities of my own ego." With this agreement, both people feel loved and valued and are willing to give their all to the other and to the partnership.

In a goal-oriented partnership, there is always the fear that one partner will value any number of things more than the other partner. That fear undermines the foundation of the partnership and sabotages the goal.

If you can and will partner with each of the important people in your life, many of the problems inherent in a relationship will disappear. You will have loving, empowering, long-term relationships that continue when the structure changes. You will have earned the love, respect, and trust of the people with whom you are involved.

16

LOVING YOUR FAMILY

The perfect parent exists only in the mind and writings of Sigmund Freud. The perfect child exists only in the minds of those who have never reared a child. Many idealistic young parents think that they will be the perfect parents and rear the perfect child. What they mean is that they will not make the mistakes their parents made. They will do it right. And they will raise a problem-free child.

Good luck. That's not how it works. If you have that kind of scenario in mind, you're in for a major shock or two. You may succeed in not making the mistakes your parents made. It is wise and important to do so. But you will make your own mistakes, one of which may be thinking that there is such a thing as a perfect parent or child. You are putting crushing pressure on yourself and your child.

This is a human being you are attempting to rear. Genetics and sociology alone will combine to create problems for the child. There is no way to protect a child from life. There will be many influences in your child's life over which you have no control.

The best you can do is be the best parent you can be and attempt to ameliorate the other influences and events. If you expect your child to be perfect, the child will rebel early and often. How would you like to be expected to be perfect? What does that mean to you? A child who does not make your life miserable somewhere along the way is a child in serious trouble. It's when the child does not rebel, never gives you any trouble, is a "perfect darling," that you should worry. These children grow up to have major difficulties in life.

It is the job of every adolescent to give you grief. It is your job to allow a certain amount of it. Teenagers are difficult because we try to control them. Up to a point, it is necessary to control them. It is our responsibility to protect and teach them. If you expect or demand that they be perfect to support the idea that you are the perfect parent, they will rebel wildly, up to and including running away. Loosen the reins on them and on yourself. To think that you are never allowed to lose your temper, to be unfair, to be out of sorts, to always be even, giving, and loving, is unrealistic.

It is important for children to learn that adults cry, hurt, get tired, argue, and experience failures and disappointments. That's how they learn that it's all right to be human and to have their own feelings.

Instead of trying to be perfect, be real with them. Share yourself. Share with them appropriately your thoughts, feelings, and dreams. Listen to theirs. Encourage them to talk to you. Let them know that they can be straight with you. They can tell you anything. They won't, but it is important for them to know that they can.

We have learned a great deal in this century about the human psyche and the influence of the family on the child. It is right and good to attempt to use that information in a practical fashion to help us rear healthier adults. Healthier is not perfect. Don't expect to undo the damage of generations in one child.

Do the best you can. No one can reasonably expect more. Whatever the child is or becomes, you will love him or her. That's really the definition of a perfect parent: one who loves the child no matter what.

The perfect child is one who grows up to be his or her own person and lives all of life's experiences. To think it should be any other way is one of the fantasies of La-La Land.

MEN ALWAYS, WOMEN ALWAYS

There are certain gender-related behaviors which drive the opposite sex crazy: Men never want to pay for parking. They will drive around forever, making everyone late for the concert, in order to find a spot on the street. Women always go to the ladies room in groups, like they're off to their own secret summit meeting. There are a number of such behaviors which are inimical to men or to women and which create great distress in their partners. One of the frequent tasks of the therapist is to interpret the opposite sex in a way that makes it understandable for the mate.

Without going into the specifics of why each sex does the things that it does to drive the other crazy, it is important that you understand what amounts to the facts of life. When we explain the facts of life to children, we should include things like men won't go to the doctor without a fight, and women will want to color coordinate his tool box. Women cry for what looks like no reason, and men will never stop to ask for directions.

Do these kind of things drive you to distraction? Do you swear you will never understand the opposite sex? They frustrate you to the point of mayhem and are unreasonable beyond belief? Is it the little things that totally threaten the relationship? You'd be surprised how big an issue these things can be in therapy. They become big issues because they are misunderstood and misinterpreted.

The first rule is, don't take it personally. If he won't park in the paid parking lot, he's not a cheapskate. He's just male. If she cries when the leaves change colors, it doesn't mean she's leaving you. She's just being female. Why do you take it so personally?

Attempt to understand what is beneath the behavior. Men don't want to go to the doctor because it interferes with their macho image and because they're not allowed to ask for help. They don't want to see themselves as needy or fragile. They're tough. They can handle it.

A man once came into group therapy late because he had been looking for a parking place. He had nearly lost a finger in an accident that day. His hand was bandaged and he had a cut that went to the bone. When the group inquired about his physical and emotional feelings, he allowed as to how it was nothing. It just took some stitches and it was nothing. He had refused even a local anesthetic. The women in the group had fits. The men admired him. Aside from what the incident said about how the man felt about himself, it was typically male: "I don't need help. I can handle it."

It is difficult not to become frustrated with someone you love who isn't taking proper care of himself. It's also difficult to deal with a weepy woman when you are doing everything in your power to make her happy.

The lesson is to not take the behavior personally. It has to do with the emotional, gender-related make-up of the individual. It doesn't mean anything. Whether it's genetic, socio-cultural, or electromagnetic doesn't matter. What does matter is that you attempt to allow, tolerate, and understand it, and don't take it personally. That's just how they are. It has nothing to do with you or with the relationship. On the other hand, it is the opposite quality that draws us to each other. The femininity or masculinity of the mate is very attractive. So there are some drawbacks. She will hang curtains in your workshop. He will break your favorite pitcher while washing the car. Is it grounds for divorce?

Hardly. Remember that it is those wonderful masculine or feminine qualities which make you love him or her so much. Viva la difference!

YOUR FAMILY MAY NOT BE YOUR FAMILY

The "new age" idea that the individual chose either the circumstances or time of birth flies in the face of scientific reality. Study biology and it will become clear that it is not possible for us to have had choice in the matter. We do not choose our families. It is an accident of fate. It is possible to consider your family as the only available bus at the time you made the trip, but you did not decide when or if to make the trip.

Whatever we manage to learn from our life situations could be learned in easier circumstances. It's not even a roll of the dice. It's just what happened. If you don't like your family, if they are consistently mean to you, if they don't love you exactly as you are, if being around them makes you miserable, give them up.

Give up your family? Blood is thicker than water. Now what is that supposed to mean? Your family has blood in its veins and other people have water? Of course you are going to feel closer and more loyal to your family than to other people, if it is at all loving and empowering. If it's not, you have the right to say, "Goodbye, have a good life."

You have no responsibility to continue to be part of a system which does not support you. Your family won't like it because they want and need to keep you involved in "The Game." You don't have to play.

You will meet people along the way: friends, lovers, teachers, and mentors, who may be more your family than your family ever was. Love them, treasure them, use them to make your life happier and healthier. You will find sisters, brothers, parents, aunts, uncles, cousins. You can have grandchildren when you have not yet had children.

If you are estranged from your family, you can still have a wonderful, loving group of supportive and accepting friends who can be your family. Not everyone is lucky enough to come from a family to which they want to belong. It doesn't mean there is anything wrong with you. Be willing to let all abusive relationships go, even if they're "family." You don't have to choose to continue to allow yourself to be abused, used, or mistreated in any way.

You don't have to sever all communication with your family, unless to continue contact results in the destruction of your identity or self esteem. You can choose how you want it to be. You can spend twenty minutes a month having coffee if you want to maintain a relationship. You can go home once a year for only twelve hours if that's all you can handle without disturbing your equilibrium.

You don't owe your family anything. It was their responsibility to rear you. Beyond that it is necessary to decide whether you want to continue the relationship. Most of you will want to continue to be allied with your families. Family is important and powerful in everyone's life. If you can work out a nurturing and loving relationship, by all means do so.

But if your experience of your family leaves you feeling devastated, abused, used, mistreated, unappreciated, and conditionally accepted, you are free to hang it up. Go find the group of friends who will love and support you unconditionally. It is your right to do so. If may even be necessary to your health, growth, and development. To do so is to be compassionate with yourself.

COMPASSION

Compassion is love expressed as understanding. Rather than judging, the compassionate person empathizes with and tries to know what it would feel like to be in the other person's shoes. Compassion is a very great gift to self and to others.

What may be less clear is that compassion may not always look like sweetness and light. Sometimes compassion means taking a hard stance with someone, with the intention to get them to move faster or in a different direction.

Some people absolutely won't or can't hear or pay attention until someone gets tough with them. What may look mean or cruel to others may be the impetus necessary to get someone moving.

Helping someone does not always look like patting him or loving him up. It may be necessary at times to kick butt. The person doing the kicking is clear that it is not from anger or meanness, but from a profound desire not to let the person stay where he is.

Setting limits and making them stick does not make one popular. With the level of manipulation practiced in this culture, it may be next to impossible to set appropriate limits. Whatever rule is made, someone will find creative ways to get around it. The limit has to be set again. Only if someone is willing to make you toe the line will you learn the lesson. If he buckles and lets you win, you lose.

In a group session, a patient was asked to leave the group when it was learned that the patient had been regularly violating the group rules. The group was aghast. They couldn't believe that the therapist would take a hard stance and stick by it. For the two years that the group remained intact, the expulsion of that member remained an issue. They used every means at their disposal to get the therapist to recant. Rules are rules and there are consequences for breaking them. The fact is that too many of us think the rules don't apply to us.

A therapist and a group represent a microcosm of the world and of each person's life. What goes on in therapy and in the group is what goes on in the person's life. If they violate the group rules, they violate society's rules. There are consequences for both. Not punishment, just consequences.

Do you set your limits? Do you make people respect and abide by them? Do you respect the limits set by others? Do you allow them to set any?

After an especially upsetting group session, a famous psychotherapist stepped over the body of a woman who had apparently fainted in front of the elevator. He saw it as manipulation and refused to play. Does that sound hard-hearted to you? It may have been. It may have required him to steel himself not to fall into the trap. He was well-trained enough to know that there was no real medical emergency. He had to face the wrath and judgment of the other clients. He did what he felt was necessary. Are you willing to go that far with your limits or do you let yourself be manipulated out of them?

If you ground your child and two hours later give them money to go to the mall, what are you teaching them? Consequences and punishment are not the same thing. Make the distinction.

A restaurant has rules. You may not enter without a tie and a jacket. You must behave properly, respecting the rules of the establishment and the rights of other diners, and pay your bill, or you will be asked to leave. Why should your friends and family put up with less respect? Why should you be allowed to misbehave or to treat others badly when even a restaurant has a code of behavior? Wake up! You do not own the world. And no one owns you. You must respect others' rights and limits and set your own.

Once you have learned to do that, you may be able to learn compassion. Compassion is love expressed. Letting people walk all over you is not compassion, it is lack of self-esteem.

People may cry and say you've hurt their feelings or offended them. The fact is you may have taught them an important lesson. This is not an excuse to be mean to anyone. It is a call to the arms of love.

Children need this kind of compassion. They need to know there are rules and consequences. If they don't get their homework done, they can't go out to play. If they don't get their chores done, they don't get to go to the movie. That is how they learn about rights and responsibilities.

One of the reasons people end up in therapy is that no one taught them the rules. No one taught them that if they don't do the job, they will get fired. No one taught them that if they don't pay their bills, they will have legal and financial problems. No one taught them that if they drink too much, they will get sick; or that if they eat too many of the wrong things, they will be fat and unhealthy.

Someone has said that a spoiled child is an unloved child. That is true to the extent that every time an adult gives in to a child rather than requiring him to deal with reality, he has taught the child that he can get his way and do as he pleases, or that the way to get what he wants is to have a tantrum.

We continue the patterns in our adult lives by either not knowing how to behave properly or by allowing others to run rough-shod over us. The person who leaves a marriage after twenty years has simply gotten tired of fighting for his or her rights. No one listened or took him or her seriously and he/she did not require it.

Clearly the consequences of not setting limits in one's personal life can be severe. If you don't know how to do that, let someone coach you. You can learn. You're not stupid. It's just that no one ever explained it that way.

HAPPY HOLIDAYS?

Holidays are often anything but happy. Not just the major holidays, but all of them offer up a Pandora's Box of unexpected emotion.

In a psychotherapy practice it is a guarantee that major issues will come up around every holiday. Holidays are national events touted in the media as happy, playful, family times. Advertisements abound with all of the items needed to have a "joyful" holiday.

What makes holidays so hard? Yom Kippur, Rosh Hashana, Thanksgiving, Chanukah, Christmas, and New Year's Day are obvious in the great expectation held of them. It will be fun, the family will be together, the food will be extravagant, gifts will be the stuff of fantasy, and children will be cherubs.

It rarely turns out that way. Expectations of that proportion are doomed to disappoint. The children are whiny, demanding, and hyper. The family isn't all together, you're away from home by yourself, or you have no family. Family members fight and long-buried resentments suddenly smoulder on the surface or break into active hostility. Family members who have died or otherwise left the family embody the empty chair syndrome and are mourned silently if not verbally. The ghost of Holidays Past appears to remind us of past disappointments, upsets, hurts, and loss. Instead of feeling cozily warmed by the family fires, loneliness and sadness may be more acute than ever.

Family problems, adolescent acting out, separations, divorce, and suicide rise dramatically through the winter holidays. Families and individuals who have been under great stress begin to unravel under the added pressure of the season. Emotional problems of every sort increase and bubble to the surface during this period.

Mother's and Father's Days are also important. All people have feelings about their parents. Many negative, unresolved issues nudge their way into semi-consciousness urged on by the focus of these holidays. Feelings surrounding the loss of a parent may become more acute and harder to suppress than is ordinarily the case.

Other holidays, such as the Fourth of July, Memorial Day, Labor Day, and Veteran's Day, also bring on deeply buried emotional matters. They are thought of as family times. When attention is focused on the family by the holiday, problems, sadness, unfulfilled longings, angers, and resentments become harder to ignore and control.

All holidays, even Halloween, traditionally a playful holiday for children, trigger unconscious reactions at a symbolic level. If would be interesting to investigate, for instance, what Easter and Passover mean to you at that level.

Don't be surprised if you find that you are depressed, angry, sad, lonely, or forlorn around holidays. Many people are. Try to isolate exactly what is making you unhappy around any particular holiday. Be conscious of your feelings as a holiday approaches so that you are not overwhelmed by them. Work with them so that you can know them and unload the baggage that belongs to that time. Forewarned is forearmed. You will have a much more enjoyable time.

Most importantly, make sure that you and all your friends are included. *Do not spend major holidays alone.* Ask a friend to invite you over. Invite others to be with you. One of the most devastating experiences of any holiday is to feel left out. Work to ensure that this does not happen to you or to anyone you know.

17

LOVING YOUR BODY

Your body talks to you all the time. What is it saying to you? Are you listening? Your physical feelings, state, and condition are what your body is saying to you. How does that work?

Pain, discomfort, and illness are messages from your body that something is wrong. Pain is literally the brain's communication to the rest of the nervous system that something is amiss.

How do you listen? How do you know what the body is saying? By what you are feeling physically. It's easy. Identify the pain or illness. What is the metaphor of the illness? Keep coming up with the metaphors until it "clicks" and you know that that is what is causing the problem. For instance, if you have diarrhea, try "Am I pushing the s—— out of myself?" or "What am I scared s——less about?" What metaphor can you think of that might be specific to your problem?

Your physical body is expressing an emotion you have repressed. It may also be telling you that your current health practices are hurtful to it. If you wake up every morning with a hacking cough, have frequent colds and sinus problems, sore throats and flu, your body could be telling you that it can't handle all the nicotine you are pouring into it. A hangover is the body's way of saying, "Alcohol hurts me." Are you going to listen? Or are you going to have "a hair of the dog that bit me?"

A runny nose and teary eyes may be all the sadness you are not feeling or acknowledging. What are you all stuffed up about? Where in your life are you feeling out of control? Are you literally being snotty?

In generalizing, we could say that heart attacks are broken hearts. What is closing your heart down? How easily do you express your love?

If you have a chest cold and a cough, what is it that you need to get off your chest? What can't you cough up? What's stuck in your craw?

Got the idea? Keep creating your own metaphors until you have unlocked the secret of the disease. This will work for most diseases. It doesn't mean that you don't need medical attention or shouldn't use the usual remedies. It does mean that you can shorten the course of the illness and be more in touch with yourself.

JUST BECAUSE YOU ARE LEARNING TO BE IN TOUCH WITH YOURSELF DOESN'T MEAN YOU'RE NOT SICK

Fortunately, many people are very aware of the emotional components in illness. In the early part of therapy, however, as clients learn to look at what is literally making them sick, they can be inclined to carry the concept too far.

Patients are sometimes inclined to ignore dealing with the symptoms of the illness altogether, and spend days trying to figure out what the underlying emotion is. Their desire to use their therapy and work with it independently is admirable. It seems to be difficult to draw the line and remember to balance emotion with intelligence.

In other words, don't be stupid. Just because you are becoming en-lightened doesn't mean you're not sick. The fact that you have some things to learn emotionally, or that you may tend to convert your feelings into physical symptoms, does not mean that you should eschew the ministrations of a medical practitioner. If you have a root canal problem, no amount of therapy is going to heal it. It hurts. Have it healed.

If you have symptoms, treat them. If they are severe or persistent, get yourself to the doctor. Forget what it means emotionally. You have not failed. Your body is telling you that you need help.

Clients sometimes think that if they do therapy right, they will never be sick again. At a very theoretical level, that may be correct. But don't risk your body to find out. Our defense mechanisms are so automatic and so fast that only the most "processed" person on the planet would be able to do that. Are you there yet? If not, behave sensibly. Take care of yourself. Get the medical or dental attention you need.

This attitude usually shows up in people who were not taught to take care of themselves, who think they don't deserve it, who were neglected, who were taught that it is "bad" to be sick, or whose family was angry when they required caretaking. Other people will refuse to get help because their parents dragged them to the emergency room if they sneezed. They are just replaying their family scenario and living out of what they have been taught. If any of the above is true for you, pay special attention to how you treat your body. What are your attitudes about health and illness?

Men in particular are inclined to resist going to the doctor. It is one of the things that drives women crazy. In reality, men may need closer medical scrutiny than women. Statistically, they do die younger. Perhaps if they made it a habit to get the medical care they required, that pattern could be turned around. Just because you think you are macho, Rambo, big and strong, you can still be smart and take care of yourself.

MY WIFE HAS PMS AND A GUN

Is that how you feel when your spouse has a period? Do you make your husband and the people around you want to run for cover?

Premenstrual Syndrome, or PMS, as it is currently called, can be frightening for everyone concerned. Women have long had difficulty with their menstrual cycles. It is nothing new. But because we have named it, it has now taken on an entirely new reality. We can buy pills directly from the shelf for PMS.

Do you have PMS? Do you have headaches, cramps, nausea, bloating, urinate frequently, crave chocolate, get cranky, moody, weepy, or easily angered? It's a real problem. Some women have very painful periods. It is real. They are not faking. Many women experience some if not all of the symptoms of PMS.

There are two issues to deal with about PMS. The first is—and you may not like this—what does what you go through each month say about how you feel about being a woman? Do you think of your period as "the curse"? Dig in and explore your feelings about being a female. Gender is a loaded topic in this culture, and has been for a very long time. We have reasons not to feel good about being women.

PMS is not all a function of attitude. Your general health can play a very important role in counteracting PMS. Some helpful suggestions are included in Workbook *Exercise 21*.

Don't make your period a reason for misery in your life and everyone else's. Explain to your friends how it feels. Help them understand that you really feel bad and need a little space and understanding. Ask your doctor to give you a prescription for some of the excellent products on the market to make your period more livable. They really help. Try anything your friends recommend to see if it helps. Check out your feelings, check out your general health, and see if you can make a difference in the severity of your menstrual pain.

The other issue to be aware of is that there are real hormonal changes which occur during your cycles that have a powerful effect on your emotions. Try to keep track of your period, when it is due and when you are ovulating, in order to understand what is going on with you.

If you find yourself being unreasonably angry, sad, easily upset, crying copiously for little or no reason, check your calendar. Adjust your reasoning accordingly. How you feel during your period is a good indication of how you feel generally. Deeply buried emotion, unrealized consciously, can appear on the surface during a time of great hormonal flux.

Do you feel sorry for everyone on the planet? Do you feel unbearably sad, full of grief? Are you woefully angry? Do you hate everything and everyone? Does your anger get out of control? Guess what is burning there all the time.

There are two useful ways to deal with your period. One is to pay careful attention to your thoughts and feelings during that time to discover what is going on with you at a deeper level. It is a good indication. The other is to turn your mind off and refuse to listen to yourself during that time. If what you say to yourself is all trauma and drama—everything is wrong, nothing is ever going to be right, no one loves you, ever has or ever will, you'll be broke forever, no one understands, or some version of all of the above—refuse to listen to it. Understand that those are your hormones talking and refuse to take them seriously.

You can really refuse to let your emotions carry you away into unnecessary fights and upsets. Turn the volume down, and refuse to listen. Your hormones are out of control, but you don't have to be. Watch yourself and your interactions with others carefully. Lock yourself in the bedroom, go for a walk, take yourself shopping, or to a movie. Do anything you can to avoid taking your hormones out on the people around you.

Be good to yourself, give yourself presents, treats, tenderness. Ask someone to pat your head, rub your back, get you a malted. Curl up in bed and read novels.

Most importantly, don't blame yourself. You are not sick and hurting and crazy because you've done something wrong. Your body is out of whack and is making your mind weird. Ride it through like a bucking bronco. You can stay on. You can maintain control.

Fella, take heart. It's only one week a month. Be compassionate and understanding. Don't take her behavior personally. Her hormones really are going crazy. She's not making it up. She has less energy and more emotion. Life is harder for her to cope with at that time. She's not just being dramatic, she is uncomfortable. There is one advantage. Just before and after, or at the beginning of the period, many women feel decidedly more sexy. Their body is saying, "Impregnate me. Do it now." Use that information however you choose.

LET THE PRESSURE OFF

In today's fast-paced, high pressure world, it is important to remember to let the pressure off. It is easy to get caught up in all the things that have to be done, and forget about yourself. If you don't take care of yourself, none of those things will get done. The system (you) will break down.

We have come to expect entirely too much of ourselves. We have lost the balance between being and doing. It is necessary to have both in our lives, in a balanced, reasonable way. No one can work all the time and stay healthy, physically, mentally, or emotionally.

Learn to make a time budget. List all the things you have to get done. In a complicated lifestyle, budget money to hire some of those things out. It's difficult and ridiculous to be the president of a company and try to do everything yourself. Hire someone to clean the house, mow the lawn, and do the family accounts.

Only you can decide what you have to do and what can be delegated. Budget your time and your activities so that you have some time for yourself. Educate the people in your life to understand that you need "down" time. You can't run at full speed all the time.

Don't expect yourself to be able to handle a difficult job, run a family, redecorate the house, travel, and participate in community and family affairs without space for yourself. Someone else can fix the leaky faucet.

A time budget might include absolute must work projects, absolute must home projects, social obligations, medical and dental appointments, shopping, haircuts, manicure, and recreation. If you find yourself suddenly in a heap because all you want to do is read a magazine and have a beer, just a few minutes to yourself, you are pushing too hard.

Let the pressure off or you will explode. Literally. You can't do it all. Make time for yourself. Have your hair done, play a round of golf, read, take a nap. Time for you to do just what you want to do will help keep you sane and will prevent you from blaming your family and friends for making you a slave to their needs. If you are being a slave, who did that to you?

Remember to factor you and your personal needs into the equation. Make sure that your family understands that you need to do that. You cannot be all things to all people at all times. They need to understand your right and need for time for yourself. So do you.

PART FOUR
CULTURAL
REVOLUTIONARIES

18

PROFESSIONAL HUMAN

Most people never figure out that it is necessary and important to go about their personal lives with the same planning, discipline, control, and focus they would apply to their business or professional life. Consider the possibilities.

What if you approached your personal relationships and problems in a professional manner? "But that wouldn't be real. It wouldn't be authentic," you say. It could be both real and authentic. It might actually be more real and authentic than the hair trigger reactions you have when you take something personally.

Business people know that it is necessary to manage up as well as down. In other words, you don't just manage the people who are in your charge, but you manage your boss and other higher ups. What if you applied the same rules and tricks of management to all of the areas in your life? For instance, just as you would empower your employees, you would empower your boss. Take it a step further. What if you saw your job in life as nurturing and empowering everyone with whom you came in contact?

Interesting idea. When dealt with in this manner, conflict, competition, and power struggles, are minimized. Problems are no longer seen as making or breaking the relationship, but as the impetus for working things out for both of you.

There will, of course, still be people and situations that require very firm boundaries. You may have to say no to them just as you would to projects or proposals that do not work in your favor in the business place. However, in this context, there is no over-riding anger or feeling of powerlessness. Rather, you simply look to see what works and firmly set your limits.

Anger and conflict are no longer necessary. You either are or are not willing and able to deal with the situation. It's not personal. You don't have to hate anyone or think they're the enemy. You simply manage the situation to your own satisfaction and good, as well as to the other party's.

What are some of the skills you use at work which could be transferred to your personal life? Let's take a look.

> *I have a professional attitude. I'm here to manage this situation so that the job gets done and everyone wins. I neither take what people say or do personally nor insert my personal problems or feelings into the mix. I leave my ego at the door.*
>
> *I am firm and clear about what I will tolerate in others and in a situation. I set my boundaries accordingly. I refuse to work with anyone who does not respect me. I recognize that if I turn down business from abusive, manipulative, customers, more and better business will immediately come my way.*
>
> *I am clear with myself and with others that my services and my time are for sale. I am not. I am unwilling to put up with abuse or other destructive behavior for the sake of a dollar.*
>
> *By honoring myself, I honor my customer or client. I refuse to deal with those who have no honor.*
>
> *I listen carefully and openly to all co-workers, with an ear to hearing what they're really saying. I communicate openly, attempting to discover how I can empower them to do their job with maximum benefit to everyone.*
>
> *I approach each problem encountered with a willingness to work it out for the benefit of everyone.*

I want everyone to win and no one to lose.
I am unwilling to compromise my standard for approval,
*   acceptance, or popularity.*
I see myself as a team player. I am willing to cooperate fairly
*   with everyone who will treat me in a similar fashion.*
I am willing to encourage, support and sympathize with all
*   problems. I won't allow any problem to derail the work.*
I see it as my job to empower and nurture everyone in my
*   environment, including myself.*
I do not take the behavior of my co-workers or any problems that
*   arise personally. I simply see it all as matters to be dealt with*
*   in order to further the work.*
I attempt not to judge my people or their products. Rather I assess
*   them to discover how to improve the work that is done.*

If you can and will take these attitudes and apply them to your life and to your relationships, your life will be different indeed. You will be clear about what is a problem and what is not, what needs attention and what is just mind chatter. Conflicts will no longer be major conflagrations but simply matters to be resolved. When there is cause for anger or upset, you will handle it fairly and evenly.

If you want your personal life to be happy and successful, apply the same rules and logic that you would in your work. Far from leaving you out of the equation or being truly impersonal, it will allow you to show up in a truly authentic way that will heal many of the problems in your life.

By being a professional human, your home, your friendships, and your recreation can be as successful and satisfying as your work.

SUPPORT SYSTEM

Do you have a support system? Do you have any idea what that is? Each person's support system will be different depending on her circumstances. There are a few basics.

Everyone needs a few good friends with whom he can talk about almost anything, share secrets, fun, evenings out, weekend hobbies, and adventures.

A good doctor, dentist, and gynecologist are also essential. If you are sophisticated, live in a big city, and have any money, your list may include: yoga teacher, therapist, chiropractor, masseuse, accountant, lawyer, nutritionist, non-specific healer, astrologer, psychic, pharmacist, hairdresser, and dog groomer. Someone living in the country may need a good feed store, a farrier, lawn doctor, veterinarian, plant nursery, pool boy, tennis or swim coach. The "cleaning impaired" may need a housekeeper. Perhaps you need a handyman, errand person, shopper, or corps of baby sitters.

What do you need to run your life easily and effectively? What can you afford? What do you want? What do you need to delegate in order not to feel overwhelmed by your responsibilities?

Everyone needs a support system. If you are of the hardy I-can-and-should-do-it-myself mentality, all this may seem silly to you. But wait a minute. Why should you do it all yourself? Where did you get that idea? Who taught you you're not allowed to ask for help or support? Is that really how you want to think and be? Does it serve you?

If we look at the job of life as being as functional as possible, then the importance of a support system becomes clear. It cannot be over-emphasized. Most people don't think they deserve it and don't want to spend the money for it because they're not worth it. If you think the idea of a support system is silly, what does that say about your attitudes? Are you really supposed to be able to do everything yourself? Do you want to?

Hiring others to help you with your load spreads the wealth around, and allows you more room to do the things that you're good at and enjoy. You can make choices about what you want to learn and what new experiences you want to have. It can be important and valuable to dig the garden or mow the lawn yourself, but when you are under crushing pressure, does it makes sense to do that? All of this comes under the heading of being nice to yourself. If you can't be nice to yourself, you need to question why. Are you required to be a major martyr and carry that cross all by yourself? Is that one of the ways in which you manage to suffer?

Hiring someone to clean the house once a week can give you more time with your family as well as make you easier to be around. Regardless of our circumstances, most Americans live complicated lives. We schedule ourselves non-stop. It is important to figure out how and what you can afford to have done for you and what you are willing to let go. If you are working 80 hours a week, you don't have to do your own ironing.

Even if you have relatively little money, and in this country that includes a lot of people, there are ways to lighten your load. A support group exists for every conceivable problem. There are agencies and organizations designed to help you. Let them. There is no shame in that. That is why you paid all those taxes. Or you can lean on your pastor, your church group, your next door neighbor. Have you ever helped a friend fix a car or clean house for a party, or taken food and supplies to a sick relative? That's support. Be willing to allow others to support you.

> *Organize your friends to help each other plant your*
> *gardens and do the canning.*
> *Take turns with other parents chauffeuring the kids to and fro.*
> *Arrange with your friends and your children's friends to*
> *trade sleepovers to give you some privacy.*
> *Have a neighborhood block sale to get the garage cleaned*
> *out and earn money for camp or music lessons.*

There are all kinds of deals that can be worked out among friends, neighbors, and co-workers. How can you support each other in getting life's jobs done and staying sane? It is also all right to let a friend do something for you without reciprocating. That is called friendship. Let them do it because they want to support you without expecting anything in return. You'll do something for them sometime.

We end up feeling unloved and alone because we are not allowing ourselves to be supported. Be willing to ask for help, for favors. You'll return them. It all balances out in the end. Be willing to accept help that is offered. People like to be helpful. It makes them feel good and less alone.

We all need each other. No man is an island and no woman is a full-service cleaner. Lighten the load by sharing it, and by identifying what is not absolutely necessary to your survival. Buy clothing and household items that do not need to be cleaned or ironed. Shop at discount stores and buy in bulk to save money for that new suit you need to feel presentable.

The pioneers had barn raisings and quilting bees to help each other.

They helped one another harvest crops before they ruined. WE can do that. WE can assist and support one another in the very stressful, complicated world in which we live. It's important. What ideas do you have about how you and friends can support each other? What can you do for them? What can they do for you? For the terminally helpful, remember, this is supposed to work both ways. Let them help you, not just the other way around. A good support team can help you develop coping strategies that will help you be prepared for whatever events or situations come along. *Exercise 22* in the Workbook offers some helpful suggestions for organizing the basics in your life.

WAKE UP

People who live with constant stress have to develop strategies for coping with it. A child who is in an angry, abusive, threatening environment does not have many choices. There are only so many adaptive maneuvers available.

What would you do if you lived in this kind of household?
What did you do?

One option is to "fuzz out," in popular parlance. This means the individual goes unconscious, not physically, but emotionally. In practical terms, it means that she shuts down her feelings and her ability to perceive what is going on around her. She simply does not see it. She disconnects from her environment.

Being unconscious can look like withdrawal, day dreaming, dawdling, distraction. Any behavior that allows the individual to go to sleep emotionally is designed to blot out what is going on in that particular household. It is the only way the child has found to live with the situation.

Do you wear glasses or contact lenses? Good chance you decided you couldn't bear to see what was going on around you. How old were you when you got corrective lenses? Try to remember what was going on then. What didn't you want to see?

In the same way that your eyes require glasses, your consciousness is unfocused. At an unconscious level, you work at not being aware of what is happening in your life. Again, you can't block out the pain without blocking out everything else. You can't focus on the nitty-gritty details of your life if you are trying to ignore your pain.

You can become more focused by being willing to see what is going on around you. Begin to work at having your feelings and being conscious of your life. Ask yourself what you're not willing to see. It will come up. It might show up in dreams or in a thought or in your feelings. Pay attention. What can you think of that would help you be more organized? Think about what you have to do and keep track of it. Then do it.

BARGAIN OR BURDEN?

A lack of self-esteem or self-worth often shows up in settling for what you think is a bargain. Instead of being clear with yourself about what it is you need and want and refusing to settle for less, your eye is on the dollar amount and what you will get for that. You're putting money ahead of your need.

For instance, a New York career woman took a truly wonderful apartment in one of the boroughs. The apartment was large and airy with high ceilings and abundant storage space. Especially in New York, those are highly prized and unexpected attributes for an apartment. She did not take into account that the apartment was in a terrible neighborhood. The noise in the building and outside on the street was deafening. She was afraid to walk her dog at night. She was a yuppie in the midst of a ghetto. She felt alienated and isolated. She had moved out of the city for this "great bargain" apartment, but now had to commute an hour on the subways. In the city, she could walk to work.

Crime was rampant in the neighborhood. She once opened her front door to the pounding of police officers who ran through her house and out her kitchen window in pursuit of an armed thief. Where is the bargain in that?

Another couple visited a large discount store on a holiday sale weekend. The store was a crush of people, noise, and confusion. They had gone to save money on a small appliance. When they left, both were over-stimulated and upset. Was it worth the small amount of money they saved?

A very tall woman with very long legs booked her first trip to Europe on a little known airline for its low fare. Apparently everyone in that airline's country of origin is short. She spent twelve hours with her knees literally under her chin, abjectly miserable. But it was a bargain.

What example of this attitude can you think of in your life?
In what ways do you put other considerations ahead of your needs?
What does that do to your self-esteem?
What does that say about your self-esteem?
What problems are created in your life by always putting money ahead
    of what you need or want?

There are ways to economize. There are times when a "false economy" is created by not taking into account the emotional aspects of the situation. Redefine your idea of a bargain by considering all of the factors involved, including your needs and feelings.

IT MAY NOT BE YOUR JOB

It may not be your job or your fault, but change it, fix it, do it anyway. Have you ever been frustrated over someone's not-my-job attitude? It is an attitude that is rampant in this culture. Government and business have become so huge and impersonal, it has become nearly impossible to accomplish anything. No one is responsible. The buck doesn't seem to stop anywhere.

If you will adopt an attitude that says, "The buck stops here," it will take you very far. When a question or a problem arises, it may not be in your job description, your department, or your expertise. You can still be responsible for finding out whose responsibility it is. You can help to that degree. Being willing to do things that are not in your job description will make you an invaluable employee. A sense of responsibility and willingness to participate are sufficiently rare that it would make you very unusual and therefore very valuable.

If each of us saw it as our job, our responsibility, to serve each other and the planet, collectively, we could create a different world than the one that exists today. What if each and every one of us took it upon ourselves to heal society and the planet?

As an individual, it would be possible to choose to intervene in a variety of ways. One person could start a tree-planting project in his community, spend one day a month picking trash up off the highway, or volunteering hours in the organization of his choice. It isn't necessary to join an organization. Just do it. Do whatever you feel needs to be done.

All those things that we are inclined to think of as someone else's problem shortly become our problems. Drugs used to be someone else's problem. Pollution and ecology was once the province of a few weirdos. It is all our problem and our responsibility.

It is true that it seems hopeless for one person to try to do anything. It is not. One person can do a great deal. One person can make a difference. That one person could be you.

If you find yourself sitting around complaining about the state of the world, ask yourself what you could do about it. Break it down into component pieces. You might not be in a position to fight the corporations that are killing the rain forests, but you can plant a tree. If you helped one child with contraception in order to protect them from pregnancy, social diseases, or AIDS, that would be a major contribution. Donating vegetables from your garden to the homeless would make a difference. There is something to do that you would enjoy and feel good about. Go find it.

Clearly no one individual can solve the world's problems single-handedly. But each person taking on a problem about which she can do something could alter the course of the planet drastically. The world we live in requires a major change in attitude regarding responsibility. We must quit acting like slaves or children and take an active part in the day-to-day workings of the world. This requires both clarity and commitment from each one of us.

CHOOSE A GOAL AND COMMIT TO IT

It is not difficult to be successful in life. It's actually easy. There are two necessary ingredients: clarity and commitment.

Do you know what you want? It's hard to get it if you don't. A young unemployed high school graduate was once asked what he wanted to do with his life. He responded that he wanted to do very little, if any, work and be very rich. He won't get what he wants.

It is necessary to have a specific goal in mind. You must be very clear that you really want it. To sorta, maybe, kinda want it doesn't work. The kind of commitment necessary to achieve goals doesn't come from "maybe."

Are you passionate about it? Do you want it more than anything else? Are you willing to give up other things you want in order to have it? If the answer to these questions is no, then you won't make it.

If you want to be a doctor, lawyer, or Indian chief, find out what it takes to be one and then go after it. Be willing to do whatever it takes. You can't be a doctor if you're upset by the sight of blood. If you have a problem with some aspect of your chosen goal, either handle it, resolve it, or choose another goal. To begin to organize your time to achieve your goals, do *Exercise 23* in the Workbook.

Once you have chosen a goal, and are sure that's what you want, commit to it. Commitment means you do it no matter what. It doesn't mean you do it if it's easy, everyone helps, there are no problems, and it's smooth sailing. You should have learned enough from this book by now to know that life is rarely about smooth sailing. It is, rather, more often about overcoming the obstacles in the way of achieving your goal. You do whatever is necessary to win. You put in whatever amount of time, energy, money, effort, sweat and brain power is required. If you really want to succeed, shine, make A's, be way out in front of the pack, you will put in more of everything than is necessary.

> *Define what you want.*
> *Choose a goal.*
> *Commit.*
> *Do whatever is necessary, and more.*

If you take each of the steps above, carefully and clearly, you will succeed beyond your wildest dreams. Good luck.

THE WAY TO BE ACCOMPLISHED AND COMPETENT IS TO BE COMMITTED

Don't try it. Do it. You can do anything. Anything. You are limited only by your beliefs and attitudes. You can do very little if you are not committed. The people who achieve and accomplish their goals are committed to the result. They have an attitude that says, "I'm going to do it or else. No matter what."

There are always excuses, reasons, and circumstances that look quite valid for why you can't achieve your goals. It's easy to be a victim here. Yet others with the same excuses and circumstances succeed in recognizing their vision. Why, then, can't you? If you say, "I'll try," that's not commitment. If you really want to do something, it doesn't matter what it is, you will do it. No matter what. Remember: "Where there's a will, there's a way."

It's wonderful to be a dreamer. Visionaries are necessary and important. But it's not enough to be visionary. That vision will require action, elbow grease, strength, fortitude, common sense, and commitment. Sitting around visualizing will not make it happen. Get behind your idea, your dream, with all the force of your will. Be willing to go the whole nine yards. Otherwise your dreams will collect dust, be forgotten, or become frustrations and disappointments. It's completely up to you. Inspiration is divine. Perspiration gets results.

The most phantasmagorical vision in the world is nothing without willpower. There is a trick here: realizing a dream is not nearly as much fun as the process of making it come true. It's the process, the trip, that is exciting, fun, and rejuvenating. Achieving the goal can be something of an anti-climax. But the trip—the trip is everything. It is during the journey to your goal that you learn, grow, develop new insight, wisdom, clarity, have adventures, challenge yourself. When you reach the top of the mountain, it is important to have another mountain in view.

Have an idea of what it is you what to achieve next. What is the next challenge? The next mountain top? If you are genuinely committed, you will develop the competence necessary to do anything you want.

It is not always the brilliant or the illuminated who do the special. It is often the plodding, determined, passionate person who achieves more than she had ever dreamed. Which would you rather be?

PARTICIPATE IN YOUR LIFE

Participate in your own life. Be willing to do something about your problems. Are you being passive? Are you caving in to a sense of being overwhelmed by all that you need to do in your life?

The busier you are, the happier you will be. You will have less time to wallow in self-pity and fear. If you are busy, actively working on your life, interacting with others, you will have a sense of involvement with others and with life that is very satisfying.

If you are alone, who are you shutting out? When people invite you to do things, do you automatically say no? Do you prefer to stay at home and watch tv or listen to music and brood? Why? Are you wallowing in your misery and suffering? Being busy and active will allow you to make friends, socialize, and participate in new ways. You will learn new things about yourself and about the world. You'll feel alive, expectant, invigorated. Does that sound better than the way you feel right now?

What is it that you could do right now, this minute? You could start by identifying the problem, making a list of alternative solutions, and then a list of steps to take to achieve one of the solutions.

> *You could discuss your problem with a friend.*
> *You could do something creative to take your mind off the problem.*
> *You could go out and be in the world to get away from it*
> *for a while.*
> *You could contact a group or an organization which*
> *specializes in your problem.*
> *What are their recommendations?*
> *What do they have to offer you?*
> *What do you have to offer people with the same issues?*
> *What have you learned from your problem that you could share with*
> *others?*
> *How could you do that?*

Take action. Take charge of your life. That's one of the ways you can create joy and eliminate fear and anxiety. Call an old friend. Call someone you've just met and get to know her better. Give a party and invite the new friends you've just made through your participation in an organization or community activity. Get off your duff and get moving. Being a couch potato isn't accomplishing much. Be willing to move. Go on. Get going.

19

RESPONSIBILITY
ISN'T AS BAD AS IT SOUNDS

How do you hear the word "responsibility"? What are your immediate thoughts? It is almost guaranteed that you think of responsibilities as duties or burdens. They are the things you have to do for yourself and others. You have no choice. No wonder they feel like burdens.

Everything that you want in life has responsibilities attached: relationship, job, marriage, home, children, money, things. If you see all those things as burdens, you will resent them and perhaps get them out of your life as quickly as possible.

The problem is that we don't make a conscious choice to accept the responsibilities of life. We feel victimized by them. They are often the tyrants who make us suffer. It is often a big disappointment to discover that all those things we wanted require time, effort, attention, and energy. No wonder our families are falling apart. They're a burden. We forget that we chose to have those people and things in our lives.

Being responsible is simply making a conscious choice to do the things YOU need to do for YOU to be happy and have a workable life. If that includes doing for others, make the choice to do so. Be honest about your choices.

Giving up the victim/tyrant game requires becoming responsible. That doesn't have to mean being burdened by your needs or anyone else's. If you choose to do it, then it becomes a joy. It is an opportunity for you to express yourself as a full-fledged champion.

Being responsible does not mean that you are guilty. If you choose to take responsibility for what is going on in your life, you are taking the first step toward becoming a champion. That does not mean you are guilty or bad or wrong or stupid. It means that you are willing to do whatever is necessary to take control of the situation and quit being victimized by it.

Responsibility is your friend. To be responsible is to be powerful. It is a gift. It will lift you out of the realm of guilt and burden into the champion's circle. If it helps you, you could substitute the word "powerful" for responsible. It is all the same thing. To be responsible is to be powerful over your life.

If you are powerful, you do your homework and get an education. By being powerful, you do a great job and get raises and promotions. A powerful person can hold a family together and experience great happiness. Now read these last three sentences and substitute responsible for powerful. You see, it really is the same.

YOU DON'T OWE ANYONE YOUR LIFE

It's your life. You have the right to live it the way you want to. There may be many people in your life, important ones, who will attempt to convince you otherwise. They need you for their game. You don't have to play.

Other people will always try to enslave you. They can't help it. It's the nature of life on this planet. All cultures have their own methods of controlling the individual to serve the society. It comes with the package. If you have a family, a job, a school, a neighborhood, someone will try to control you.

Isn't it interesting how people who clearly can't run their own lives know how to run you? And they will be adamant. It is amazing to see a father who has been unhappy in his work and his marriage guiding his children into the same path. It's what he knows. He might have been unhappy, but he's been safe and secure and—that awesome word—"stable."

You don't have to do what you're told or what's expected. Do the unexpected. If you want to do what's expected or demanded, go for it. But if your heart and soul rebel at the idea, then don't.

Others will exert lots of pressure. Your own sense of responsibility and guilt and desire to please will exert lots of pressure. Don't listen to any of it. If it doesn't feel right, don't do it. It's that simple. You don't have to do it.

Think. Feel. This is the only life you have. What do you want to do? How do you want to live it? We've been taught to be slaves. Be willing to stand up and be an individual. That's loving yourself and loving life. You're entitled. You are a free agent. You don't owe anyone your life.

NEVER DO ANYTHING YOU WOULDN'T WANT TO SEE ON THE FRONT PAGE OF THE NEW YORK TIMES

That's a good rule of thumb to follow. If you ever have a question about whether something you are about to do is right or wrong, ask yourself if you would want it made very public. If you would be ashamed to see it on the front page of your local newspaper, don't do it. Be honest with yourself about it. How would it really feel? Would you be ashamed for your friends and family to know? Would it hurt your professional standing or your social credibility? It's a very useful guideline.

THE REASON NOT TO VIOLATE YOUR INTEGRITY IS THAT YOUR SELF-ESTEEM WILL SUFFER

Are you inclined to be guilty? Are you harsh and judgmental with yourself? Do you have a hard time forgiving yourself? Then, if you violate your integrity, your self-esteem will probably suffer badly.

Even if your answer to these questions is no, tread carefully. You are dealing with the human psyche. You may be able to break man's law or even God's law. You cannot break your own. Although you may have no conscious discomfort, it will show in your face, in your posture, and in what happens in your life.

Your self-esteem rules everything that happens in your life: how much money you make, your creativity, health, and even your accidents. One or even all of these areas may be sabotaged until you have managed to clear it with yourself. That may take a long time.

Do you really want to do something badly enough to hurt yourself like that? Moralists will have a problem with this view. They would say something like "Virtue is it's own reward." White-knuckle virtue is not a reward, it is impossible. Real virtue, honor, comes from loving yourself.

If you violate your integrity, will you still love yourself? Probably not. After all, a violation of your integrity is an indication that you don't love you. When you violate your integrity, ultimately you hurt you. If you loved yourself, you wouldn't do that, any more than you would consciously hurt anyone else you loved.

If you add a lack of self-love to a guilty conscience, you get stomach aches, headaches, sleepless nights, frustration, and anxiety. Do you really need another reason to hate yourself?

Clearly this is not about morals. This is about what's practical, what works, what's real. Morals are not real. You didn't choose them. Someone taught you that view of what is right and wrong. But what's true for you?

If you make the decision on the basis of what supports your self-esteem, you will not have a problem. If, on the other hand, you do something that damages your self-esteem, then you will learn the lesson.

IF YOU DECIDE IT IS NECESSARY TO COMPROMISE YOUR INTEGRITY TO ACCOMPLISH YOUR GOAL, BE SURE YOU CAN LIVE WITH THE LEGAL AND EMOTIONAL CONSEQUENCES

Be careful. It is always your decision. Everyone compromises. You have to decide for yourself. Therapy isn't about morals. You make up your own mind. No one can tell you what you should or shouldn't do. You will have to face this question many times in many different situations. Integrity and honor are life-long issues. How you deal with yours is entirely up to you.

No one can rightfully tell you what is right or wrong. The fact, is you may have to do something others would judge as wrong, in order to learn. That may be your path.

The question is, can you live with it? There are many grey areas in ethical or moral considerations. People do things every day that others may consider deeply unethical or immoral. How do you think the planet feels every time we get in a car?

The lines are not always so clear. Especially if you have emotions which drive you in a particular direction, they may be very unclear. But when there is clearly a question in your mind about what to do, consider very carefully whether you can live with the emotional implications. If there is a legal penalty, are you prepared to pay it?

If the idea makes you anxious, if you are afraid someone will find out, if you take legal matters very seriously, don't do it. Don't even consider it.

If you have weighed all of the factors very carefully and thoughtfully and you know you can live with it, then it's up to you. But don't kid yourself. At least be honest with you.

HONOR

Honor can be defined as esteem, respect, or reverence; personal integrity maintained without legal or other obligation. Have you given any thought to the concept of honor recently? The idea of honor seems to be a thing of the past, both politically and socially. What about your personal honor?

There is a clear and powerful connection between the honor of the individual and the honor of a country. If the honor of each politician was absolute, or even somewhere in the vicinity, he would conduct himself in a way that conferred honor upon the nation. Clearly that is not the case.

Our politicians are a reflection of the body politic. That's us. There are very few of us who operate with honor, or who can say that we have lived an honorable life. Feeling guilty about it isn't helpful. Recognizing the reality and making conscious decisions about it may be.

At a personal level, a dictionary definition of being honorable, or living an honorable life, may be as simple as "maintaining personal integrity." That can be difficult given the flaws characteristic of most Americans. How can we rectify that? How can we learn to value honor in ourselves and in others? It is especially difficult to deal with the concept of honor without becoming judgmental and moralistic.

Keep it personal. You are the only person involved at this point. Is there any particular part of your life which is without honor? Are there other places in your life where you exhibit honorable behavior regularly and automatically? Identify each area. Be specific. Be honest with yourself.

Honor has nothing to do with being "good" or "right." Use the dictionary definition. Do you treat yourself with esteem, respect, reverence? Do you treat other people with the same esteem, respect and reverence? If your answer is yes, good for you, but be careful. Are you sure? Did you check every nook and cranny?

This may seem redundant, but if you don't love yourself, which we assume you probably don't, then how is it that you treat yourself with esteem, reverence and respect? Do you really treat yourself that way? You have learned enough by now to know that if you don't love yourself, you don't love others and don't treat them that way, either.

We can redefine the definition. For our purposes, we could say that to honor yourself is to live as if the most important thing in life is to love yourself. If you love yourself, you will not behave dishonorably.

Violation of personal integrity becomes a cycle that is difficult to break. It works something like this: You don't love yourself. Something about the way in which you don't love yourself causes you to violate your integrity. You do something which you and or others consider to be dishonest or dishonorable. Because you have been dishonest in that regard, you then have more reason not to love yourself. The problem is now compounded. Because you now love yourself even less, you violate your integrity in more serious ways, creating new lows in self-esteem. Each time you revisit this cycle, it reinforces itself.

We are a nation of people who have taught ourselves that it is more important to win and to be right than to be honest. We have an economic situation that makes it hard for everyone to stay even, much less get ahead. We have come to value things more than personal virtues. We admire wealth, glamour, and power. Combined with a miserly sense of self-love, these factors help create a consciousness that says the ends justify the means.

We violate our integrity when there is something that we want or think we need more than our own self-respect. It is when we are under pressure that we are most likely to throw honesty to the winds. Be honest. What is it for which you would sell your soul? If you say nothing, you are not being honest. Everyone really does have a price. What, where, is yours?

Don't look at this as a moral issue. Leave that to the moralists. See it as a love issue. If we loved ourselves, we wouldn't have to ask any of these questions. Under what conditions would you hurt yourself (esteem) in order to get what you want, or to look good in the eyes of others? Is the esteem of others more important to you than your own?

The answers to these questions may not be apparent yet. There may be issues you have to face and resolve in the crush of emotion and crisis. Knowing that they may have to be faced can help you be prepared.

If there are times or areas in your life when you have abandoned honor, how does that feel? How would it feel to rediscover your honor?

It is possible to recapture honor. It has not disappeared. You have not damaged it so badly that it no longer exists in you. It can be resurrected. In some future or current situation, where you have a strong desire amounting to a compulsion to cheat, to be dishonest with yourself or with others, dig those heels in and refuse. No matter what it costs you, refuse to give in to your self-hate or to the need to get ahead at the expense of your self-esteem or self-respect.

Be smart about this. Define honor for yourself. It's not about good and bad or right and wrong. It's not helpful to become rigid about anything. Honor comes from the heart. It is, in part, a desire to feel good about yourself and your actions.

How would it feel to refuse to gossip? How would it feel to refuse to lie, cheat, or steal? How would it feel to refuse to break your personal honor code regardless of the potential benefit?

It is not a violation of honor to park illegally. Or is it? If it represents an attitude that says, "I care only about myself and my own needs, and I am above the law," then it is a violation. To park in such a way that it creates impediments or dangers for others is dishonorable. Caring about yourself is caring about everyone else as well.

It is not dishonorable to reach for an apple when you are starving, unless it's the only food the other person has.

It's not dishonorable to refuse to talk to someone who would use the truth to hurt you. It may just be none of his business.

Does this sound like splitting hairs? It is. Honor is personal. It is your definition. You are the one who has to live with the consequences. Honor cannot be legislated. It helps to think about it from the point of view of the other person. Would you want to punish someone who was so hungry she took an apple from your orchard or grocery? Do you think she should punish herself? Don't attempt to be honorable to make a point. That's rigidity and possibly masochism. Be honorable because that's what makes you feel good, because there is a longing deep inside you to know that you are honest.

If you win by cheating, have you really won? You may never be found out, but will you get the rush of self-love when you know you have cheated? If you do the absolutely best you can, full-tilt boogie, nothing held in reserve, and you don't win, you have the satisfaction of knowing that you participated with honor. That holds true for every area of your life. Ultimately, that is what really counts.

A useful way to determine what is honorable and what is not is to think about whether, in pursuing a certain course of action, you are selling out on yourself or on anyone else. If you are, and you will feel it in your heart, then you are violating your honor.

Make a distinction between what is legal and what is honorable. They are not the same thing. Do understand that if you break the law, you have to be prepared to pay the price.

The bottom line is whether you love yourself enough to honor and respect yourself. Do you? For more work on this issue, use *Exercise 24* to clarify your thoughts and feelings.

GOSSIP

Gossip is a major violation of honor and respect for ourselves and others. It is also one of the most delicious treats we have. Most of us can't wait to get together personally or on the phone to "dish it out."

It is an integral part of the Victim/Tyrant game. "He's so bad... she's so awful...can you believe that he would do something like that...and then she...." The game teaches us to delight in telling each other the worst about everyone we know. We relish the petty details of other people's troubles, foibles, and weaknesses. If we don't have the details, we make them up: they're probably more interesting that way, anyway.

Most people are willing to gossip at the drop of a hat. We think nothing of it. We hypocritically befriend someone to his face, then talk about him behind his back. Everyone does it. It is accepted procedure.

Have you ever given any thought to the effects of gossip? What is the result of gossip?

It is noteworthy that we often feel uplifted and exhilarated by a good game of gossip. We have spent a period of time with a friend tearing down everyone else we know, comparing how good we are with how bad they are. Our friend agrees with us about all their bad qualities and deeds and has infinite sympathy for our suffering at their hands. What a relief. What joy.

Gossip is a habit. It is an addiction. We come to be as dependent on gossip as we are on being victimized. There is a "high" that comes with gossip, and a withdrawal of sorts if there is no one to talk to who wants to play the game. Our friendships are often based on large part on our agreement to gossip about the same people and the same things in the same way. Relationships break up when those agreements break down. If there are disagreements about the quality and quantity of the gossip, or if one person chooses not to play the game, there is no longer a basis for discussion or relationship.

What do you think of the idea that you spend a good portion of your time being critical, judgmental, and destructive of others? What does that say about how you treat you? How do you feel when others gossip about you? It hurts, doesn't it? It's unfair. What they say may be largely untrue and certainly distorted. People look at you strangely. You feel embarrassed, ashamed, betrayed.

Other people feel the same way when you talk about them. It hurts them too. Does it really gain anything for you? It may make points for you in the game, but what does it really get you? Does it make you feel good about yourself?

Gossip is very destructive. It can destroy any relationship. It can lay waste a business. It can damage credibility and reputation. It is a major waste of time and productivity. One really good poison peddler in an office or an organization can create chaos.

There are two kinds of gossip. One is, "I am angry at you, but I'm going to tell everyone else how awful you are rather than work it out with you." The other is, "I'm full of venom and I'm going to poison everything in my path with negativity, judgment, innuendo, and outright lies."

If you sit and judge this, back up and remember some of the times you have gossiped very unfairly, when you have hurt someone's relationship with someone else by what you have said. It is extremely unlikely that you are immune to this.

There are some easy solutions to the problem:

> *Refuse to listen to or to participate in gossip. You don't have to be haughty about it. You can say no thank you just as you would to an extra helping.*
> *Take your problem directly to the person who can solve it.*
> *Work out conflicts with the person involved, instead of spreading news all over town.*
> *Keep your mouth shut. When you start to say something destructive about someone else, think, and then stop yourself.*

If someone insists on gossiping to you, you stop her by "detriangling." That means that the next time you and this person are with the person who is being talked about, you say "Jane, Susan tells me you're sleeping with the boss." That will stop the gossiping to you forever. She will never want to tell you anything again. If you are loathe to take any of these steps, look at your own addiction to gossiping. Are you that dedicated to The Game?

LIVE IT, DON'T TALK IT

If you do not live what you have learned, it is useless. It will not make a difference in your life. It's easy to talk a good game, to brag about how transformed and enlightened you are. It's possible to sound very knowledgeable, to tell everyone else how to solve their problems and live their lives. Cocktail party Freud will not make a difference in anyone's life, except possibly to make you sound pretty weird.

If you read this book and put it back on the shelf, it will have made no difference, nothing will have changed. Use the book, make the lists, use the Workbook, think, feel, and challenge yourself all along the way. It's hard work, but then it will have been useful.

Live your life in the same way if you want to produce change and results. Don't just talk about what you think or feel, put it to use. Follow through with action. Then your learning will be powerful.

Ideas, thoughts, and philosophies are entertaining. We can amuse ourselves for hours on end with this theory or that. Does anything change as a result? Are we better people for the experience? No. We have wasted time talking to ourselves inside our capsules with no results, visible or otherwise.

In order to change and to grow, commitment is necessary. That commitment is seen in what you do. It is seen in how you live your life. It is easy to say, "Be more loving. That's what everyone needs." But are you? Do you live it?

Work with your judgments of yourself and others. Work with your feelings, your attitudes, thoughts, interpretations. Work with your personal issues as rigorously as you would exercise, as regularly as you would brush your teeth, eat, breathe.

If you can take what you learn intellectually and apply it to reality in an emotional way, your life will take a dramatic turn for the better.

Sometime around the third grade, we are taught to apply what we have learned in one area to other areas: to apply what we learn in reading to spelling, grammar, and writing. It is very helpful to learn to apply what you learn across the board. To translate what you read or hear from information into learning, apply it. Use it. Make it work for you. Ask yourself how that information or that idea applies to your life. Then use it.

The people who get the most out of therapy are the people who work at using what they learn and applying it in every area of their lives. For them, therapy is not an hour a week. It is an on-going exploration of themselves and the world, with results produced by living what they have learned.

20

THE ROAD TO MASTERY

The changes that occur in life are often accompanied by great sorrow and upset. Most people hate and dread change. The human being struggles always toward a stasis in the self and in the environment. Changes are often met with a deepening sense of failure and defeat. There is an idea or a belief that we should be able to maintain the status quo.

It is somewhat mind-boggling that we hold on to the idea that we control life and hold it steady. Where did we get that idea? It flies in the face of observable reality. The idea that life situations should remain steady and constant does not reconcile with experience.

Carefully review your life experience. When did anything remain the same for any length of time? Although we resist them, changes occur naturally and frequently.

Fritz Perls, the father of Gestalt Psychotherapy, said, "You can't stop the river." When you stand in the river, the river moves around and past you. You are never standing in the same river you stepped into. It has moved on downstream.

If life is an ever-changing, on-going process in which little if anything remains the same, it may be said that much of our pain and sorrow is a result of resisting change. Somehow, change is always a surprise, a betrayal of sorts. We have worked so hard to maintain the status quo. We have gotten things set up just the way we want them, and then it all falls apart.

Biologically the body is in a constant state of flux, sloughing off old skin, creating new cells, growing, decaying. It does not stand still. Observe nature. Is it static, steady? Never.

All laws of nature, biology, and physics apply to the human being. We are part of the larger universe of physical laws. Given enough time, you will begin to realize that the only constant is change. The only thing you can ultimately count on is that everything in your life will change. Part of the job in life is to learn to adjust to and manage the change that comes, not to stop change.

If the laws of change are acknowledged and understood, one can learn to flow with the river. It is possible to understand the process of change, to anticipate and to prepare for it. Change then becomes part of the growth process: expected, inevitable, and nurturing. Like the willow which bends in the wind, we learn to bow to the exigencies of change with a recognition of its value and ultimate power for good in our lives.

TRANSITIONS

Each change requires a transition. Each transition requires an adjustment of the psyche and the environment. Transition periods can be some of the most emotionally strenuous exercises in life.

What do we mean by transition? There are the easily recognized ones: starting school, graduating from high school or college, taking your first job, marriage, moving, having a baby, a child going off to kindergarten, children going off to college, changing jobs, or the death of a parent.

We are often so excited by the obvious transitions like going to college, getting married, having a baby that we forget that these can also represent major upheavals in our usual way of life. Everything is going to be different. Our foundations will be shaken. It is important to factor in the problems that accrue at these times as well as celebrate the excitement.

There are other transitions which are harder to identify as transitions. They may look like your life is just in a great deal of chaos. Feelings may be at the fore and challenges will arise that are unexpected. "The empty nest syndrome" is recognized as a time of difficult emotional adjustments for a woman. These are transitions from one emotional level to another. They are a sign of spiritual and emotional growth. There is little support for them in the culture because they are not clearly defined.

Life could be described as one long series of transitions. No sooner is one transition complete than another begins. It is very important to understand that nothing ever stays the same. The honeymoon is over again and again and again. Enjoy, revel, wallow in the excitement. But keep track of the changes necessary on an inner level to accelerate your conscious growth through them.

Welcome the transitions. Celebrate the chaos. It means you are growing, changing, evolving. Your life is proceeding apace. You are not stuck, stultified, rotting away in a rut. You have accepted the challenge of life to grow or to die. Changes and transitions, hurtful and upsetting as they may be, mean that you have chosen to live. You have made the painful personal decision to take the next step, to have the next adventure, to experience the next potential.

Transitions signal the next leap into the unknown. To be willing to venture into the unknown is the greatest single act of heroism and courage a human being can exhibit. We avoid the unknown in favor of the known. We will even take the known pain over the unknown solution. But the power and majesty of life is in the unknown. As an artist creates a painting or a symphony, each human being who tremulously enters the unknown creates something from nothing: a life out of chaos, a reality previously unlived. What more could one aspire to than to explore the unknown?

Where is your courage?
Where is the fire that burns in you to know the unknown?
Where are the dreams you once had?
What stops you?
What are you afraid of?

Be willing to throw it all to the winds, and start over again, to begin the process anew. That is where the fun and the accomplishment lies; not in safety and stagnation.

TURN IT AROUND AND MAKE IT WORK FOR YOU

Whatever your problem may be—anger, stubbornness, fear—turn it around and make it work for you. If you have the power to make it work against you, you also have the power to make it work for you.

In one sense, self-defeating behaviors are caused by using enormous amounts of energy and concentration to create havoc in your life. You have been doing that for a long time with great efficiency. You may have become quite proficient at creating disasters in your life. You can use the same energy and concentration to create success, joy, love, and peace in your life. It is up to you.

Stubbornness is a common trait. It can and usually does create a great deal of sabotage in one's life. "I'm going to do it my way, I don't care what anyone thinks." The problem with that is that your way may not work. Learn to stop in mid-reaction long enough to consider what works rather than what you are driven to do. For instance, you may want to defy yourself and everyone else by having another drink. You can do that. No one can stop you. Stop and think, though. Will you like the result?

Defiance and stubbornness are handmaidens. They are likely to create results you don't like. Let us say that you take that next drink. You'll show them, whoever they may be. But you will also have the hangover as well as many of the other complications of excessive drinking. Is that what you really want? Is that what works for you?

Learn to think about what you want in the long run, not the short run. Yes, you may feel angry and defiant enough to have another drink now. Right now, that's what you really want. But is that going to get you what you want tomorrow or the next day? If you have that drink will you make a good impression on the people you are with? Will you be able to go home and take care of the needs of the day effectively? Will you be able to go to work in the morning clear-headed.

Use your stubbornness and defiance as your allies. Stubbornness can become determination and persistence. It can be a very valuable asset. Defiance can become a willful commitment to have a better life. Defy self-defeating behaviors. Anger can become the fuel to push you on to achieve your goals. It can become a refusal to continue self-destructive patterns. You can make any trait which has up to now been in your way work for you. You can make it a positive force in your life. You can turn your weaknesses into strengths. Go ahead: make a silk purse out of a sow's ear. It can be done.

BE A MASTER, NOT A SLAVE

Archeologists and anthropologists tell us that we have a history of being slaves. The attitude of the slave is easily seen in our behavior. Other cultures are dependent on totalitarian forms of government, such as dictatorships or monarchies. True independence of spirit and freedom of will are not options.

Americans talk about how independent we are, but in reality we are dependent. We rely on corporations, the church, and the state to take care of us. You don't like that idea? That's understandable. It contradicts our most treasured myths about ourselves. But look at the facts.

It is clear that an employer should be expected to pay the agreed wage for work done. They are also expected to provide paid vacations, bonuses, "benefit packages" including medical and dental coverage, pension plans, profit sharing, maternity leave, sick leave, and educational benefits. That is all very expensive to the company and to the employee.

How is it expensive for the employee? It makes him dependent. She can't leave the job because she needs the money, the insurance, the benefits. It is not a system which teaches independence. What if the corporations gave their employees the money spent on benefits as part of their salary and let them make their own decisions about how to spend it?

The church tells us what to think and how to act. The government tells us what is legal and what isn't. Everything is nicely and clearly laid out. We don't have to think or act for ourselves. You may bridle at these suggestions, but think about it. It is very clear what is acceptable and what is expected. We are a nation of people who want to be taken care of. When something goes wrong, we turn to God or the government to fix it. If we have no power and no responsibility, then we are slaves and victims.

All three institutions—the corporation, the government, and the church—treat us like dependent children because that is how we behave. We are willing to give our power away in order to be taken care of. We do not want to be responsible at the level necessary to take control of our lives.

The media, the marketplace, and private citizens gather about with complaints and criticisms of our government: the national debt, the failure of the banking system, farmers in crisis, the AIDS epidemic, inflation, the environment—there are so many issues of such major proportion it seems almost impossible to grapple with any of them effectively. What can one person do? You can't fight city hall, you say.

You can fight city hall. In fact, we had better fight city hall. The world in which we live desperately needs our attention. Each and every one of us needs to adopt the attitude of the master rather than the slave. We can then master our destiny. By giving up dependency and taking responsibility on an individual basis, we can make a difference. One master can make a big difference. A great place to start is with your own heart.

IF YOUR HEART IS RIGHT, YOUR MIND FOLLOWS

Many of the concepts and ideas discussed in this book can be clarified under the general rubric "If your heart is right, your mind follows." It seems simple enough. Now, how do you apply it to your life, and to the concepts in this book which are about your life?

"If your heart is right" is another way of saying, "Be true to yourself," "You come first," "Do what you want or feel you need to do," "Your feelings are your power to create," and many of the other encapsulating phrases in this book. If you are clear about what is in your heart, you will not be the slave of guilt or self-sabotage under peer pressure. You will be free to live your life as a being of impeccability and integrity.

If you follow the real, deepest dictates of your heart, your mind will tell you exactly what your heart requires. The requisites of the heart are not necessarily easy. But if you will make them your first priority, they will lift you out of the ordinary and the mundane into freedom and joy.

There is a choice to be made in life that must be made on a daily basis, often on a situation by situation basis. It's not a decision that is made once and then forgotten. To live from the heart is to live in truth. It is not easy. There will be many pressures to deviate from that path and to follow in the footsteps of the demands of the culture.

The choice is whether to be your own person living up to the needs of your own soul, or to be a victim tossed about on the tides of cultural games. Neither choice leads to an easy life.

To be a victim is to be constantly at the beck and call of everyone and everything in your life. There is no real power or autonomy in that choice. It is what is expected. It may be demanded of you. Much force is exerted at every level to require the individual to stay in the accepted cultural modes. You will not necessarily be encouraged to strike out in the direction of greater health and joy. This culture is addicted to suffering and you must do your share. To stray off that path in the direction of greater health, autonomy, and growth may be seen as a deviation verging on perversion by those who are still chained to their suffering.

The price for attempting to be all that you can be may be very high. You may lose friends and be alienated from family. It is likely you will be largely misunderstood, for how can others understand what they have not experienced? There may be major uproar in your life when the people around you decide that what you are doing is selfish, perverted, or dangerous. They will try to rope you back into the corral to be a member of the herd, to be the way you have always been. Your own mind and feelings may long to take you back to belonging and to the safety of approval and acceptance. The road to personal freedom may be long, hard, lonely, fraught with danger and despair. You may be plagued by doubts and insecurities. Are you making the right choices and will you ever get where you are going? Compared to the responsibilities and demands of freedom, victimization may look easy and desirable.

If both paths are difficult, why buck the system? Why attempt to be extraordinary rather than ordinary? There is one very clear reason. The path of the victim is limited. It leads nowhere except to more pain and suffering. Your heart will never be at ease. While following your heart may be difficult at times, it will lead you to greatness of being, understanding, wisdom, enlightenment, and joy.

THE ANSWER IS INSIDE OF YOU

All of the work you ever do on your emotional life should teach you how to access the answer to your problems from inside you. Therapists, teachers, and coaches can help you find the doors and unlock them, but the answers come from you.

That is the power and richness of emotional work. To discover that you have a depth and intensity of feeing that will answer all of your questions is the point of the exercise. You know that something is true by how you feel about it. When you find that feeling, you will know with a certainty that is absolute. With that feeling and knowing come wisdom, clarity, and peace.

Old hurts and confusions exist inside us like boils that are too painful to touch. It is partly for that reason that we need someone to help us. Who wants to lance that boil? Who can? If it is painful enough, we may even deny that it is there. A therapist can assist you in identifying its existence and location. The boil can be lanced and you will feel and know what you have hidden from yourself. The idea of emotional boils is not an attractive metaphor. If you are in touch with yourself at all, you will be aware that it is quite apt.

Those areas you have been unwilling to identify and deal with are painful sores afflicting your functioning in every area. To open them and release the poison is a relief. Would you rather be hurt or healed? There is a beauty in the therapeutic release of pain that transcends all art forms. It is a beauty that cannot be spoken, written, painted, or sung. It is the lightness of a soul healed and uplifted. The creativity necessary to produce such beauty exists inside of you. The therapist is the facilitator. You are the healer.

An artist of great talent can study with a master teacher and learn nothing if she is unwilling to dig down inside and find her own creative juices. The only person with a magic wand is you. The way to grab onto that wand is to know yourself, and be willing to feel, to plumb the depths of your feelings and your life. Then you can wave the magic wand and it will all go away in the twinkling of an eye. When the answer comes from inside you, it will be yours forever.

Frequently, a therapist will tell the client the same thing ten times, a hundred times. Eventually, the client will walk in and say, "Guess what I have discovered," and repeat in essence what the therapist has been saying all along. The client has finally been able to see the truth in his own terms. It is then his truth, not something the therapist taught him.

When it is your answer, it is the right answer. It doesn't mean you can't learn from others, or that they have nothing to tell you or to teach you. It means that the most powerful learning occurs inside you with or without help.

It is empowering to know that you have the ultimate answers. Then you are dependent on no one. You have simply chosen to consult with someone to help you access and know what those feelings and answers are.

As any creative person takes lessons in her chosen area, so therapy is lessons in feeling and knowing. It is a way to find your magic wand and make it work for you.

I'D RATHER BE ME

Who would you rather be? Michele Pfeiffer? Princess Di? Donald Trump? Kevin Costner?

Why? Why would you want to be someone else? Most people do. We envy the lifestyles, the achievements, the glamour of others. But what is it about you that would make you want to be someone else?

> *What is it that you don't like about you?*
> *What have you done that you wish you could hide?*
> *What is it about you that you think prevents you from*
> *being what you want to be?*

You can be and do anything you want to be or to do. What is more important and more valuable is to like yourself just the way you are. To be able to celebrate the very wonderful person that you are is a result of knowing that you have learned from everything you have done.

When you know, really know, that everything you have done, everything that has happened to you, has been turned into learning and wisdom, then there is no one else you would rather be. How could there be? When you can think and feel that you'd rather be you than anyone else, you've arrived. That's when the fun begins.

With that kind of understanding comes great joy. There is a sense that life is a huge cosmic joke that only you understand. The sadness, the anger, the despair created by the events in your life disappear. If everything has a purpose, if wisdom has been garnered from it, then it wasn't a tragedy. At that moment, it is absolutely clear that you have never done anything wrong.

This does not mean that everything that has happened to you had a conscious purpose. You did not choose your parents, your country, your social setting. There are many things that happened to you with which you had absolutely nothing to do. The point is what you have done with all of that? If you still see yourself as a victim of those circumstances, you have not used them to make yourself wiser. Learning from them is the purpose. There is nothing cosmic or aerie-faerie here. This is not metaphysical mumbling. It is a very simple and clear equation: *Event = victimization or event = learning.* It is your choice. You can transform the worst things that happen to human beings into absolute joy. You can do that by looking at what you can learn from it. How can you turn those lemons into lemonade? Not as a Pollyanna, but as a wise person who knows that "there's juice in them thar cactus." Cacti are not necessarily pretty. They have thorns. But, in the middle of a desert the water in them can sustain you. In the desert of your soul, finding the wisdom, the learning in your experience, will sustain and nurture you.

When you have wrung every little bit of wisdom from your life experience, when you have owned it all and earned it all, there is more joy, more freedom, more lightness than you could ever imagine. You don't want to be anyone else, because no one else has had your experience. Your experience has brought you to exactly where you need to be. Your experience is heaven on earth.

WHAT CAN YOU DO FOR HEAVEN ON EARTH, THE PLANET?

Not just today, but every day? Because we have not loved ourselves, we have also not loved this planet. It is our home and we are in danger of losing it.

What can you do to save your home? Start seeing the planet as your responsibility. We clearly can't leave it up to the government or the corporations. We are the government. We have failed to take care of our beautiful earth. Don't leave it to someone else. Make it your responsibility.

There are many books out on this subject. Some of them are listed in the bibliography.

Here are a few practical suggestions:

Plant a tree.
Pick the trash up off the street.
Recycle.
Carpool.

What else can you think of to do? Hurry. It may already be too late. It is a part of loving you.

THE TREE OF LIFE

The Portable Therapist is a book about life. It is about living life more abundantly. Part of growing and changing is becoming involved with the world around us and doing what we can to better it.

As everyone is well aware at this point, our planet Earth is in serious trouble. Without Mother Earth, we will not have a place to have problems or to solve them.

There are many steps that all of us can take to help our planet. One of the easiest and most productive is to plant a tree. If you don't know how to plant a tree, visit a local nursery and ask for help.

If you live in an apartment or are otherwise unable to plant a tree on land of your own, contact civic leaders, neighbors, and friends. Find a way to plant trees in your area. Trees can be planted in parks, along roadsides, at public schools, and near churches. Make it a community project in which all can participate.

Each tree planted will significantly reduce the "greenhouse effect" by producing oxygen and consuming the CO_2 produced by humans and their machines. Consider planting fruit or nut bearing trees which can also be a source of sustenance.

Give a tree as a gift. What better gift could you give the people you love than the gift of life? Planting a tree in their name can be a holiday or special event treat, with far greater benefits than any ordinary gift.

If each person who reads this book would plant a tree for each person on their gift list for an entire year, we could make a major difference. If everyone who buys a Christmas tree would buy a live tree and then plant it, think what an enormous difference that could make in our environment.

It is not even necessary to buy a tree to plant. Trees give off their own seed. Plant the seed. Nurture it. It will grow. It is a lovely thought to think that as you grow, you can help the planet grow and change as well. To Life!

EPILOGUE

It is not possible to say everything that needs and wants to be said in the scope of one book. There is a great deal left unsaid. To have attempted to say it all would have resulted in a book that is not portable. When a child goes out into the world to make his or her own way, the parents think about all the things left unsaid, all the ways in which the child is unprepared. It is simply not possible to tell the child everything he or she will need to know.

There are some things that don't translate. The learning comes only through experience. *The Portable Therapist* is meant to be a guide, a partial map, a talisman to assist the traveler along the path. The rest must be learned through trial and error, experience, and feeling. The student will make and learn his/her own lessons. New, undreamed of wisdom will result. It is good and right that this is so.

If someone could tell you everything you need to know, where would the fun, the excitement, the adventure be? Life is full of surprises for which no one has an easy or handy solution. Each generation pushes out the edges of knowledge, experience, and wisdom.

We all stand on the shoulders of the last generation. The shoulders of this book are strong and steady. Stand on them to go as far and as fast as you can. Don't reach for the gold ring. Reach for the stars and you will see your own grandeur and beauty.

With all my heart I wish you well. I hope that you can use this book in a way that is empowering and strengthening. That is its purpose. Take my love for you and build on it. Join me in being an engineer of love, building and constructing love in everything we see and do.

Let your purpose be to love yourself and the world. Love yourself so much that your love pours over onto everyone and everything around you. That is ultimately the message of this book. "All we need is love" may be true, but we need lots of it. I invite you into the Corps of Love Engineers. You will always have a job.

THE PORTABLE THERAPIST
WORKBOOK

This Workbook section is designed to enhance your learning. By using the exercises in the Workbook, it is possible for you to make the lessons in *The Portable Therapist* work for you so that your learning becomes emotional, not just intellectual. It will help to make the information in the narrative section concrete and real for you. It will help you learn how to incorporate the insights you make into your life. If you will use the Workbook, this will not be just another self-help book that ends up on the shelf, vaguely remembered. Instead, you can participate in making real changes in your life.

Use this section to let the book make a real difference in your life. Be absolutely honest in your answers. No one else will see your work, unless you want to share it. This is private for you. Use a notebook and copy the exercises if you don't want to write in the book. Imagine that I am sitting with you, if you need to talk to someone. Talk to me. Only by being as honest as possible, by doing some soul-searching, and by being willing to face your own truths, can you make this a powerful tool for your own growth.

A word of caution: go easy on yourself. Play. Have fun with it. If you do an exercise and become emotional and upset, leave it for a while and go back to it later. Remember to love and forgive yourself every step of the way—throughout this Workbook, and in your life.

EXERCISE 1: CREATE YOUR LIFE THE WAY YOU WANT IT NOW

Some people begin the process of getting what they want from life by using a technique called "visualization." Others simply start by making comprehensive lists, adding to them and refining points as they go along. Be willing to do a little of both. Just sit down and give some real thought to how you want it to be. Then start making lists. Start focusing on and thinking a lot about what you do want. Dream about it. Feel how it would feel to have all those things you want. Then do everything you can on a conscious level to make those things happen.

There are many good books available to help you with this process. Some of them are listed in the reference section in the back of this book. To begin this exercise, start naming what you want. For every category in your life, write down how you want it to be.

Health

_____

_____

_____

_____

Relationship

_____

_____

_____

_____

Personal Growth

_____

_____

_____

_____

Money

_____

_____

_____

Lifestyle

_____

_____

_____

_____

Spiritual Growth

_____

_____

_____

_____

Work

_____

_____

_____

_____

Friends

_____

_____

_____

_____

Activities

_____

_____

_____

_____

Hobbies

_____

_____

_____

_____

Travel

_____

_____

_____

_____

EXERCISE 2: **HOW MUCH ENERGY AM I SPENDING TO MAINTAIN WHAT I DON'T WANT IN MY LIFE?**

Now make a list of what you DON'T want in each category. Add your own categories and write what you want and don't want for each. Take a long hard look at how much energy you are giving to keeping in place the things you do not want to keep. What you focus on and give great thought to is what will be in your life. Have you ever noticed that all, or most, of those things you are afraid of or do not want to have happen, do? It is because you focus on and think about them a lot. You invest a lot of emotion in them. In the following areas of your life, what are you hanging on to that you really don't want in your life anymore? Be very specific.

Health

_____

_____

_____

_____

Relationship

_____

_____

_____

_____

Personal Growth

_____

_____

_____

_____

Money

_____

_____

_____

_____

Lifestyle

_____

_____

_____

_____

Spiritual Growth

_____

_____

_____

_____

Work

_____

_____

_____

_____

Friends

_____

_____

_____

_____

Activities

_____

_____

_____

_____

Hobbies

_____

_____

_____

_____

Travel

_____

_____

_____

_____

EXERCISE 3: PATTERNS

Patterns are those things that you do over and over until you have learned the lesson and don't do them anymore. Give serious thought and attention to the patterns in your own life and in your family history. They will tell you a great deal about you, how you function, and the areas where you need to get to work on yourself. For example, if you have been molested, it is almost a guarantee that others in your family line also have been. What causes that and how can you stop the pattern? What are the patterns in your life? They are there. Identify them. Write them down. Then look for similar patterns among family members. The following are just a few examples to get you started. Check off those that apply to you and/or to family members.

☐ *Do you see yourself as always being abandoned by men or by women? Did any of them abandon you?* _____

Were any of these family members abandoned?

☐ Mother   ☐ Grandmother (P)
☐ Father   ☐ Grandfather (P)
☐ Sister   ☐ Spouse
☐ Brother   ☐ Other_____
☐ Grandmother (M)   ☐ Other_____
☐ Grandfather (M)   ☐ Other_____

☐ *Do you have difficulty keeping a job?*

Did any of your family members frequently change jobs?

☐ Mother   ☐ Grandmother (P)
☐ Father   ☐ Grandfather (P)
☐ Sister   ☐ Spouse
☐ Brother   ☐ Other_____
☐ Grandmother (M)   ☐ Other_____
☐ Grandfather (M)   ☐ Other_____

☐ *After a major achievement, do you get drunk and make a mess of your life?*

Does this sound like:

☐ Mother	☐ Grandmother (P)
☐ Father	☐ Grandfather (P)
☐ Sister	☐ Spouse
☐ Brother	☐ Other_____
☐ Grandmother (M)	☐ Other_____
☐ Grandfather (M)	☐ Other_____

☐ *Do you have serial relationships?*

Was committment an issue for:

☐ Mother	☐ Grandmother (P)
☐ Father	☐ Grandfather (P)
☐ Sister	☐ Spouse
☐ Brother	☐ Other_____
☐ Grandmother (M)	☐ Other_____
☐ Grandfather (M)	☐ Other_____

☐ *Do you attract abusive people and situations?*

Who gets abused and who are the abusers?

☐ Mother	☐ Grandmother (P)
☐ Father	☐ Grandfather (P)
☐ Sister	☐ Spouse
☐ Brother	☐ Other_____
☐ Grandmother (M)	☐ Other_____
☐ Grandfather (M)	☐ Other_____

☐ *Do you consistently let yourself be used? Who used you growing up?*

Who else in your family seems to get used?

☐ Mother   ☐ Grandmother (P)
☐ Father   ☐ Grandfather (P)
☐ Sister   ☐ Spouse
☐ Brother   ☐ Other_____
☐ Grandmother (M)   ☐ Other_____
☐ Grandfather (M)   ☐ Other_____

☐ *Are you incapable of completing anything?*

Is this true of:

☐ Mother   ☐ Grandmother (P)
☐ Father   ☐ Grandfather (P)
☐ Sister   ☐ Spouse
☐ Brother   ☐ Other_____
☐ Grandmother (M)   ☐ Other_____
☐ Grandfather (M)   ☐ Other_____

☐ *Do you get mad and drop people, making long-term relationships impossible?*

Do any of your family members practice "emotional amputation?"

☐ Mother   ☐ Grandmother (P)
☐ Father   ☐ Grandfather (P)
☐ Sister   ☐ Spouse
☐ Brother   ☐ Other_____
☐ Grandmother (M)   ☐ Other_____
☐ Grandfather (M)   ☐ Other_____

☐ *Did you, your parents, or your grandparents "have" to get married?*

☐ Mother   ☐ Grandmother (P)
☐ Father   ☐ Grandfather (P)
☐ Sister   ☐ Spouse
☐ Brother   ☐ Other
☐ Grandmother (M)   ☐ Other
☐ Grandfather (M)   ☐ Other

☐ *Has someone in the last three generations committed suicide?*

What does that say for you and your siblings?

☐ Mother   ☐ Grandmother (P)
☐ Father   ☐ Grandfather (P)
☐ Sister   ☐ Spouse
☐ Brother   ☐ Other_____
☐ Grandmother (M)   ☐ Other_____
☐ Grandfather (M)   ☐ Other_____

☐ *Are you an alcoholic, drug, or other substance abuser?*

Are any of your family members substance abusers?

☐ Mother   ☐ Grandmother (P)
☐ Father   ☐ Grandfather (P)
☐ Sister   ☐ Spouse
☐ Brother   ☐ Other_____
☐ Grandmother (M)   ☐ Other_____
☐ Grandfather (M)   ☐ Other_____

☐ *Are you chronically ill?*

Who in your family is always sick?

☐ Mother   ☐ Grandmother (P)
☐ Father   ☐ Grandfather (P)
☐ Sister   ☐ Spouse
☐ Brother   ☐ Other_____
☐ Grandmother (M)   ☐ Other_____
☐ Grandfather (M)   ☐ Other_____

What are some other behaviors and events that tend to recur in your life? What things always seem to happen to you? How do your current relationships reflect your family relationships? How are they the same? How are they different? Are all the oldest children in the family super-achievers? Are the youngest unable to commit to an adult relationship? Use the blanks and add more sheets to list other patterns and match them to you and your loved ones.

My pattern is to: _____

☐ Mother   ☐ Grandmother (P)
☐ Father   ☐ Grandfather (P)
☐ Sister   ☐ Spouse
☐ Brother   ☐ Other_____
☐ Grandmother (M)   ☐ Other_____
☐ Grandfather (M)   ☐ Other_____

My pattern is to: _____

☐ Mother   ☐ Grandmother (P)
☐ Father   ☐ Grandfather (P)
☐ Sister   ☐ Spouse
☐ Brother   ☐ Other_____
☐ Grandmother (M)   ☐ Other_____
☐ Grandfather (M)   ☐ Other_____

My pattern is to: _____

- ☐ Mother
- ☐ Father
- ☐ Sister
- ☐ Brother
- ☐ Grandmother (M)
- ☐ Grandfather (M)

- ☐ Grandmother (P)
- ☐ Grandfather (P)
- ☐ Spouse
- ☐ Other_____
- ☐ Other_____
- ☐ Other_____

My pattern is to: _____

- ☐ Mother
- ☐ Father
- ☐ Sister
- ☐ Brother
- ☐ Grandmother (M)
- ☐ Grandfather (M)

- ☐ Grandmother (P)
- ☐ Grandfather (P)
- ☐ Spouse
- ☐ Other_____
- ☐ Other_____
- ☐ Other_____

My pattern is to: _____

- ☐ Mother
- ☐ Father
- ☐ Sister
- ☐ Brother
- ☐ Grandmother (M)
- ☐ Grandfather (M)

- ☐ Grandmother (P)
- ☐ Grandfather (P)
- ☐ Spouse
- ☐ Other_____
- ☐ Other_____
- ☐ Other_____

Now we're going to take this a step further in the next exercise, by developing a family map.

EXERCISE 4: CREATING A FAMILY MAP.

A family map is a very clear visual representation of the patterning process over generations. This exercise may require that you do a little family sleuthing in order to fill in the blanks.

To begin family mapping, simply list each member of your family as far back as you or anyone in the family *remembers*. Use full names (first, middle, last) whenever possible. After you have filled in the name blanks, underneath each one's position on the map list as many attributes, characteristics, or experiences that you know they had. Here is a sample:

William A. Smith
Great Grandfather (P)
unapproachable
wealthy   *Edward R. Smith*
died of a heart attack   Grandfather (P)
                                   mean old man/curmudgeon
                                   heavy drinker   *William E. Smith*
                                   died of heart disease   Father
                                                                charmer
                                   MaryAnn (Jones) Smith   *macho self image*
                                   m.Grandmother (P)   *hyper-critical*
                                   independently wealthy   *heavy drinker*
Susan (Braun) Smith   *heavy drinker*
Great Grandmother (P)   *died senile (Alzheimers?)*
German immigrant   *great wit*
had eight children
died young

Now complete your own family maps on the next pages. When you have completed the lists, go back and begin to link traits that flow through the family. Notice how many times a particular characteristic reappears. Do all the women get cancer? Are all the oldest children successes? Are all the men alcoholics? How many people were in trouble with the law? How many suicides, divorces, remarriages, bachelors or spinsters? Be creative about your questions and do this for all attributes, both "negative" as well as "positive."

Begin with your father's side of the family.

Great Grandfather (P)

          Grandfather (P)

Great Grandmother (P)

                Father

Great Grandfather (P)

          ---
          m.Grandmother (P)

Great Grandmother (P)

Now map your mother's side of the family.

——————————————
Great Grandfather (M)

        ——————————————
        Grandfather (M)

——————————————
Great Grandmother (M)

                ——————————————
                Mother

——————————————
Great Grandfather (M)

        ——————————————
        m.Grandmother (M)

——————————————
Great Grandmother (M)

Here is a blank map that you can duplicate to do this exercise for other significant people in your life. Very few of us come from "normal" nuclear families. We have step-parents, adoptive parents, and adopted siblings with their own histories. It is also helpful and important to include in the map those people who were intimately involved in the family who were not blood relatives: your mother's best friend who is your Aunt Bessie, etc. However, be careful not to go too far afield with who is included in the map. Only people who are considered "family" should be included.

_____
Great Grandfather

_____
Grandfather

_____
Great Grandmother

_____
Person - *(relationship to you)*

_____
Great Grandfather

_____
Grandmother

_____
Great Grandmother

EXERCISE 5: YOU'RE TRAPPED BY YOUR LIMITS

What limiting beliefs, interpretations of past events, feelings, ideas do you have? Where did they come from? What makes you think you can't do anything in this particular situation? Anything is possible for you. Where have the limits come into play? Are they societal? Are they a function of gender, class, race, family rules and beliefs, or religious tenets? What would you like to do that you think is not allowed or unacceptable? Who made that rule? Do you think you are not good enough? Do you think there is someone outside of you who won't let you or will prevent you doing what you want? Who gave him that power? What is your vision? How would you like your life to be?

Be determined about revisiting those past areas of your life that have continued to limit you, even now. Then deal with the source of your limits. Make new interpretations. If you find obstacles along the way, find a way to get beyond them. You created the obstacle. It is a function of what you think and feel. Find out what it is in you that insists on keeping you limited and get rid of it. Here is an example.

Past Event: *When I was fifteen, I used to have to do the dishes every night. I was the oldest girl. My parents always used the same wine glasses, special crystal goblets from their honeymoon in Europe. One night I accidentally broke one of the glasses in the kitchen sink and was severly reprimanded by my father for being so thoughtless.*

Interpretation (why did it happen): *Like all the other mistakes in my life, I believed this one happened because I was self-absorbed, not paying attention to what I was doing and deliberately thoughtless about what was important to our family.*

This belief or interpretation came from: *My parent's desire for me to do the right thing and not make "stupid" mistakes.*

Another way of looking at it is: *Accidents happen. Even with "priceless" family crystal.*

Use the sheets on the next pages to delve into your past events and create reinterpretations of them.

Past Event:

_____

_____

_____

_____

Interpretation (why did it happen):

_____

_____

_____

_____

This belief or interpretation came from:

_____

_____

Another way of looking at it is:

_____

_____

_____

Past Event:

_____

_____

_____

_____

Interpretation (why did it happen):

_____

_____

_____

_____

This belief or interpretation came from:

_____

_____

Another way of looking at it is:

_____

_____

_____

EXERCISE 6: EXPLORING YOUR CAPSULE

The inside of your capsule is a hodge podge of all of the things you've been taught. It contains your beliefs, presuppositions, and feelings, all of which are probably inappropriate to your life at this point. How do they limit and defeat you?

If you will put some real effort and attention into doing this exercise, you will begin to see what makes up the fabric of your life. You live your life out of all those beliefs. You may never have questioned any of them. They are so ingrained that you may not even have realized that they were there. For example, some people actually believe that children should be seen but not heard; or that money is the root of all evil.

Making these lists will help you become conscious of the beliefs and attitudes that are running *your* life. You can then begin to decide whether a particular belief works for you. Do you want to keep it? If not, simply erase it. What do you want to believe? What really works for you? What are your "automatic" judgments in the following categories:

Health

_____

Children

_____

The Professions

_____

Religion/God

_____

Marriage

_____

Money

_____

Family

_____

Status

_____

Work

_____

Success/Failure

_____

Education

_____

Relationship

_____

Creativity

_____

Men

_____

Women

_____

Dress/Wardrobe

_____

Sports

_____

Weather

_____

EXERCISE 7: I DO WINDOWS

In order to make some windows in your capsule, you need to think about the areas in your life that may be shutting out the view. Make a new set of lists that addresses these issues. Go through each of the following categories and any others you deem necessary and important. Be thorough. Be precise. Remember you are installing and cleaning windows. Get off all the smudges.

For instance, guilt. List everything you can think of about which you are guilty. Even if you think in the listing that it is ridiculous, list it anyway. Try not to dramatize or judge. For example, say "I cheated on my tenth grade exam," not "I am a cheat."

Then go back through the list and deal with each item separately. Have your feelings about it. How do you feel that you cheated on that exam? What have you done with those feelings? How have they muddied up your life? Take as long as you need with each item in each category.

Don't back off because it's emotional. It's not going to hurt you to do this. It will help you. Categories for these lists might include:

Guilt

_____

Shame

_____

Unworthiness

_____

Inhibitions

_____

Inferiority

_____

Negativity

_____

Judgments

_____

Jealousy

_____

Insecurity

_____

Complexes/Phobias

_____

Disabilities

_____

Sexuality

_____

Substance Abuse

_____

Others:

_____

_____

_____

_____

_____

_____

EXERCISE 8: **DREAMS**

To "gestalt" a dream, you simply imagine yourself being each part of the dream. Consider that each symbol in the dream stands for a part of you. Then become that symbol and speak as if you are that symbol. For instance, if you dreamt about being in a beautiful apartment with a sofa in it you would say: "I am the sofa. I am big and soft and colorful. I am supportive and comfortable, strong, and reliable. I sit in the corner, against the wall, and am there if anyone wants me. I ask for nothing and am accustomed to being ignored. I enjoy having people use me."

After you have been each part of the dream, reflect on what you have said about yourself. What do you now know about yourself that you did not know before? What does your gestalt of the dream say about a problem you have been having or trying to work out?

Describe your dream:

_____

_____

_____

_____

_____

_____

_____

List the items you noticed in your dream and describe them as though you were describing yourself:

I am:

_____

I am:

_____

I am:

_____

I am:

_____

I am:

_____

I am:

_____

I am:

_____

I am:

_____

I am:

_____

I am:

_____

EXERCISE 9: WOULD YOU RATHER BE RIGHT THAN HAPPY?

Do you know someone who is more concerned about being right than about being happy or getting along with people? Are you that way?

The Know-It-All Checklist

☐ *Do you have a habit of insisting that you're right?*

☐ *Do you find yourself being right all by yourself a lot?*

☐ *Will you fight to the death to prove your point?*

☐ *Do co-workers try to avoid open-ended discussions with you?*

☐ *Does your boss seem to always want to cut you off just when you're getting warmed up to your subject?*

☐ *Do your loved ones eyes glaze over when you talk for more than a a few minutes on any one subject?*

☐ *Would you rather argue than eat?*

☐ *Are you absolutely certain that you are right and that it's important that other people acknowledge that?*

☐ *Does winning an argument at the time seem more important than anything else?*

☐ *Do you refuse to admit the possibility that you might be wrong and spend days after the argument is over trying to "document" your position?*

☐ *Have you ever discovered you were wrong after the fact and still couldn't admit it? (This is for the hardcore know-it-all!)*

If the answers to any of these questions is yes, you are going to have a miserable life. You will fight with other people endlessly. You will be upset about absolutely nothing of any import. People will avoid you rather than deal with you.

It is important to get off the idea that you have to be right. What is it in you that makes being right so important? Are you that insecure? Do you think you're that stupid? Are you that controlling? Why do you require others to acknowledge and accede to your superiority? What difference does it make anyway?

Most of all, what is it costing you to be that brilliant, that self-important, that determined to win out over others? Take some time to recall incidents where being right took precedence over everything at the time. Write down in a few words what the argument was about. Then write down what was gained and lost as a result of the argument.

We argued about:

_____

I gained:

_____

I lost:

_____

We argued about:

_____

I gained:

_____

I lost:

_____

EXERCISE 10: **WHO ARE THE VICTIMS/TYRANTS IN YOUR LIFE?**

We love victims and despise tyrants. Why not the other way around? The victims are very powerful. They get all the sympathy and support. Everyone wants to help them. The tyrant is the bad guy everyone dislikes and is angry at. It's like a petri dish for judgment: it can grow wild and unchecked and everyone will agree with you. "Yes, that bad person did that to that poor little thing." "I never liked him anyway." The judgment, anger, and blame are all clearly justified. He's bad and that makes us right. How many examples of this game can you see in your own life and in the lives of the people around you? Who are the oppressors in your life? Who do you think it is who makes you into a victim? What are the tyrannical acts, circumstances, agencies or conditions which victimize you? List them here:

The tyrants and tyranical forces, (i.e. those place or things to which I feel enslaved) in my life include:

People:

_____

_____

_____

Places:

_____

_____

Things:

_____

_____

Now ask yourself, "Why did/do I (the victim) put up with it?" When these questions are asked and answers sought, the game becomes both more interesting and less seductive. The game is now conscious. For each of the items listed above, try to sketch out options by using the following checklist:

Is there a choice? What could it be?

_____

_____

Is it possible to end the game? How?

_____

_____

If I give up playing the victim/tyrant game, what would I lose?

_____

_____

What would I gain by giving up the game?

_____

_____

How would I respond to others who are still playing the game?

_____

_____

Would I lose friends if I stopped playing the game? How do I feel about this?

_____

_____

Five good reasons for giving up my victim status are:

1._____

2._____

3._____

4._____

5._____

If you will approach your life as though everything that happens, whether good or bad, is an opportunity to learn, your own victimization will disappear. By asking yourself the following questions about events in your life, you are beginning to think like a champion, and not like a victim. Jot down a few examples from real life and apply the formula presented on the following pages.

My Experience Is/Was:

_____

_____

_____

What is the purpose of this event or this person in my life?

_____

_____

_____

What can I learn from this experience?

_____

_____

_____

How can I view this experience in a way that will bring me good, healing, happiness?

_____

_____

_____

EXERCISE 11: **FIRST THINGS FIRST**

Achieving clarity in your life will help you know where you really are and what you can and can't realistically do. Check in with yourself. How is your health? An unhealthy body can complicate problems and create others. Here are some things to think about in getting your daily living situation up to par. Check the item if the answer is affirmative and then take a look at the areas that you could improve on. After a month or two, do this exercise again and see if you've made any progress. Developing new habits takes time. Be patient.

☐   *Have you had your annual physical? If not, schedule one today. It's important to know exactly what kind of shape you are in.*

☐   *Have you had junk food for dinner more than one night this week?*

☐   *Do you consciously limit sweets and fats in your diet?*

☐   *Do you smoke? How much?*

☐   *Have you tried to quit during the last year?*

☐   *Do you smoke or drink coffee in lieu of one of the three basic meals?*

☐   *Do you get the vitamins that you need through your meals or in high-quality nutritional supplements, particularly if you live in a city?*

☐   *Do you include a leafy green vegetable in at least one meal a day?*

☐   *Do you have an alcoholic beverage every day? More than one?*

☐   *Are you taking any prescription drugs for longer than one refill? Substance abuse tends to lead to enormous dietary abuses.*

☐   *Have you been to the dentist during the last 6 months? Make an appointment for a check-up and a cleaning.*

☐   *Do you get any exercise at all?*

☐   *Are you sleeping through the night? All the time? Most of the time? Not at all?*

☐   *Have you balanced your checkbook this month?*

☐   *If you are a woman, have you had a gynecological exam during the last 12 months? Do you know how to check your breast for lumps? And have you done this during the last month? If not, learn how and do it monthly. It's easy and it could save your life.*

EXERCISE 12: **WHEN LIFE GETS YOU DOWN, REMEMBER THE GOOD TIMES, TOO**

Nothing is forever, not even the pain of the moment. Life is incredibly sweet. There is so much to enjoy and savor. Think about it. When you're upset, life may seem like cardboard: flat and tasteless. That's you, not life. If you can't think of anything that you would enjoy right now, think of things you have enjoyed in the past. Following are some memory "joggers." Use them to trigger your own memories of special times and write them down. Then, when the blues strike, you can always turn to this page and remember all the special reasons why you're life is worth living.

I remember having a wonderful time:

swimming

_____

wading in the waves

_____

eating Mexican food

_____

gardening

_____

watching football games

_____

gathering fresh flowers

_____

hunting

_____

traveling

_____

dancing

_____

taking long drives in the country

_____

There are a million—probably more—wonderful and enlivening things to do. What do you like to do?   What would you like to feel alive enough to enjoy again?

My Special Chase-The-Blues-Away List of
Things I Have Loved Most In My Life

_____

_____

_____

_____

_____

_____

_____

You can do all these and much, much more again.

EXERCISE 13: ADDICTIONS

The idea that we are addicted to suffering cannot be over-emphasized. Many of us have a broken record of what is wrong with our lives that we play over and over again like an endless loop tape in our heads. How much do you suffer? Check off those items that apply to you on the "Suffering Index."

☐ *Does most of your life/time revolve around your trauma and drama?*

☐ *If things get too good, do you seem to find a way to stir up trouble?*

☐ *Do you find a way to suffer even when you're happy, i.e. every silver lining has its cloud?*

☐ *Are you always upset or unhappy over something?*

☐ *Do you focus on what's wrong rather than on what is right with your life?*

☐ *Are you always waiting for the "other shoe to drop?"*

☐ *Do the negative things people say to you stick in your mind far longer than the positive messages?*

☐ *Do you often feel powerless to control many of the situations in your life?*

☐ *Is "Why bother?" a frequent response to difficult tasks?*

☐ *Do feelings of fear or inadequacy keep you from even trying to do some of the things you'd really like to do?*

☐ *Do you often have trouble getting started at tasks, waiting until the situation has reached crisis proportion?*

☐ *Do past "failures" significantly influence plans for the future?*

If you've checked off at least five of the above items, you can consider yourself a member of the "Suffering Society," dues payable daily!

EXERCISE 14: **ANGER IS ANOTHER NAME FOR FEAR AND INSECURITY**

Insecurity is a kind of fear that leads to anger. If you are often angry, if you fight with everyone you know, take a long look at your fears. If you are very angry, you may be very frightened. To get a sense of how anger works in your life to cover up your feelings of powerlessness or fear, give as close to an automatic response as possible to the following statements:

The things I fear most are:

_____

_____

_____

_____

_____

The things I believe I cannot live without are:

_____

_____

_____

_____

_____

I am powerless over the following parts of my life:

_____

_____

_____

_____

In what ways do I sometimes still feel like a dependent child?

_____

_____

_____

_____

What do I do that reinforces that feeling?

_____

_____

_____

_____

What could I do differently? What's the truth?

_____

_____

_____

_____

_____

My personal strengths are:

_____

_____

_____

_____

I demonstrate my power in the following ways:

_____

_____

_____

_____

The source of my power actually comes from someone or something outside of me: (spouse, job title, material possessions, children):

_____

_____

_____

_____

My internal sources of power are:

_____

_____

_____

_____

Redefine the word 'power' for yourself. My definition of power is:

_____

_____

_____

_____

_____

What would you have to give up in order to feel independent?

_____

_____

_____

_____

_____

_____

_____

_____

_____

_____

_____

_____

EXERCISE 15: CONQUERING FEAR

The way to conquer your fear is to get clear about what's real and what's not. Make your list. List everything you can think of that frightens you. Work on it for a couple of weeks, adding new items as they come up and as you think of them. Go through the list. Look at the reality of each fear. Try to isolate what it is you're most afraid of instead of being globally frightened. What is the real underlying fear? Is that really likely to happen? Would you survive it? What makes you afraid of that consequence? Where did you learn to be so fearful? Who taught you that? Think about your family. How fearful is each member, and in what way? Are their fears realistic or unrealistic?

I am afraid of:

_____

_____

_____

The likelihood of this happening is:

_____

_____

_____

An underlying fear may be:

_____

_____

_____

I am afraid of:

_____

_____

_____

The likelihood of this happening is:

_____

_____

_____

An underlying fear may be:

_____

_____

_____

EXERCISE 16: PROCRASTINATION IS PUTTING OFF UNTIL TOMORROW WHAT WILL MAKE YOU ANXIOUS TODAY

What makes you continue to create situations that become messy and difficult? Take some time to answer the following questions and see if you can discern a pattern here.

What was it like at home? What was your family life like? How did your parents deal with you?

_____

_____

_____

_____

_____

Were your parents often angry? Were you often or always in trouble? Did your mother threaten you that your father would get after you when he got home?

_____

_____

_____

_____

_____

Did your home environment create a lot of stress and anxiety for you? Did you live under the constant threat of parental anger, disapproval, or abuse?

_____

_____

_____

_____

Was one or more parent alcoholic?

_____

_____

_____

_____

Were you required to be the caretaker of the household or of the younger children or even of the parents?

_____

_____

_____

_____

EXERCISE 17: **PREJUDICE**

In order to locate and identify your particular prejudices, you are going to have to reach out to others in this assignment. Find and relate to a person representing the group you feel prejudiced about. Get to know him. Talk to her. Share your humanity with him. You do not have to like her, but at least get to the basic principal that we are all human beings.

When you have completed the assignment, look to see what it is on which you have based your thinking and feelings regarding a particular group. Are they your thoughts and feelings? Or have you merely taken on the attitudes of your family or of the culture? Are your beliefs true? Accurate? Based on observable fact? Write down what you did, and how you felt.

_____

_____

_____

_____

_____

_____

_____

_____

_____

_____

EXERCISE 18: WHAT HAVE YOU DONE THAT'S SO AWFUL

Stop floating around in your guilt and self-hate long enough to take a realistic look at what you've done. What was it? Do you have a list of things you feel guilty about? What are they, specifically? Take some paper and sit down and write it out. Be very clear. Write only exactly what you have done. Don't judge it. Don't dramatize it. Just the act itself. For example:

1. Stole a lipstick from a department store when I was fifteen; NOT, "I'm a shoplifter and a thief."
2. Kissed my neighbor in the kitchen during a block party; NOT, "Broke my marriage vows. Adulterer."
3. Drank heavily for twenty years; NOT, "I'm a no-good drunk."

Now, take a look at who you hurt. You and who else? Anyone? Have you really hurt anyone? Not unless you believe in victims and tyrants. Quit guilt-tripping long enough to look at the reality of the situation. When you take away the judgments and interpretations, it becomes pretty simple. Maybe now you can let it go.

What did you do?

_____

_____

Who did you hurt?

_____

_____

How can you reinterpret what you did?

_____

_____

What did you do?

_____

_____

Who did you hurt?

_____

_____

How can you reinterpret what you did?

_____

_____

What did you do?

_____

_____

Who did you hurt?

_____

_____

How can you reinterpret what you did?

_____

_____

EXERCISE 19: WHAT'S YOUR SECRET?

Your secret may be that you have only had sex in the missionary position. Believe it or not, some people are embarrassed by that admission. What kinds of other sexual secrets do people have? Here's a list of some of the more common ones:

- ☐ Lost virginity very early.
- ☐ Lost virginity very late.
- ☐ Have never had sex at all.
- ☐ Had a shotgun wedding.
- ☐ Have been promiscuous.
- ☐ Had interracial sex.
- ☐ Molested a child.
- ☐ Incest victim.
- ☐ Perpetrator of incest.
- ☐ Am homosexual.
- ☐ Am bisexual.
- ☐ Am asexual.
- ☐ Have been raped.
- ☐ Have raped someone.
- ☐ Have had sex with animals.
- ☐ Had an affair while married.
- ☐ Involved with married person.
- ☐ Watch porn movies.
- ☐ Made porn movies.
- ☐ Have had group sex.
- ☐ Have been a prostitute.
- ☐ Frequent prostitutes.
- ☐ Fantasized about others while having sex with mate.
- ☐ As adolescent, fondled member of own sex.
- ☐ _____
- ☐ _____
- ☐ _____

Now, forgive yourself.

EXERCISE 20: **TO BUILD SELF-CONFIDENCE, THINK OF ALL THE THINGS YOU'VE DONE SUCCESSFULLY**

Sit down and list everything you've ever done; as much as you can possibly remember. Let the knowledge that you did all those things well build your self-esteem and self-confidence. If you did it once, you can do it again. If you've done something similar, you can do this, too. Don't decide that if *you* did it, it doesn't count. It does! You earned the grade, the promotion, the raise. Recognize your achievements. Acknowledge yourself.

1._____

2._____

3._____

4._____

5._____

6._____

7._____

8._____

9._____

10._____

11._____

12._____

EXERCISE 21: MY WIFE HAS PMS AND A GUN

There are two issues to deal with about PMS. First, what are your specific feelings and thoughts with respect to your sex? Check off those attitudes that best describe your feelings:

☐ *Do you think you have fewer options, are less powerful, more helpless?*
☐ *Do you think it's a man's world?*
☐ *Do you like women?*
☐ *Do you prefer men as authority figures?*
☐ *Do you see women as victims? As competition? As the enemy?*
☐ *Do you think a woman is less than a man?*
☐ *Do you think having a period makes you unsexy, undesirable, even dirty?*

Second, PMS is not all a function of attitude. On the purely physical side, think about the following:

How healthy are you?
How long has it been since you had a gynecological examination?
Do you have other health problems that impinge on your cycle?
Do you drink enough water? Much of the cramping and emotionality of the menstrual cycle can be a result of dehydration. Eating less salt and drinking lots of water can make a difference. You retain water because the body doesn't have enough.
Do you exercise too much, putting a strain on your reproductive organs?
Do you eat nutritional, well-balanced meals?
Are you getting all the vitamins, minerals and nutrients you need?

Now use this space to write down your ideas for coping more effectively with your next bout with PMS.

EXERCISE 22: DO YOUR HOMEWORK

If you are prepared, you won't be worried. Homework doesn't end when you finish school. If you do what you need to do to be prepared to deal with any situation successfully, that's doing your homework.

Successful people do their homework. They show up prepared for the job at hand. They are properly groomed. Their life is in order and they have what they need to get the job done. What is some of your homework?

- ☐ *To be appropriately dressed for the occasion and the weather.*
- ☐ *To arrange your life so you are on time.*
- ☐ *To make sure that you have enough money to care for your needs at a particular time.*
- ☐ *You always have bus or carfare home, and a quarter for a phone call.*
- ☐ *You have the directions and know where you are going and how long it will take to get there.*
- ☐ *Your bills are paid, your laundry is done, there is food in the house, so that you can focus on what you are doing.*
- ☐ *You spend some time each day organizing what you will need for the next day and have it with you when the time comes.*
- ☐ *If you can't meet a deadline, renegotiate it, don't just disappear.*
- ☐ *Keep appointments and make phone calls as agreed.*
- ☐ *Don't leave everything to the last minute.*
- ☐ *Know what you need and if you can't provide it, make sure someone does.*
- ☐ *If necessary, read up in the field you are currently working in. Take a class that will help you in your job. There are very few jobs that will not benefit from education.*
- ☐ *Do the best job you can, and ask for help in areas you don't handle well.*

What can you think of for which you need to be prepared? Teach yourself to pay close attention to yourself. What are you feeling, thinking, dreaming? Thoughts and feelings are not random. They are related to each other and to your life. Investigate them. Think about what you have to do and keep track of it. Then do it.

☐   *Begin to pay attention in an organized way to details.*

☐   *Think about what you need to do on a daily basis and make a list.*

☐   *Write down on your calendar what is due on what day and check the calendar daily.*

☐   *Have a work area set aside with paper, pen, envelopes, and stamps.*

☐   *Have work areas and equipment for laundry, lawn, cooking, and other projects set up and organized with all of the things you need to accomplish the job. Make them attractive so you will want to spend time there.*

☐   *Make a detailed list of what you need from the grocery store. It will save money and you won't have to make daily trips.*

EXERCISE 23: **DO IT ANY WAY**

There are always many reasons and excuses to postpone doing what you need to do. If you want to have a successful, manageable life, you must learn to do it anyway.

Yes No

☐ ☐ *Are you always behind on things?*

☐ ☐ *Are you often late with projects and assignments? Do you never complete them at all?*

☐ ☐ *How many incompletes do you have in your life?_____*

☐ ☐ *Did you finish high school?*

☐ ☐ *College?*

☐ ☐ *Graduate School?*

☐ ☐ *Is there a half-written novel on the closet shelf?*

☐ ☐ *Do you have projects laying all over the house unfinished? What about the dresser you were going to refinish, or the car, appliance, or sports equipment you meant to fix?*

☐ ☐ *Are your bills laying around in piles somewhere untouched?*

Make a list of the things you have left undone and incomplete. Mark off the ones which are no longer necessary or interesting. Make a new list of the things you would like to complete.

Projects left undone and incomplete:

1._____

2._____

3._____

4._____

5._____

Now cross out those incompletes which are no longer relevant to your life. Make a new list of the things that you do want to complete and assign a date by when it should be done. Some things might be done by tomorrow, others might take years.

1._____By:_____

2._____By:_____

3._____By:_____

4._____By:_____

5._____By:_____

Now check off the excuses you habitually make to avoid completion of projects:

☐   *I don't feel well (have a cold, cramps, headache, toothache)*
☐   *I'm tired.*
☐   *Too many other things to do.*
☐   *Too many distractions.*
☐   *Not enough time.*
☐   *Not enough money.*

Complete this list with your excuses. All of them.

_____

_____

_____

If you will apply the same creativity and energy you use in making up excuses, you will complete your projects in no time. No matter what the reasons for postponing, do it anyway.

EXERCISE 24: HONOR

How can we learn to value honor in ourselves and in others? It is especially difficult to deal with the concept of honor without becoming judgmental and moralistic. Keep it personal. You are the only person involved at this point.

What does personal honor mean to you? Define it. Honor is

_____

_____

_____

_____

Is honor important to you?_____

Why?

_____

_____

_____

Why not?

_____

_____

_____

_____

It is when we are under pressure that we are most likely to throw honesty to the winds. We violate our integrity when there is something that we want or think that we need more than our own self-respect. Be honest. What is it for which you would sell your soul? If you say nothing, you are not being honest. Everyone really does have a price. What, where, is yours? What do you do under pressure?

_____

_____

What do you value?

_____

_____

Under what conditions would you hurt yourself (esteem) in order to get what you want, or to look good in the eyes of others?

_____

_____

Is the esteem of others more important to you than your own?

_____

_____

How did it feel at those times when you abandoned honor?

_____

_____

How would it feel to rediscover your honor?

_____

_____

Is there any particular part of your life which is without honor?

_____

_____

Are there other places in your life where you exhibit honorable behavior regularly and automatically.

_____

_____

Be sure to use this exercise to learn to love yourself more, not less. Look for the opportunity to learn, not to condemn.

FURTHER INFORMATION

BOOKS

Anderson, U.S. *Three Magic Words.* New York: Thomas Nelson & Sons 1954.

Bry, Adelaide. *Est.* New York: Avon Books 1976.

Campbell, Joseph. ed. *The Portable Jung.* New York: Viking Press 1971.

Fox, Emmet. *Around The Year With Emmet Fox.* New York: Harper & Row 1958.

Fromm, Erich. *The Sane Society.* New York: Fawcett Books 1977.
———. *Escape From Freedom.* New York: Avon Books 1971.
———. *Man For Himself.* New York: Fawcett Books 1978.

Hay, Louise L. *You Can Heal Your Life.* Santa Monica: Hay House 1987.

Horney, Karen. M.D. *The Neurotic Personality of Our Time.* New York: W.W. Norton & Co. 1965.

Hugo, Victor. *Les Miserables.* New York: Penguin 1982.

Jampolsky, Gerald. *Love is Letting Go of Fear.* New York: Bantam 1982.

Keyes, Ken Jr. *How To Enjoy Your Life In Spite of It All*. St. Mary, KY: Living Love Publications 1980.
———. *Taming Your Mind*. St. Mary, KY: Living Love Publications 1975.
———. *How To Make Your Life Work, Or Why Aren't You Happy?* St. Mary, KY: Living Love Publications 1976.

May, Rollo, *Love and Will*. New York: W.W. Norton & Co. 1969.

Peck, M. Scott, M.D., *The Road Less Traveled*. New York: Simon & Schuster 1985.

Perls, Frederick. M.D., Ph.D., Hefferline, Ralph F. Ph.D., Goodman, Paul. Ph.D., *Gestalt Therapy*. New York: Dell Publishing 1969.

Ramtha, *Ramtha The White Book*. Eastsound, WA: Sovereignty, 1986.
———. *Love Yourself Into Life*. Eastsound, WA: Sovereignty 1983.

Sitchin, Zecharia. *The 12th Planet*. New York: Avon Books 1978.
———. *The Stairway to Heaven*. New York: Avon Books 1983.
———. *The Wars of Gods and Men*. New York: Avon Books 1985.
———. *The Lost Realms*. Santa Fe, NM: Bear & Co. 1991.

Thoreau, Henry David, *Walden And Civil Disobedience*. New York: Signet Classic, New American Library 1973.

VIDEOS

Dead Poet's Society.

Pump Up The Volume.

The Color Purple.

INDEX

Abuse 66, 85-94, 174, 216
Acceptance 32, 108, 164, 217, 245
Achievement 9, 132
Adaptive maneuvers 22, 220
Addiction 7, 168, 235, 236, 99-106
Adolescents 136, 167
Adulthood 28, 66
Affection 91, 133, 136, 164
"Age of Anxiety" 116
AIDS 131, 134, 140, 223, 244
Alcohol 71, 80, 85, 115-116
Alcoholics Anonymous 7, 44, 70, 84
Anger 26, 42, 107-111, 175, 210, 216
    guilt as a cover for 121-124
    headaches from 143
    repressed 143
    out of control 145, 210
    turned in on oneself 175
Anxiety 71-72, 102, 113-119, 226,
    as substance 102
    elimination of 226
Approval 32, 64, 108, 174-175, 217,
Autonomy 245

Battering 87
Beauty 3, 164, 246, 251
Beliefs 18, 29, 35, 40, 54, 83, 120,
139-141, 224
Betrayal 93, 240
Blame 121-122, 192-193
    your parents 24

no one left to 27
others 42-44, 54
children are not to 86
Brutality 86
Burdens 163, 227

Cancer 26, 93, 175
Capsule 35-37, 40, 57, 107, 156, 190
Caretaking 161, 176, 178, 209
Champion 50, 53-55
Change 17, 19-23, 37-39
    only you can 191-192
    commitment is necessary to 237
    in life 239-241
    the planet 250
Childhood 28, 75, 91, 193
Children 54, 203
    abuse of 86-91
    incest with 92
    molestation of 92-94
    guilt of 121
    loss of innocence 132
    sexuality of 136
    unwanted 141
    transitions of 240
Choice 22-25
    "pro—" 141
    mate of 186-187
    homosexuality as unconscious 135
Clinical social workers 6, 7, 57
Clinics 7, 71

Co-dependence 99, 100, 173-177
Comfort 84, 169, 176, 178, 187
Commitment 134, 223-224
  to life 29
Communication 151, 155-157, 171-172
  basics 207
  in marriage 189
  in partnership 194
  poor 9
Community 222-223, 249
  support of 83
Compassion 76, 82, 163, 201-203
Compromise 54, 185, 189, 217, 230
Condoms 140
Conflict 6, 9, 121, 151, 194, 215, 216
Confusion 4, 52, 75, 78, 144, 221
Conscience 33, 128, 140, 230
Control 145-146, 191-192, 215, 228
  out of 11
Cooperation 189, 190
Courage 17-18, 30-31, 102-103, 193,
Creativity 129, 146, 166, 168, 230, 246
Crisis 11-14, 69-84
Cry 81, 102, 198, 203
  babies who 90

Debtors anonymous 72
Demanding 65, 179-180
Denial 48, 77, 182
Dependency 174-178
  in marriage 188
  giving up 244
Depression 30, 71, 81, 99, 102, 146
Deprivation 142
Despair 75-76, 81-82
Destructive behavior 154, 216
Determination 9, 20, 28, 153, 242
Disabilities 6
Disappointment 43-48, 54, 79, 114, 227
Divorce 25, 43, 81, 184, 200, 204
Drama 105

life 86
Dreams 41-42, 168
  giving up 100-102
Drug abuse 93

Ego 194, 195, 216
Emotions 29, 210-211, 231
  blocked 36
Empower 39, 54, 177-178,
  partnership 195
  your boss 215
Encouragement 187
Erhard, Werner 39
Excuses 8, 10, 61, 224, 225
Expectations 62, 166
  other people's 18
  giving up your 110
  of yourself 162
Experience 130
  failures and disappointments 198
  learn the lesson of 51-53, 109
  of yourself 154
  sexual 132
  traumatic 74

Failure 58, 130, 162, 239,
Faith 71, 83
Family 8-11, 197-205
  alienated from 245
  suicide survivors of 78
Fantasies 62, 87, 113, 116, 190, 198
Fear 29-31, 108-109, 113-120
  attempt to control 145
  in partnership 195
  make it work for you 242
Feelings 58-63, 143-154, 164
Finances 24, 71, 89
Flexibility 189
Fortitude 73, 225
Freedom 53-55, 243-245, 248
  allow others their 64

of choice 141
of will 244
Friends 62, 194, 219
    as support system, importance of 217
    lose 245
    loving, supportive 201
Frustration 45, 65, 91, 109, 194, 230
Fun 47-48, 168-169

Gender 7, 198, 200, 210
Gestalt 239
    a dream 41
Goals 162, 223-225
    in partnership 194-195
God 82-84, 167, 177, 189, 229
Gossip 154, 233-236
Gratification 65, 72, 109, 131, 133
Gratitude 25, 178
Grief 80-82
Group therapy 7, 129, 199
Growing pains, 137
Growth 21, 241
    process of 240
Guilt 121-123, 125-127
    homosexual 135

Handicapped 10, 29
Hangover 207, 242
Happiness 19, 23, 92, 101, 228
Harmony 192
Headaches 143, 209, 230
Healer 218, 246
Healing 94
    12-step programs for 99
Health 71
Heart attacks 208
Hidden agendas 61, 194
Homosexuality 120, 135
Honesty 194, 232
Hope 8, 62, 72, 77, 105, 122, 176, 252
Hostility 42, 87, 135, 138, 204

Identity 50, 188, 201
Illness 48, 54, 78, 81, 146, 207-209
Incest 8, 92, 99, 134
Individuality 9, 26, 166, 168, 183
Infantile behavior 177
Inferiority 36, 164
Inhibitions 36, 123
Innocence 53, 82, 93, 132
Insecurity 194
Insensitivity 190
Insight 127, 225
Inspiration 225
Integrity 54, 183, 194, 229-232, 244
Interpretations 29, 37-39, 146, 152, 237
Intimacy 131, 133, 146, 172, 187
Isolation 31

Jealousy 108
Joy 102-103, 145, 242, 244-245,
    create 242
    in life 164
    sex, of 132
    shut off 145
    source of 169
Judgments 135

Learn 45-46, 130-132
Lie 184, 233
Life 13-15, 17-22, 49-65
    nothing is as important as 72
    participation in 225
    tree of 249
    you don't owe anyone your 228
Life experience 239, 248
Light-heartedness 102
Limits 28, 56, 202-204, 216
    inability to set 31-32
Listen 32, 155-158, 171-173
    refuse to 236
    to others 46-47
    to your feelings 92

Loneliness 31, 81, 145, 182, 204
Loss 22, 43, 54, 73, 79, 81, 89, 204,
Love 159-170
    body 207-214
    communication is 151
    family 197-205
    making 132-133
    others 171-195

Manipulation 28, 175, 202, 203
Marriage 184-191
    loss of a child in 82-83
    problems with 24
    trouble in your 9
Masochism 100, 234
Masturbation 138, 139
Medication 6, 7, 72, 73, 115
Men 29, 198-200
    can cry 29
    homosexuality and 135
    marriage and 189
    perfect mate and 186
    PMS and 209
    sex and 132
Menstruation 136
Mirrors 45, 55, 56, 58, 76, 189
Miserable 23-28, 32, 183
    life 109, 197
    time, having a 175
Mistakes 24, 62, 113, 130, 197
Molestation 92, 134
Morality 141
Mourning 182, 191

Neglect 9
Negotiations 151

Obligation 64, 231
Obstacles 29, 70, 74, 136, 224
Opportunities 7, 153, 166
Options 22, 39, 49, 74, 100, 243

Orgasm 132, 140

Pain 143-145
    emotional 79-81
    ignore the 220-221
    more than necessary 169
    physical 207-212
Panic 75, 116, 147
Paranoid projection 60, 62
Parenting ethic 87
Parents 23-24
    bereaved 82
    children take care of 176
    marrying people like 28
    may not be your family 201
    perfect 197
Partners 17, 132, 140, 181, 189, 193
Passion 96, 102, 132, 133, 186
Passivity 52, 65, 87
Pathology 4, 29, 49, 99, 167, 182
Patience 66, 189
Patterns 9, 154-156, 182, 204, 243
Peace 103, 118, 134, 242
    "at-any-price" person 26, 173
    in relationships 43
    in your heart 120
    protect your own 92
Perls, Fritz 41, 239
Personality 6, 105, 109
Perspective 3, 35, 73, 75, 124, 126
Play 168-170, 188
Poverty 54
Power 49-57, 116-118
    feelings are your 146
    higher 83-84
    interpretation and 38-39
    personal 108-109
    struggles 215
Powerless 28, 86, 87, 152
Pre-menstrual syndrome 209
Pregnancy 136, 139-142, 223

Prejudice 119, 120, 135, 138, 144
Projection 30, 60
Pro-Life 141
Psychogenic illness 146
Psychotherapy 3, 6, 73, 146, 204, 239
Punishment 5, 128, 202,

Rage 65, 83, 88, 93, 96, 135, 145, 188
Rape 94-98, 134
Reality 35-39
    checks 59
    fit your 64
    observable 239
    of your life 166
    thoughts and 165
Recreation 129, 212, 217
Rejection 7, 26
Relationship 171-193
    abusive 201
    break up 235
    committed homosexual 135
    personal 215
    sex is more important than 131
    threaten the 199
    with God 84
Relatives 28, 78, 81, 83
Religion 84, 141
Resentment 64, 191, 194
Respect 33, 133, 166, 202, 216, 231
Responsibility 227-229, 243-244
    accept 122
    definition of 166
    for your own life 27, 43, 193
    parental 93
    to protect children 198
    to participate 222
Rights 153, 203, 204
Rigidity 234
Risk 78, 79, 184, 187, 209
    take a 33
Roles 6, 42, 167

Sado-masochistic culture 100
Sanctions 29
Satir, Virginia 151
Security 35, 65, 89, 108, 117, 185
Self-defeating behavior 119
Self-esteem 93, 139, 174, 203,
    integrity and 229
    low 85-89
Self-righteousness 173
Self-sufficient 177, 189
Self-worth 36, 59, 108, 221
Separations 204
Sexuality 131-136
    secrets of 134
    homosexual 135
    adolescent 136
Shame 36, 75, 93-96, 125, 137, 219
Slave 62, 103, 142, 183, 212, 243
Sneaky 16, 87
Sorrow 22, 23, 50-54, 69, 100, 105, 239
Soul healing 3
Spirituality 84, 129, 147, 173
Stability 71, 117
Status 58, 73, 81, 117, 166, 188, 216,
Status quo 26, 174, 239, 240
Street savvy 93
Stress 71, 118, 161, 182, 194, 204, 220
Substance abuse 28, 66, 81, 144, 146
Success 31, 35, 58, 59, 101, 167, 242
Suffering 99-103, 108
    addicted to 105, 168
    committed to 104
    guilt and 127
    misery and 226
    needless 129
    over secrets 134
Sugar 28, 71, 85
Suicide 73, 74, 77-79, 126, 204
Support 7, 139
    for loss of a child 82-83
    of friends 201

support system 217-220
Support groups 135-136
Symptoms 143, 208, 209

Team player 179, 217
Temper 173, 198
Tenderness 84, 95, 178, 179, 211
Transference 57-57, 194
Transformation 173
Transitions 240-242
Trust 61-63, 83, 117, 121, 172, 186
12-step programs 8, 99
Tyrants 49, 51, 54, 55, 227

Unconditional love 163, 164, 180, 192
Unconscious desire 86
Unhappiness 73, 100, 110, 156, 193
Unresolved feelings 43
Unresolved issues 181, 205
Unwanted children 94, 137, 139, 141

Values 9, 54, 167, 195
Victim 14, 100-105, 180, 234, 245, 248
    game of 49-53
    of incest 92
    of molestation 92
    of rape 94
    playing the 42-44
    Victim/tyrant game 50, 189, 228, 234
Violence 85, 87, 120, 131
Vision 28, 45, 74, 225

Wisdom 19, 58, 91, 182, 225, 245-248
Women 29, 35, 39, 198
    abortion and 140
    and birth control 139
    and PMS 209-211
    and rape 94-96
    and sex 132-136
Worthless 32, 46, 47, 160, 162, 188

You're the boss 161
Young parents 197

Zombies 27, 146

Order Your Own Copy Of
THE PORTABLE THERAPIST

Name: _____

Address: _____

_____

City: _____

State: _____ Zipcode: _____

Telephone: (_____) _____

THE PORTABLE THERAPIST $16.95*

Number of Copies: _____

Total Order (price x number of copies): _____

New York State Residents Add 8.25% sales tax: _____

Shipping and Handling**: _____

TOTAL ENCLOSED: _____

Send Your Order To: BYWOOD PUBLISHING COMPANY
P. O. Box 227, Grand Central Station, New York, NY 10163-0227.
Phone or Fax: (718) 797-5170
BOOKSTORES AND LIBRARIES:
Please contact us for rate sheets and discount information.
*Special Introductory Discount.
**Shipping and Handling:* First book $3.00; each additional book 50 cents.